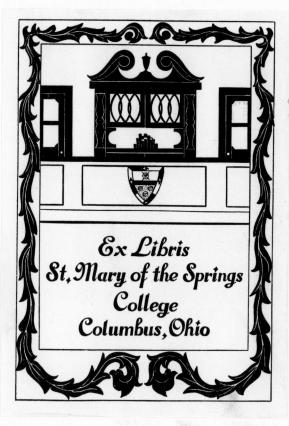

# THE POET AND HIS FAITH

A. S. P. WOODHOUSE

# THE POET
# AND HIS FAITH

*Religion and Poetry in England*
*from Spenser to Eliot and Auden*

THE UNIVERSITY OF CHICAGO PRESS
CHICAGO & LONDON

Library of Congress Catalog Card Number: 65-24428

THE UNIVERSITY OF CHICAGO PRESS, CHICAGO & LONDON
The University of Toronto Press, Toronto 5, Canada

TO

DOUGLAS  BUSH

*not for, but in memory of*
*forty years of friendship*

# PUBLISHER'S FOREWORD

At the time of his sudden death, in October, 1964, Professor Woodhouse had nearly completed his revision of these lectures. He had in effect rewritten the text as originally delivered, without, however, substantially altering its form and scope. Some revisions, suggested by colleagues who read part or all of the manuscript, and considered and approved by the author, have been made and a few minor slips have been corrected. Except for these relatively unimportant changes, the text remains as he had prepared it for publication.

For permission to use copyrighted material, we wish to acknowledge the co-operation of the following:

Oxford University Press, by permission of the Clarendon Press, Oxford, for quotations from:
Matthew Arnold: Poetical Works, edited by C. B. Tinker and H. F. Lowry (1950)
Testament of Beauty, by Robert Bridges (1930)
Coleridge's Poems, edited by E. H. Coleridge (1912)
The Metaphysical Poets, edited by Helen Gardner (1961)
The Poems of John Donne, edited by Herbert Grierson (1963). Oxford Standard Authors series
The Poetical Works of Edmund Spenser, edited by J. C. Smith and E. de Selincourt (1924). Oxford Standard Authors series
The Poetical Works of John Milton, edited by Helen Darbishire (1958). Oxford Standard Authors series
Poetry and Selected Prose of Henry Vaughan, edited by L. C. Martin (1957). Oxford Standard Authors series

# PREFACE

A series of public lectures which must thereafter be printed presents to its author some peculiar difficulties, and these are enhanced if the lectures are the first to be given on a foundation, so that one has no predecessor to whom one can look for guidance or warning. In taking for my subject religion and English poetry from the last decades of the sixteenth century to our own day, I had in mind both the terms of the Frank L. Weil Institute and my own limitations. It is a large subject—I now think too large. The dangers are of falling into a mere catalogue of poets and poems, and of too hurried and superficial a treatment. I hope that I have escaped the first danger by rigorous selection, at the risk no doubt of omitting names one might reasonably expect to find; to the second I fear that I have sometimes in the later reaches of the subject fallen victim. At least I have made no mistake, I think, in limiting comment and letting the poets speak for themselves.

The lectures are here presented substantially as they were written, though in the delivery a degree of compression was of course necessary. I have preferred, however, to let the subject fall into its natural divisions, rather shorter and slightly more numerous than those imposed by the requirement of six lectures.

Anyone attempting so large a subject inevitably falls under some obligations to his predecessors in different parts of the field, however much the point of view may be his own and the criticism based on no consciously borrowed opinions but on his reading of the texts. A bibliography and footnotes seemed inappropriate in such a semi-popular effort, but two works may be mentioned here. Professor Douglas Bush's lectures, published under the title *Science and English Poetry*, give special and valuable attention throughout to the bearing of science on traditional religious and ethical beliefs, and incidentally supply a model of rapid and lucid survey of a large field, which one despairs of emulating. I acknowledge also the direction to some poets and their work afforded by Professor Hoxey N. Fairchild's massive history *Religious Trends in English Poetry*, covering the period from 1700 to 1920, though the point of view and mode of treatment are, as he would be the first to detect, very different from my own.

I am deeply sensible of the honor of the invitation to give the first series of Weil Lectures, and I have most vivid and grateful memories of the kindness of the many friends I made in Cincinnati, of whom I can mention here by name only a few: Dr. and Mrs. Samuel Sandmel, Dr. and Mrs. Nelson Glueck, and Mr. and Mrs. William A. Mitchell.

A. S. P. WOODHOUSE

UNIVERSITY COLLEGE
UNIVERSITY OF TORONTO

# CONTENTS

# CONTENTS

# I

## DEFINITIONS: RELIGION,
## POETRY, HISTORY

AMONG THE LESS TANGIBLE hazards that beset our civilization
today is the danger that we may find important parts of our cultural inheritance inaccessible to us. If we are to preserve our ac-
cess to the inheritance of Western history, philosophy, and
literature, we must keep fresh our understanding of three major
traditions which have shaped it: the Hebrew-Christian, the classical, and (most recently) the scientific. The exploration and
exposition of these traditions, as they bear on the life of man,
are the special duty of the humanities today. This is a vast un-
dertaking, which can be carried out only by a co-operative effort.

These lectures will attempt some historical account of religion
and English poetry during the past four hundred years—that is,
they will try to examine the influence of one tradition on one
facet of the culture of one major Western nation. There are
many other facets of English culture which have responded to
the influence of religion—for example, the political—which
would bring into view quite other considerations. Poetry and
politics are poles apart; one must be careful to respect the character of the second entity brought into the discussion, whatever
it may be.

We must decide what we mean, in the present context, by religion, by poetry, and by relevant historical data.

Religion is not identical with theology, being primarily (and nowhere more so than in religious poetry) a matter of experience rather than of dogma; but neither can it be entirely divorced from theology, since it supposes some element of dogma. Religion in the West has always entailed some belief in a deity, failing which the philosophy of life, however exalted, would be classified as a form of ethical humanism. The minimal dogmatic requirement appears to be the recognition of a power, anterior and superior to man, which serves to explain to man himself and his universe, and to give a measure of meaning and guidance to his life, and which therefore becomes the object of his worship, or, in Matthew Arnold's formulation, "a Power not ourselves making for righteousness." We must allow for considerable variation in the firmness and constancy of such recognition, so long as it is sufficient to give rise to a genuine experience, without which religious poetry worthy of the name is impossible.

With these facts broadly established, it becomes possible and necessary to draw certain distinctions which will aid us in understanding the different types of religious poetry we encounter: the distinction, for example, between natural religion (which rests its case on the evidence of God in the world and in the mind of man) and revealed religion (which supplements this by a particular revelation—in our context, the Christian revelation); or, within revealed religion, the distinction between the order of nature and the order of grace; or, again, between the kinds of religious attitude which Lovejoy has designated the "this-worldly" (whose emphasis is on action) and the "other-worldly" (whose emphasis is on contemplation). Further, we must be prepared to recognize (as we approach our own age) that reli-

2

gion can tolerate a considerable infusion of what Tennyson called "honest doubt." What it cannot tolerate is indifference, which is another name for a secular view of life; from such a view, it is clear, religious experience, and hence religious poetry, cannot be generated.

To attempt now a working definition of poetry, in this or any other context, is inevitably to invite controversy. The theory of poetry in our own day has undergone something like a revolution. Responding to a variety of modern influences, ranging from the techniques of imagist verse to the findings of psychology and cultural anthropology, and haunted by the aesthetic equivalent of the epistemological problem, our theorists have sought to redefine poetry in the light of some or all of these influences. The four cardinal dogmas arrived at appear to be: that the poetic process is in every instance identical; that it issues in the poem, an artifact existing in its own right, detached—not to say insulated—from every other entity, including the poet himself; that its essence resides not in thought but in language, and its effect depends on patterns of imagery and the reverberations which these may set up in the mind of the reader; and that, in consequence, every extraneous reference in criticism, every historical consideration, including the poet's intention (however clearly avowed), is irrelevant and, if invoked, misleading. The result has been to sharpen our perception of patterns of imagery as elements of artistic form and vehicles of poetic meaning, but at the same time to divest the poem of its immediate contact with human thought and experience, leaving it at best a sort of remote radar-like communication therewith, particularly with the ground swell of primitive apprehensions and beliefs, and, further, to remove poetry from its central place in the humanities and assign to it a favored position indeed, but a position on the side lines. In our modern age it is taken for granted that the sole criterion of truth is furnished by science. But the affirmations of poetry are not susceptible of scientific verification. They can be proved on no computer, but only on our pulses. This has led to a flight from affirmation in favor of more indirect modes of suggestion and to an assertion that where affirmations occur they are in fact pseudo-statements to be judged solely by their emotive power and with no reference to their assumed truth or falsehood. This theory has rescued the critic and also the modern poet from the necessity of commitment, and this, one suspects, is among its underlying motives. But it seems impossible that religious poetry can be written without some degree of commitment. Whatever the adequacy or inadequacy of such a theory of poetry considered in itself, nothing could be clearer than the fact that, as an instrument of criticism, it is fully applicable only to the poetry of our century written under the very influences mentioned above and sometimes in response to the critical theory itself. The mistake is to apply the theory to the great body of traditional poetry, where it is patently insufficient to unlock the meaning or surprise the secret of power. When poems written to this prescription emerge, we shall recognize them. Meanwhile we had better attempt an account that does less violence to traditional poetry, its intentions and effects.

Let us say, then, that a poem is a work of art, and shares with the other art forms—sculpture, painting, music—certain characteristics, such as structure and design, and what has been called alternatively "aesthetic pattern" or "significant form." Not less important, according to Aristotle, was the fact that each work of art was an "imitation of nature"—that is, a representation of some aspect of reality as apprehended by the artist. It is clear that if the formal characteristics point to the integrity and sufficiency of each work of art in itself, the idea of "imitation" assumes a reference to something outside the work, and that the successful work of art must be one in which the two principles are united. What differentiates one art from another is the medium employed. The medium of poetry is words. This gives it a command over time, allowing it to present the development of an action, situation, character, or theme. Further, it puts at the poet's disposal all the resources of image, simile, metaphor, and the very ambivalence on which the new criticism has fastened. And, finally, words bestow on poetry a power of formulating (as distinct from merely suggesting) ideas, a power of comment, and even a power of expounding the poet's meaning. If poetry is an art, it is also, by virtue of its medium, a form of knowledge, and occupies some common ground with philosophy, with history, indeed with the whole range of knowledge communicable by—and only by—words. When Aristotle declared that poetry was more philosophical than history, he recognized this fact, and suggested (though it was Sir Philip Sidney who completed the formulation) that poetry dealt not with particular facts but with general truths, which, however, by a resort to fable or fiction, it was able to present in the guise of particulars.

We do not abandon our sense of reality when we read a serious poem: we are given a deeper insight into it; and this applies as much to the emotions which it arouses as to any other feature of the work. Occasions of pity and terror are not, alas, confined to the theater; but the emotions are aroused by tragedy under special conditions which allow them to be experienced and at the same time contemplated, and with pleasure. Among the various explanations of this seeming paradox, the most cogent, perhaps, is that which invokes the Aristotelian emphasis on form. We are moved to pity and terror by a significant action; we can experience the emotions with aesthetic satisfaction because that action is embodied in significant form. Tragedy as such will not enter very largely into what I have to say about religious poetry. I choose this illustration simply because it offers the most unmistakable example of the relation of traditional poetry to life, and of poetic to what I will call experiential emotion, and at the same time emphasizes to the full the pervasive power of poetic form. Nor do I cite Aristotle to invoke his authority, but because his theory, or some modification of it, underlay all the more serious practice of poetry from the Renaissance to within our own century. Such poetry always represented some aspect of reality as the poet apprehended it; and no one who took poetry seriously supposed that its affirmations could be dismissed, much less accepted, as pseudo-statements. The extension in poetic subject matter and appropriate form meant the emergence or development of descriptive, reflective, and lyric poetry; and this in turn entailed an extension of critical method, in which nothing of permanent importance was abandoned but new areas of exploration came into view. From the poem as imitation the critic proceeded to the poem as the record of an experience, and from its structure and its effect upon an audience to the emotional experience of the poet himself as explaining the poem's power. It is not impossible, of course, to bring this—the lyric or subjective type of poetry—under the rubric of "imitation": in such poetry, what is represented is not an external action but the mental experience of the poet himself. And even where the vehicle is dramatic or quasi-dramatic, one may—and sometimes must—associate the poet with the audience in considering the effect. Milton was still thinking primarily of the effect upon the audience when he claimed for poetry a power

6

"to allay the perturbations of the mind and set the affections in right tune." But one cannot go very far in the study of Milton's poems without discovering that where they manifest this power, the first to experience it was the poet himself. In religious poetry, this can be quite simply illustrated from Milton's famous sonnet on his blindness ("When I consider how my light is spent"). Its starting point is a fact in the poet's own life (in his extra-aesthetic experience), a fact which gives rise to a problem, and the problem breeds emotional tension. What the poem does is not so much to solve the problem as to raise it to a level where self-regarding thoughts are irrelevant, and thus to effect a resolution of tension. But it achieves this resolution of tension by, and in the very act of, imposing on the whole an aesthetic pattern, uniting significant content and significant form. In this act, religious experience and aesthetic experience unite—indeed coalesce—and this is the indispensable condition of all great religious poetry. The poem is not a mere record of an experience; it is the realization of the experience: the poem is the experience. This is the answer to Dr. Johnson's objection that religious poetry is a contradiction in terms, since one who is in a genuinely religious attitude "is already in a higher state than poetry can confer."

In dealing with religious poems, the question of the relation of poetry and belief is inescapable. Nowhere perhaps is it more necessary to distinguish between the attitude required in the poet and that in the reader. In the poet, the affirmation uttered (which includes, of course, whatever reservations he introduces), whether as initial assumption or as conclusion reached by virtue of (that is, by means of) the poem itself, must, at least at the moment of utterance, command his wholehearted belief and response; for this is the condition of that merging of religious

7

and aesthetic experience which is the mark of religious poetry. George Herbert phrased it in his own way: "The fineness which a hymn or psalm affords / Is when the soul unto the lines accords." From the reader, fortunately, much less is required: what is demanded is not assent but receptivity and a sufficient exercise of historical imagination.

This lends added urgency to our third decision: What do we mean by relevant historical data? Again I am conscious of running counter to a current in contemporary criticism, which has set strongly against historical method, which proceeds on the absurd assumption that attention to history necessarily means inattention to the text, but which originates of course in the theory of the poem as a phenomenon unique and isolated, already discussed. It seems evident, nevertheless, that poetry may be considered in its relation to history in two different ways: first, as it supplies data for depicting and explaining the age in which it was written; secondly, as forces operating in the age can be shown to have had their influence upon its poetry. In both divisions, it is necessary to recognize the complexity introduced by the personal factor—as indeed it is wherever history concerns itself with individuals, and especially with individuals of talent or genius; but here to be forewarned is to be at least half-armed. It has been argued that "literature is no document," simply because it is literature and an imaginative creation, not a literal transcript. The truth is that literature is a document, but that, as with other documents, one needs to know the language in which it is written and how to deal critically with the data it presents. At the very least, literature will tell us much of the sensibility of an age, of the assumptions it makes, and of the effects it enjoys. In its other relation to history—namely, the way in which historical considerations may help to elucidate it—

8

the poem can be considered first in its purely literary aspect, as standing in some relation to a tradition, either a positive relation as accepting the tradition or a negative one as reacting against it; and, secondly, it may be considered as responding to extra-literary influences which have contributed to shape the poet's mind and outlook or provide the assumptions which underlie his work. It is almost as inconceivable that the *Divine Comedy* or *Paradise Lost* should have been produced in any other periods as that anyone but Dante and Milton should have been able to produce them. They are the products of certain states and conditions of religious belief not peculiar to the poets, as well as of individual qualities of experience, sensibility, and genius. All these are worthy of consideration as the most immediate of historical data and in closest relation to the text. More remote but still relevant are other data, such as the tone and temper of the prevailing organization of religion, or of the dissident group to which the poet may belong, and, beyond this again, the inheritance transmitted by education and, modifying that inheritance, such current developments in philosophy and science as may have their effect on the religious outlook of the poet and audience—at which point, one recognizes that the distinctive influences of the classical tradition and of the philosophy of science come into play. English education, with its emphasis on the classics, and pursued as it long was under the auspices of religion, resulted in a strongly entrenched, if not always very vividly apprehended, Christian humanism. But the progressive secularization of English culture, supported by the steady advance of science, weakened both elements in this compound; and the discoveries of science, with their philosophical implications, at the same time altered the accepted pictures of man and his world, with profound consequences for religion. The example which will spring to everyone's mind is the effect of the Darwinian hypothesis, and it will be readily imagined that religious poetry, especially that which moved on the level of natural religion, must inevitably have felt its impact. In a word, then, whatever has a definable bearing on either religion or poetry may supply relevant historical data for the elucidation of the religious poem.

## II

## ELIZABETHAN RELIGION AND POETRY
## SPENSER AND SOUTHWELL

Some date about 1580 is a natural starting point; for by this time in the reign of the first Elizabeth, English religion, culture, and poetry had taken, or were about to take, decisive new directions, which were to leave their mark on subsequent history.

If the Protestant Reformation had not come to England, or if it had come in another form, above all, if it had not issued in the Elizabethan Settlement in the Church, the whole course of English history, and certainly of English religion and culture, might have been quite different. In the union of Church and State, which after many vicissitudes continues to this day, the end in view was political: to secure the unity of the nation and escape the disruptive effects of the religious struggle elsewhere. In this it met with, at most, partial success. The via media, the middle way which it offered, was rejected by Papists on the one hand and Puritans on the other; and the ideal of a comprehensive national Church remained in part an unrealized ideal. Indeed, if anyone had been called to give judgment, say in 1650, when the Church lay in ruins, its ministers evicted, and its liturgy proscribed, he must have pronounced the Settlement an unqualified failure; but he would have been wrong, not recognizing the resilience and flexibility of its underlying ideas and the peculiar relation which they bore to the national temper —how, springing from that temper, they were able at once to fortify and to mollify it.

The Elizabethan Settlement, then, bestowed upon the English Church the principle which was to become uniquely its own: the principle of the *via media*. Hostile critics might regard the *via media* as just a fine name for compromise; but Paul Elmer More was perhaps nearer the mark when he described it as an application of Aristotle's doctrine of the mean, and went on to remind us that in this doctrine the mean does not simply reject the two extremes but reaches out to comprehend so much of their content as it can assimilate to itself. Thus the Church has embodied a principle which has gradually and increasingly come to dominate the thought and action of the nation. In a matter of this kind it is not easy to distinguish cause and effect. Suffice it to say that, while other religious bodies, reacting against the principle, have made their contribution to English religion, and in lesser degree to English culture, the national Church has expressed, and in expressing has helped to mold, the temper of the nation. No wonder that Matthew Arnold, who was born into it, called the Church of England the most national and natural of institutions, or that T. S. Eliot, who was irresistibly attracted to it, called it the oddest. It is both, by virtue of this single principle of the *via media*, which (if I may snatch from its context a couplet of Pope's) makes it at once

> Papist or Protestant, or both between,
> Like good Erasmus in an honest mean.

And this result of the Elizabethan Settlement extends far beyond the sixteenth century, and will be felt in every period as we proceed.

The Settlement early found its ideal exponent in Richard Hooker, whose *Of the Laws of Ecclesiastical Politie* is one of the great classics of English prose—eloquent, luminous, and humane. The first book of the *Laws* is devoted to laying a foundation in the reign of law throughout the realm of nature (as the Elizabethans understood it), in the life of man, where it expresses itself as the rule of reason, and finally in Scripture, where God, the source of all law, has revealed the means of man's salvation but has neither prescribed every detail of his life and action nor called upon him to renounce nature and his own rational being. For if nature has need of grace (and Hooker never doubts that it has), grace (as he says) has use of nature. On this foundation, and in opposition to the Scripturism of his Puritan opponents, and to their ruthless depreciation of nature and man's reason, Hooker erects his theory of a comprehensive Church. Into the further steps of his argument we cannot pause to go, and anyway it is his first principles that are specially important for us. We see at a glance that they are the principles of Christian humanism and Christian rationalism. Every moral act, as well as every exercise of right reason, has its divine sanction, and is a step on the way to prayer and praise. If Hooker insists on obedience, it is a rational obedience: he refuses to submit his reason to the claimants of infallibility—that is (in his own phrase) to "Rome which cannot, and Geneva which will not, err"; and better than many of the more extreme Reformers, he recognized in the Reformation itself a principle of liberty, which he sought to preserve by uniting it with a principle of rational order. This was a matter of high importance for the life of the national Church, making it when most true to itself—that is, most true to the spirit of Hooker—perhaps the most tolerant Church in Europe. It was important, too, for the free play of mind in those poets who wrote from within the fold.

In his assumption of a rationally ordered universe, part of a divine scheme, on which he can ground his argument, Hooker is characteristic of Elizabethan culture. But here he stands rather on the extremity of the old than on the threshold of the new. His basic conception does not differ in its main assumptions from that of Saint Thomas Aquinas; nor was there need or expectation that it should. Copernicus had indeed rearranged the pieces of the stellar world, but had thereby (if anything) cleared and vindicated the impression of order. More ominously, Bacon was soon to propound a new method disruptive of traditional conceptions over a wide range, and Donne was to exclaim, "And new philosophy calls all in doubt." But for the time being—and indeed, in conservative minds and in the popular imagination, for long to come—the inherited world picture on which Hooker relied continued to hold sway; and even when the new philosophy had indeed called it in doubt, its sweep and grandeur retained their aesthetic and something of their religious appeal and caused it (as we shall see) to be revised, adapted, and still invoked. If in his conception of nature, of the relation of nature and grace, and of the office of reason, Hooker's affinity with Thomism is clear, the form of his argument is very different: it has no trace of the Scholastic dialectic: it is traditional of course, but of another tradition—that of humane letters coming down from Cicero and Saint Augustine and fortified by the precepts and example of Erasmus. One cannot easily illustrate in a short quotation the amplitude of Hooker's thought and style. But his final pronouncement on law will perhaps suggest this quality.

Of Law there can no less be acknowledged than that her seat is the bosom of God; her voice, the harmony of the world. All things in heaven and earth do her homage, the very least as feeling her care, the greatest as not exempt from her power: both angels and men, and creatures of what condition soever, though each in different sort and manner, yet all with uniform consent admiring her as the mother of their peace and joy.

The style is worthy of the conception, and the conception of the style. Religious in its origin and sanction, law thus conceived is at once the basis of all obligation and a virtual synonym for God's natural providence; and whenever poets have sought to bring man and nature together and place them under the aegis of God, they have sought for some adaptation of Hooker's world view.

The second reason for our starting point is the great and sudden flowering of English poetry in the last two decades of Elizabeth's reign, signalized by the publication of Spenser's *Shepheardes Calender* in 1579 and which continued (with internal changes and developments, but scarcely abated vigor) till Milton's day. In this flowering, religious poetry was to have its share, though at first the proportion of weeds to flowers is disconcertingly high.

By way of background, we must remind ourselves that poetry as one of the elements of a pagan culture had been a problem for the early Christian Church. Was it to be rejected out of hand or taken into the service of the Gospel? The more liberal opinion prevailed, though from time to time the problem would re-emerge in one form or other, and something of the old tension would again develop.

The main outcome was a continually augmented tradition

of specifically Christian poetry, coming down from Prudentius in the fourth century, who, adopting Virgil as his model in diction, had sought to give to Christianity a poetry of its own. Of this tradition the Renaissance was fully aware. Prudentius himself was included in Colet's curriculum for Saint Paul's School, and was probably still read there by Milton. In the *Defence of Poesy*, Sidney treats divine poetry as a distinct kind, where the poet is less a maker or creator than a *vates* or prophet, and its purpose is nothing less than to "imitate the inconceivable excellencies of God." Its prime models are the poetic parts of the Bible: the Psalms, the Song of Songs, "Moses and Debora in Their Hymns," and the Book of Job; and, interestingly, Sidney recognizes a poetry of this kind among the ancient Greeks, as, for example, in the Homeric hymns, though (as he hastens to add) "in a full wrong divinity." The great achievement of this tradition in the Middle Ages was, of course, the *Divine Comedy*, a mountain peak surrounded by a host of lesser hills. In the Renaissance there was no abatement of religious poetry, rather an increase in its volume; but new influences left their mark upon it. Protestantism directed it to Scriptural story and evangelical doctrine, while the Counter Reformation modified the character of Catholic verse; and the effects of the classical revival were visible, though intermittently, in both divisions. It is significant that the second great achievement in the tradition belongs at once to the Renaissance and to Protestantism: the only mountain peak in the whole tradition comparable to the *Divine Comedy* is *Paradise Lost*. It is very different, of course, in character and formation: the full tide of the classical Renaissance and of the Protestant Reformation have intervened. And again this peak is surrounded by lesser ranges, something of whose variety we must explore.

16

In England, we shall encounter at first a body of verse distinctively Protestant in orientation and emphasis, important mainly as a prelude to the delayed achievement of Puritanism in the next century; and confronting this, a smaller body of Catholic poetry, a product of that part of the nation which resisted the tide of Protestantism and rejected the standing ground of the Elizabethan Settlement. Finally, we shall recognize the outcome of that settlement in the emergence of a body of religious poetry unmistakably Anglican in character.

Well before the great flowering of Elizabethan poetry, we observe an obvious effect of the Reformation on English religious verse. Protestantism discouraged a type of devotion that allowed the play of imagination around the life of Christ and the saints, and this meant the loss of such poetry, not without its simple charm, as one meets in the first thirty items in the *Oxford Book of Christian Verse*. Take, for example, *The Holy Well*.

> As it fell out one May morning,
>   And upon a bright holiday,
> Sweet Jesus asked of his dear mother
>   If he might go to play. . . .
>
> Sweet Jesus went down to yonder town,
>   As far as the Holy Well,
> And there did see as fine childrèn
>   As any tongue can tell.
> He said, "God bless you every one,
>   And your bodies Christ save and see!
> And now, little children, I'll play with you,
>   And you shall play with me."
>
> But they made answer to him "No!
>   Thou art meaner than us all;
> Thou art but a simple fair maid's child,
>   Born in an ox's stall."

Weeping, the Christ child returns to the Virgin, who declares that he is King of Heaven and (rather surprisingly, surely) counsels him to "take those sinful souls / And dip them deep in Hell."

> "Nay, nay," sweet Jesus smiled and said;
>   "Nay, nay, that may not be,
> For there are too many sinful souls
>   Crying out for the help of me."
> Then up spoke the angel Gabriel,
>   Upon a good set steven,
> "Although you are but a maiden's child,
>   You are the King of Heaven!"

For this kind of poetry Protestant insistence on Scripture unadorned substituted metrical versions of Biblical stories and paraphrases of the Psalms, whose poetic quality was certainly not superior, and whose human appeal a good deal less immediate. A principal purpose was the desire to spread a knowledge of the Bible in the vernacular. But with this Protestant motive went another, not exclusively Protestant, though intensified by the Reformation: namely, that recurrent antipathy to secular song, particularly poems of gallantry and love, and a desire to replace pagan fictions and pagan morals by a content at once divinely true and morally edifying. "Tell me, is Christ or Cupid lord? doth God or Venus reign?" asks one minor poet; and another boasts,

> The vain conceits of love's delight
>   I leave to Ovid's art.
> Of wars and bloody broils to write
>   Is fit for Virgil's part. . . .
>
> But unto our eternal King
>   My verse and voice I frame. . . .

The hope was to provide a body of song for those who would (in Sidney's phrase) "follow St. James his counsel in singing

Psalms when they are merry." Metrical versions of the Psalms extend throughout the period from Sternhold and Hopkins to Milton and beyond, and prove on the whole an effective leveler of poetic talent. The other poetical parts of the Old Testament mentioned by Sidney were likewise paraphrased, with little better result, as we see in Drayton's *Harmonie of the Church*.

A new variety and vigor was, however, supplied in the naturalized work of the French Protestant poet du Bartas, who found in Josuah Sylvester a translator appropriate in every way: one sharing to the full his pious and patient industry, his boundless energy, and his prolific flow of images, and one (we must add) as lacking as himself in critical discrimination and finesse. Sylvester made the works of du Bartas a part of English literature. The poems ranged from Scriptural paraphrase in the *Job Triumphans* to an epic ordering of Biblical story in the *Judith*. But the most famous and influential effort, the *Divine Weeks and Works*, is neither paraphrase nor epic. In a series of poems combining narrative and commentary, it carries the story of God's chosen people from the Creation to the Babylonian captivity. Freed from the shackles of paraphrase, the poet can indulge his imagination and produce something that is poetry in its own right, while the spirit of wonder and worship which informs the whole bespeaks a genuine religious experience in poet and translator, and qualifies the work for inclusion as authentic religious poetry. The first six sections go to the Creation of the world and introduce into English poetry the theme of the hexaemeron—the six days of Creation—a favorite topic with more than one of the fathers, and destined to furnish Book VII of *Paradise Lost*. Of Milton's response to Sylvester's du Bartas there is abundant evidence from his early days. And it is worth while to remember that in another of his poems du Bartas converts Urania from the Greek muse of supramundane studies to the Heavenly Muse, the inspirer of Christian poetry, whom Milton is to invoke.

Even with du Bartas added, Scriptural verse does not, until we come to Milton, furnish an adequate vehicle for religious poetry. Save for some reported early efforts, never published and now lost, the greatest of Elizabethan nondramatic poets, Edmund Spenser, takes an altogether different line. He adopts no such special form, but interweaves the religious motive with the secular (the ethical and political) in *The Faerie Queene,* or couples it with the theme of love in the *Amoretti,* and finally presents *An Hymne of Heavenly Love* and *An Hymne of Heavenly Beautie* (which, of course, are not hymns in the modern sense, but rather meditations which take the form of extended odes) as parallels, completions, perhaps correctives to his *Hymn of Heavenly Love* and *Hymn of Heavenly Beautie* in a more mundane sense. These facts are significant of the degree to which religion is integral—indeed central—to Spenser's view of life and poetry.

That he is deeply engaged to the Protestant Reformation is clear from the eclogues referring to the Church in the *Shepheardes Calender,* and also from *The Faerie Queene,* but the latter leaves us in no doubt that he is also a loyal adherent of the Elizabethan Settlement. We may call him an Anglican poet with a strong Protestant emphasis, which is nevertheless compatible with a large inheritance from the Catholic Middle Ages.

In *The Faerie Queene* we come at last to poetry of a high order. But who, in a few sentences, can give any conception of its scope and effect? It is a poem of many meanings, "a continued allegory, or darke conceit" (as Spenser calls it), with, indeed, different levels of meaning—religious, ethical, political, and patriotic. The ethical is, by Spenser's own account, primary. The poem is addressed to the individual, and figures forth his experience and for him a motive and ideal. It is also addressed to the nation, and figures forth its history, past and present, and (as history gives place to prophecy) suggests the glorious future opening before it under God. Not but what Spenser is well aware of the pitfalls that beset the way: his idealism carries its necessary complement of realism.

The Faerie Queene is perhaps the most adequate symbol we possess of the spacious days of great Elizabeth—its very length and all-embracing character are themselves symbolic. There is scarcely a genre that it does not involve or draw upon—epic narrative, chivalric quest, the whole range of allegorical poetry as the Middle Ages had developed it, not to mention pastoral idyll, emblem, interlude, and masque. And within its ample confines it gathers up all the principal elements of the Elizabethan cultural inheritance: the wealth of Greek and Roman philosophy, poetry, and myth, mediated through the classical Renaissance; the treasure of the Christian tradition, mediated through the Reformation; the inheritance of medieval chivalry and romance—that entrancing and impossible world of love and adventure, which forms the staple of Spenser's narrative on the literal level, but whose values he corrects by the generous Renaissance ideal of the gentleman (for does he not tell us that his purpose is "to fashion a gentleman or noble person in vertuous and gentle discipline"?). All these things The Faerie Queene assembles and in measure co-ordinates, laying them at the feet of Elizabeth, the symbol of England's national unity, "to live" (in Spenser's own phrase of magnificent humility) "with the eternity of her fame."

What is the place of religion in this vast symbolic panorama of English and Elizabethan, but also, more generally, of human, life? The answer is that its place is nothing less than essential to the whole.

The Faerie Queene, as we have it, consists of only six of the projected twelve books and what is probably the fragment of a seventh book, the so-called Cantos of Mutabilitie. Each book is devoted to a particular virtue, whose "legend" it is called. Book I is the legend of Holiness, comprising the adventures of the Redcrosse Knight. Here at the outset Spenser places the one specifically religious and Christian virtue which he treats, as if to make it the foundation and the guarantee of all the rest. The other virtues are Temperance and Continence (both in the sense given to the terms by Aristotle in the Ethics), Chastity and Love (which go well beyond the Aristotelian scheme, but are treated without overt religious reference), Friendship (which can be in part based on Aristotle), Justice and Equity (which are almost entirely so based), and Courtesy (a chivalric virtue treated in the light of the Renaissance ideal of the gentleman); the Cantos of Mutabilitie (as their publisher, ten years after Spenser's death, observed) appear to be part of a book devoted to Constancy (that is, the Aristotelian virtue of steadfastness). It is evident that Spenser in his scheme is invoking that traditional frame of reference which distributes all existence and all human experience between the order of nature (within which these later books all, in the main, move) and the order of grace (within which alone Book I is located). This statement will require some qualification, or rather extension; but a failure to recognize the basic fact is, I believe, a first step in misunderstanding The Faerie Queene.

In Book I, Gloriana, the Faerie Queene (and heroine of the

whole poem) has assigned to the Redcrosse Knight the task of freeing the parents of Una by slaying the dragon under whose power they have fallen. To be adequate to the task, the Knight must first have achieved the virtue of Holiness; and his education for and in this virtue is presented in the long journey which he must take under the guidance of Una to the place of her parents' abode and imprisonment. Early in the journey he is separated from Una (the one, the true) by the wiles of the false enchanter Archimago, and attaches himself instead to Duessa (the double, the false), who claims that she is Fidessa, the true faith—whence come all the hero's woes, his successive errors, and at last his abject humiliation. He is cast into a keyless prison by the giant Orgoglio (spiritual pride), the ally of Duessa, from which he could never have escaped had not Una summoned to his aid Prince Arthur, the hero of the whole poem, who slays Orgoglio and, breaking by violence into the keyless prison, rescues the Knight. So far (that is, two-thirds of the way through the book) the Redcrosse Knight's achievements have amounted to almost nothing: indeed, he seems farther from the goal of Holiness than he did at the outset. By Prince Arthur he is restored to the guidance of Una, but there is one more hazard that he must encounter: stricken in conscience by his former errors, he comes suddenly upon the grim and awful figure of Despair, who brands him a sinner beyond all hope of mercy, and almost persuades him to end an errant and wasted life. But Una intervenes to strike the knife from his trembling hand. Now she leads him to the House of Holiness, a place first of repentance, then of instruction and illumination. He is taught by Faith, made acquainted with Hope, led by Mercy, the handmaid of Charity, through the active virtues to Contemplation, from whom he receives his vision of the New Jerusalem and knowledge of his own identity: for he is no elfin knight as he has seemed, but a destined saint, "St. George of merrie England, the sign of victory." Then, and only then, can he go securely forward to his fight with the dragon, the fulfillment of his task, and its reward in his betrothal to Una, at last unveiled to him in all her beauty.

Such in barest outline is the Book I of *The Faerie Queene*. As one reads the poem, one sees at a glance that it is Spenser's version of the old loved legend of Saint George and the Dragon, that it is compacted of the matter of romance, whose supreme master is Ariosto, and that with this matter Spenser has combined figures that belong rather to allegory and emblem. Even on the literal level, however, he endows this compound with psychological interest, for the Redcrosse Knight, it has been wisely said, is a type of the young and inexperienced idealist, in love with truth and goodness, but too easily led astray by false appearances. The literal narrative is, however, a base for other and deeper meanings. The book is, first and chiefly, an allegory of the individual soul in its quest for holiness, and the central idea on which it turns is the evangelical doctrine that no man by his own unaided effort can achieve this state: no man can save himself; only the grace of God can save. This the Knight must learn, and does at last learn from his rescue by Prince Arthur, who in this book represents divine grace, and whose breaking into the keyless prison represents what we may call the irresistible violence of grace. And Spenser is insistent that we too should learn the lesson:

> Ne let the man ascribe it to his skill,
> That thorough grace hath gainéd victory.
> If any strength we have, it is to ill,
> But all the good is Gods, both power and eke will.

24

Thenceforth faith and knowledge will suffice. To rescue her Knight from Despair, Una has only to admonish him:

> In heavenly mercies hast not thou a part?
> Why shouldst thou then despaire, that chosen art?
> Where justice growes, there growes eke greater grace . . .
> And that accurst hand-writing doth deface.

One will be baffled by this final line unless one recognizes that it comes straight from Saint Paul: "And you being dead in your sins hath he quickened . . . having forgiven you all trespasses, blotting out the handwriting of ordinance which was against us . . . [and] nailing it to his cross."

I have said that thenceforth faith and knowledge will suffice, but this is not quite true: in time of special need, divine assistance will not be lacking. In the fight with the dragon the Knight is almost overcome, until he staggers back into a stream of living water and comes forth restored. In Spenser, and in Milton, water is a symbol of grace, as it is in the sacrament of baptism.

On this level, then—the allegory of the individual soul—Book I is in essence a pilgrim's progress (Bunyan indeed has given us his own version of the encounter with Despair and the visit to the House of Holiness); and the slaying of the dragon is the conquest of Satan, first in the heart of the individual and thereafter in the world (for in its conclusion Spenser's Legend of Holiness is not evangelical only, but apocalyptic).

The other books of the poem move on the level of nature, and present those natural or humanistic virtues which Christianity ratifies indeed and subsumes in the very act of transcending, but their motive and sanction (unlike those of holiness) are ethical and rational and not specifically religious. Spenser recognizes, however, the limits of natural virtue. In these later books Prince Arthur represents magnanimity, the crown of the classical virtues, not grace, the foundation of the Christian. In his defense of the Castle of Alma, the citadel of humanistic virtue in Book II, the Prince encounters the most heart-shaking figure in Spenser—Maleger, who has on him all the marks of death but is possessed of the terrible resilience of the giant Antaeus: you seem to slay him, but as he falls upon the earth he springs again to life and redoubles his menace. Prince Arthur fights on, but in vain, till at last he has no resource but to cast the monster into a standing lake of water, and then the victory is his. The allegory is, I think, plain to read: Maleger is Original Sin, with which human virtue unaided cannot cope: only grace (whose symbol once more is water) can eradicate the evil, just as it fortifies the good. The other example which I have mentioned occurs in Book V: justice and even equity are part of the law of nature, apprehended and sanctioned by reason, and adequately formulated in Aristotle, whom Spenser here follows closely. But mercy, that mercy which must temper justice—mercy as a virtue, distinct from the unorganized human sentiment of pity— only religion can teach; for

> . . . in th' Almighties everlasting seat
> She first was bred, and borne of heavenly race;
> From thence pour'd down on men by influence of grace.

To state these matters baldly, as I am compelled to do, is to give no idea at all of the complexity of the poet's thought or the richness of his interlocking symbols. All that one can do is to indicate the dependence of *The Faerie Queene* on Spenser's religion and his religious experience. Into the ramifying details of his view of nature, we cannot pause to go. It is far less simple and confident than Hooker's, partly because his wider experience gave him a deeper sense of the power of evil, and especially of the natural goodness which fallen man has perversely turned to evil ends. For Hooker, the Fall meant at most some deprivation of man's original goodness, which left the great order of nature in itself unimpaired, and for which God's freely offered grace and the revealed scheme of salvation provided a ready remedy. But Spenser had responded in measure to the sterner teaching—so evident, for example, in Calvinism, which thought of the whole order of nature as sharing in the results of the Fall—and read those results, not as deprivation merely, but rather as total depravity, till, by the grace of God, the elect received from him a new nature, and were by conversion born again. There is evident in Spenser's poetry a struggle between these contending traditions. The distinction of nature and grace is far sharper than it is for Hooker, the interval between them much wider. For Spenser, the order of nature contains within itself the seeds of evil as well as of good, and its mark is, above all, mutability. But if mutability means change and decay, it also means replenishment and expansion; if mutability is the law of death, it is also, in the natural order, the law of life—thus Nature pronounces in the *Cantos of Mutabilitie*. It is something, but it is not enough to satisfy the craving of the human soul, and Nature herself points on to a time when change shall cease. The picture of a perpetually changing and decaying world induces in Spenser the mood of *contemptus mundi*, a strain with a long tradition in Christian (as in Oriental) thought, and a distinctive feature of "other-worldly" religion; under its influence he resolves to cast away the "love of things so vaine," and adds:

> Then gin I thinke on that which Nature sayd,
> Of that same time when no more Change shall be,
> But stedfast rest of all things firmly stayd
> Upon the pillours of Eternity. . . .

For, all that moveth doth in Change delight:
But henceforth all shall rest eternally
With Him that is the God of Sabbaoth hight:
O that great Sabbaoth God, graunt me that Sabbaoths sight.

These are the last words we have of Spenser's great unfinished poem, and like the first words they are about the order of grace.

Had he lived to finish *The Faerie Queene*, Spenser must by the end have attempted some synthesis of the two orders which he has so evidently discriminated, and this might have been less difficult than at first appears. For he was enough of a Platonist to conceive of nature as the shadow or reflection cast in time by the eternal verities, imperfect, indeed, as such a shadow must be, and transient, but taking whatever value it possessed from its perfect and immutable source; and he was so confirmed a Christian as inevitably to read this conception in the light of revelation. Nor was his poetry without resources for the task: it provided for different levels of allegorical meaning; it allowed him to compare earthly to heavenly things, and so to employ his images as to convey secondary suggestions beyond the limit of their immediate application. Such words as "grace" and "glory" are ambivalent, and so are many of his images. When, for example, Britomart with sword and shield braves the flames that bar her entrance to the House of Busyrane, she is, we know, armed only by her natural virtue, but her armor reminds us—and is meant to remind us—of the armor of the Christian described by Saint Paul in Ephesians, and directly utilized in the arming of the Redcrosse Knight. Thus does Spenser prepare for the synthesis of nature and grace with which he must conclude his poem.

We have said that (*The Faerie Queene* apart) Spenser's most important religious poems, *An Hymn of Heavenly Love* and

An *Hymne of Heavenly Beautie*, are coupled with two other *Hymnes* (or extended odes) to *Love* and *Beautie* in a more mundane sense. The relation of the two groups has been differently interpreted: some seeing in them a simple progression; others, a rejection of the earthly in favor of the heavenly. This is perhaps a special instance of the problem that confronts us in the relation of the two orders in *The Faerie Queene*. That *An Hymne of Heavenly Love* and *An Hymne of Heavenly Beautie* are to be regarded as a corrective to the two which precede them is strongly suggested in Spenser's dedication; yet perusal of the poems reveals unmistakable elements of continuity, and suggests the raising of the themes to progressively higher levels, with at the same time the elimination of whatever there was of error and disorder in love as initially conceived. Insofar as this idea of progression is present and operative, it relies on the conception of love elaborated by Christian Platonists of the Renaissance: first, the beauty of the individual earthly object and the emotion of love which it evokes; then, the contemplation of this beauty in a more abstracted form; thence, the generalization therefrom of the ideal beauty; and, finally, the raising of the mind to contemplate the Creator as the source of all beauty, as of every good, and the recognition that only in him is found the perfect object of love. There is perhaps here, as in every Platonic scheme of ascent from the sensible to the intelligible, not only a merging of the rational in the mystical at the highest level but a tendency at every stage to reject as lower, and as having served its only purpose, the very means by which the ascent was achieved. And this latter characteristic is certainly strongly marked in Spenser's poems.

An *Hymne in Honour of Love* moves primarily on the level of sensuous appeal, but recognizes its power to beget in the human heart aspiration and a motive of heroic action. The attitude, however, is purely pagan and, appropriately, it revives the ancient Greek myth of Love as the power which produced the world out of chaos and hence permeates the cosmos. *An Hymne in Honour of Beautie* revises this conception by referring rather to a creator who works according to a "goodly Paterne" preconceived, and this version, derived ultimately from the *Timaeus*, signalizes the presence of a more definitely Platonic note in the poem. *An Hymne of Heavenly Love* substitutes, and presents in much greater detail, the Hebrew-Christian account of the Creation, linking the Creation and man's redemption as dual manifestations of God's love, which alike demand our whole-hearted love in return: our love of God our Creator, of Christ our Redeemer, and of our brethren, like beings with ourselves, created and redeemed. These are the commonplaces of Christian doctrine, but by the poet vividly experienced. Though Spenser does not use the terms, the love of the first two *Hymnes* is plainly Eros, that of his third is less like Eros than Agape. And in this, the third *Hymne* marks less a progression than a new beginning, as Spenser is not slow to recognize.

> With all thy hart, with thy soule and mind,
> Thou must him love, and his behests embrace;
> All other loves, with which the world doth blind
> Weake fancies, and stirre up affections base,
> Thou must renounce, and utterly displace,
> And give thy selfe unto him full and free,
> That full and freely gave himselfe to thee.

In *An Hymne of Heavenly Beautie*, however, there is some return to the Platonic scale of ascent. The means vouchsafed is first to approach the Creator through his works, and thence to "Mount up aloft through heavenly contemplation" till one beholds Sapience herself, beloved of God from before the Crea-

tion. She is true Beauty, the heavenly counterpart of the Venus
of the first two *Hymnes*, and an object of love but one step below the highest. That highest is reached when one looks at last

> ... up to that Soveraine Light,
> From whose pure beams al perfect beauty springs,
> That kindleth love in every godly spright,
> Even the love of God, which loathing brings
> Of this vile world, and these gay seeming things;
> With whose sweete pleasures being so possest,
> Thy straying thoughts henceforth for ever rest.

The note is precisely that on which the *Cantos of Mutabilitie*
break off: rest and the end of change, even if change were
marked (as it seldom is) by steady and unimpeded ascent.

Whatever the degree of continuity between the two pairs of
*Hymnes*, there can be no doubt of the dependence of the second
pair on the long tradition of Christian mysticism, with its ascent,
through ordered meditation, to a vision of, and union with, the
divine. Such meditation took two principal forms: a meditation
on the love of God as revealed first in the Creation, and then
in the Incarnation, in Christ's earthly ministry and his redemption of fallen man, with the response of love which this love demands; and, secondly, a meditation on the power, wisdom, and
goodness of the Creator as revealed in the works of his hand:
commencing with the beauty of the earth and its creatures, and
ascending, through the starry heavens, the spiritual heavens, the
hierarchy of the angels, to a contemplation of the divine attributes and notably the divine wisdom which is the supreme
beauty, the source of all beauty, and the supreme object of our
love. Preparatory to either meditation were repentance and
purification; and here the experience of the Redcrosse Knight in
the House of Holiness is seen to take its place in the tradition:

with repentance followed by instruction, and ending in contemplation and a vision of the New Jerusalem. This tradition of meditation, ordered in its method though mystical in its end, had a long and complicated history. Adumbrated by Plato, developed in the *Confessions* of Saint Augustine and the *Mystical Theology* of the Pseudo-Dionysius, revived and systematized by Saint Bernard, Saint Bonaventure, and others, exemplified by Dante—it was handed on not alone to the Renaissance (where it received accessions of Christian Platonism) or to the Counter Reformation (with some accession of specifically Roman doctrine) but also to the Reformation, so that it is not at all surprising to find it prominent in Spenser, in other Protestant writers such as Nicholas Breton, and in the Anglican poets of the next century. It is in essence part of the general Christian inheritance, though, like much else, religious meditation ultimately takes on a variety of more or less distinctive forms or kinds of emphasis. For example, we shall find Protestantism concentrating on Christ's redemption of the chosen from an utterly fallen world, while natural religion meditates on nature and finds therein (as Wordsworth phrases it) "a Presence that disturbs me / With the joy of elevated thoughts," and to this natural supernaturalism Christianity replies by finding nature itself transfigured for the believer. But to return to Spenser.

We have said that *The Faerie Queene*, if completed, must have attempted some comprehensive synthesis of nature and grace. Perhaps on the crucial subject of beauty and love, the *Fowre Hymnes* give us the outline of such a synthesis. Certainly they leave us in no doubt that nature must be assimilated to grace, not grace to nature. But in the wide panorama of life and human experience presented by *The Faerie Queene* as we have it, and by Spenser's other poems, nature receives its full due.

There is in *The Faerie Queene* (after Book I) a frank recognition of how much in this world, beset with evils though it be, natural virtue may attain, but also a sense of its limits. In this very matter of love, one would have to co-ordinate with the *Fowre Hymnes* the natural virtue of Britomart, and her perfect union—perfect within its limits—with Artegall. One would also have to find a place, and a central one, for Spenser's own superb *Epithalamion*, from which all conflict seems to be banished, and for the famous Easter sonnet in the *Amoretti*:

> Most glorious Lord of lyfe, that on this day,
> Didst make thy triumph over death and sin:
> and having harrowed hell, didst bring away
> captivity thence captive us to win:
> This joyous day, deare Lord, with joy begin . . . ,

and so on, through the remembrance of Christ's redeeming blood, and his love which demands our love in return, to the dependent commandment to love others as ourselves, and the conclusion:

> So let us love, dear love, as love we ought,
> Love is the lesson that the Lord us taught.

Here too is a phrase of Spenser's experience, which, unlike the *Epithalamion*, turns on a dual reference to nature and grace; but neither is this, perhaps, a final synthesis. All that one can demonstrate with certainty is the range of the poet's experience, and of his recognition of values, and the large place held by religion therein. Indeed he challenges for poetry a religious function: the Hill of Contemplation from which the Redcrosse Knight attains his vision of the New Jerusalem is, we are told, like Sinai (the symbol of the Law), like the Mount of Olives (the symbol of the Gospel), and like Parnassus, which can only mean that poetry also can have its role in pointing on to the New Jerusalem when appearing in company (as here) with the Gospel of Christ.

The place of religion in Spenser's poetry and his dominantly Protestant outlook, which unites with his political sense and patriotic sentiment, can be illustrated by considering for a moment a secondary but still important meaning of Book I of The Faerie Queene. Spenser spoke of the whole poem as "coloured by an historical fiction"; and among the aspects of English history involved, one must recognize that Book I can be read as a history of the Protestant Reformation in England. This mode of interpretation has been, it is true, somewhat discredited by the attempts of scholars to find too many exact equivalents of particular characters and events, whereas it is clear that the historical, like the moral, allegory is general rather than particular, and moves along with it pari passu. The Redcrosse Knight (identified at last as Saint George) is the spirit of England; Una is not simply religious truth but (an identification easy to Spenser) Protestant truth. That the Knight takes service with her gives us the starting point of the allegory in the brief reign of Edward VI; their separation and his transfer of allegiance to Duessa (under the name of Fidessa), with the errors and disasters that ensue, signify the reversion to Roman Catholicism in the reign of Mary. The remarkable omission of all reference to the Marian martyrs must have been deliberate, as if Spenser would not needlessly reopen old wounds. The Knight's release by the grace of God from the keyless prison and his restoration to Una mean the reunion of England and Protestant truth at the accession of Elizabeth. The House of Holiness marks the repentance and renewed instruction which (from Spenser's militantly Protestant point of view) England must undergo for past error and sinful acquiescence; the encounter with Despair suggests the danger of

34

a national relapse into fruitless remorse and apathy, of which the evangelical emphasis on the forgiveness of sins and the Calvinistic assurance of election are the solvents. But Una's question "Why shouldst thou then despaire that chosen art?" has evidently a double meaning. For now, as the Redcrosse Knight goes forward to his task—the slaying of the dragon and the freeing of Una's parents—past history gives way to prophecy of the future: Una's parents are the Universal Church, held in thrall by the Dragon of Rome, which England must slay. In other words, the hope of Protestantism will be realized when England takes up her appointed mission—assumes leadership of the Protestant cause and marshals all its forces against the common enemy. This, I conceive, or something like it, is the purport of Book I when read as historical allegory. Here, plainly, Spenser propounds a parallel between the religious life of the nation and that of the individual; and Protestant religion and national patriotism join forces in his poetry, as they did in Elizabethan England.

But the higher reaches of both Spenser's poetry and his religion are met when he is moving on less controversial ground, and fastening on the great truths of the Christian tradition, as they prove themselves in his own experience. Thus, for example, after his striking picture of the angel standing guard over the sleeping Guyon, he exclaims, elaborating of course on the question "What is man that thou art mindful of him?":

> And is there care in heaven? and is there love
> In heavenly spirits for these creatures bace,
> That may compassion of their evils move?
> There is: else much more wretched were the cace
> Of men, then beasts. But O th' exceeding grace
> Of highest God, that loves his creatures so,

And all his workes with mercy doth embrace,
That blessed Angels, he sends to and fro,
To serve to wicked man, to serve his wicked foe.

This is Spenser at his simplest and plainest, but writing with an eloquence that comes from, and speaks to, the heart.

As Spenser was our inevitable choice among the Protestant poets of Elizabeth's day, so Robert Southwell best represents the poetry of the persecuted Roman Catholic minority. The Marian martyrs had been for the most part aged Protestant bishops and simple lay folk, and there was no poetry from that source; but the Romanists of the following reign included young men of gentle birth and nurture, of whom Southwell, but with an added portion of poetic talent and saintliness, is typical. As a poet he is of course far inferior to Spenser both in range and in achievement. Almost all his themes are religious, and he adheres throughout to his conviction:

It is the sweetest note that man can sing
When Grace in Virtue's key tunes Nature's string.

And even in religion, his range is not very wide. Nor is he, like Spenser, in any sense a philosophical poet. One of his favorite subjects is the Nativity, and in a series of poems on the events of Christ's life on earth his emphasis falls on the Saviour's childhood, confirming the assertion of another poem, A Child My Choice; it is perhaps not too fanciful to see in this a distant kinship with the later poets Vaughan and Traherne. He has verses on the Blessed Virgin and on Mary Magdalene, and his longest, though not his most successful poem, Saint Peter's Complaint, is a meditation on Peter's denial of the Lord, cast in the form of a monologue uttered by the saint himself. Southwell's religion is unmistakably of the "other-worldly" kind, with a strong vein of asceticism: nature and grace remain unreconciled, except insofar as poetry, which belongs to the natural order, can be turned to spiritual ends. Though he has two poems on the Eucharist, the Church and its sacramental system hold a smaller place in the verse of the Catholic poet, ready to give his life for that form of faith, than might be anticipated, hardly more indeed than in the Protestant Spenser and less than in a later Anglican like George Herbert; and there is at least one suggestion, in the words of Man to the Wound in Christ's Side, of an evangelical note which will be a recurrent feature of Anglican poetry, in poets as different as Herbert, Addison, Charles Wesley, Cowper, and John Keble. It would be a mistake, however, to overemphasize this fact, since there is here a broad meeting ground of Catholic and Protestant, through which the Anglican middle way inevitably passes.

Despite his very different circumstances, Southwell seems less remote from his Protestant contemporaries in poetic tradition and sensibility, and even in his religion, than one might expect. Educated from an early age at Douai, and proceeding thence to Rome, where he had to relearn his half-forgotten English tongue, he is still no alien. In his poetry, no doubt, he sometimes expresses his most solemn religious experiences in Italianate conceits. In such a stanza as the following, we encounter, perhaps for the first time in modern English, what Courthope calls "theological wit," the exploiting in poetry of the elements of paradox in the Christian faith. The subject is Christ's Nativity, and Southwell writes:

> Behold the father is his daughter's son,
>   The bird that built the nest is hatched therein,
> The old of years an hour hath not outrun,

> Eternal life to live doth now begin.
> The Word is dumb, the mirth of heaven doth weep,
> Might feeble is, and Force doth faintly creep.

In the next century we shall meet this theological wit again in Crashaw, a convert to Roman Catholicism and Italianate poetry. But Southwell has more than one style at his command. He can on occasion call up a vivid sense of natural, as well as of supernatural, objects, as in this desolate Alpine landscape:

> A Vale there is enwrapt with dreadful shades,
> Which thick of mourning pines shrouds from the sun,
> Where hanging cliffs yield short and dumpish glades,
> And snowy floods with broken streams do run.

Loud winds add their voice:

> And in the horror of this fearful choir
> Consists the music of this doleful place:
> All pleasant birds their tunes from thence retire,
> Where none but heavy notes have any grace.

It is bereft of human inhabitants, and

> Resort there is of none but pilgrim wights,
> That pass with trembling foot and panting heart.

Desolate and menacing, it is resonant of the Creator's power. All who view it must "remain aghast / Much at the work, more at the Maker's might." And this scene loses nothing of its reality when it is later revealed to us that it is all a symbol of the state of the penitent soul. Again, Southwell can approach the simple gnomic style of George Herbert:

> Shun delays, they breed remorse;
>     Take thy time while time doth serve thee;
> Creeping snails have weakest force,
>     Fly their fault lest thou repent thee.
> Good is best when soonest wrought;
> Lingered labours come to nought.

But a better example of the simple (but not gnomic) style is seen in the poem on Christ's wounded side, already mentioned:

> O pleasant port! O place of rest!
> O royal rift! O worthy wound!
> Come harbour me, a weary guest
> That in the world no ease have found!

Then, referring to the burden of his sins:

> Discharge me of this heavy load,
> That easier passage I may find,
> Within this bower to make abode
> And in this glorious tomb be shrined.
>
> Here must I live, here must I die,
> Here would I utter all my grief,
> Here would I all those pains descry,
> Which here did meet for my relief. . . .
>
> O happy soul that flies so high
> As to attain this sacred cave!
> Lord send me wings, that I may fly,
> And in this harbour quiet have!

Still better perhaps, Southwell's simpler style is illustrated in a poem on the Nativity, which elaborates one of the commonest paradoxes of theological wit and makes it the structural principle of the piece:

> Despise not him for lying there,
> First what he is enquire;
> An orient pearl is often found
> In depth of dirty mire.
>
> Weigh not his crib, his wooden dish,
> Nor beasts that by him feed;
> Weigh not his mother's poor attire,
> Nor Joseph's simple weed.

This stable is a Prince's court,
　　This crib his chair of State;
The beasts are parcel of his pomp,
　　The wooden dish his plate. . . .

With joy approach, O Christian wight:
　　Do homage to thy King;
And highly prize his humble pomp
　　Which he from heaven doth bring.

In *The Burning Babe*, Southwell's most famous poem, which is also the most moving, the basic simplicity is made to carry, without sinking under it, a wealth of vivid and daring imagery:

As I in hoary winter's night stood shivering in the snow,
Surprised I was with sudden heat which made my heart to glow;
And lifting up a fearful eye to view what fire was near,
A pretty Babe all burning bright did in the air appear;
Who, scorchèd with excessive heat, such floods of tears did shed,
As though his floods would quench his flames, which with his tears
　　were fed.
Alas! quoth he, but newly born, in fiery heats I fry,
Yet none approach to warm their hearts or feel my fire but I!
My faultless breast the furnace is, the fuel wounding thorns,
Love is the fire, and sighs the smoke, the ashes shame and scorns;
The fuel Justice layeth on, and Mercy blows the coals,
The metal in this furnace wrought are men's defilèd souls,
For which, as now on fire I am, to work them to their good,
So will I melt into a bath to wash them in my blood.
With this he vanished out of sight and swiftly shrunk away,
And straight I callèd unto mind that it was Christmas day.

I have preferred to concentrate on Spenser and Southwell rather than to illustrate Elizabethan religious verse more widely, but at a lower level of both religion and poetry. The two poets represent sufficiently the difference between the Protestant and Catholic currents in thought, feeling, and expression, while at the same time warning us not to make too absolute a dichotomy. (We speak of Spenser as predominantly Protestant, because though the Elizabethan Settlement set the stage for a distinctively Anglican poetry, this had not yet been at all fully achieved.) The two poets chosen illustrate, further, the range of religious poetry: from the philosophical, on the one hand, where religion takes its central place in a complex of perceptions and values, to the simpler, more purely experiential response, on the other, where every secular idea is banished and religion remains as the only value and motive recognized.

Such rigorous selection must not be allowed to create a false impression. The mere bulk of Elizabethan religious verse is not inconsiderable. In general we may say, however, that the dominant outlook in Elizabethan poetry, and (Spenser and Southwell apart) its best products were secular, not religious, in spirit. The golden age of English religious poetry is the seventeenth century. It is significant that the *Oxford Book of Christian Verse*, which gives only twenty-five pages to the Elizabethans, devotes well over two hundred to the seventeenth century, and might have done more, had not its editor, Lord David Cecil, decided that Milton was a great but not a Christian poet!

# ✧ III ✧

## THE SEVENTEENTH CENTURY
## DONNE AND HIS SUCCESSORS

Tʜᴇ ꜱᴇᴠᴇɴᴛᴇᴇɴᴛʜ ᴄᴇɴᴛᴜʀʏ would still be the golden age of English religious verse, even if it did not include the great, and in some ways isolated, figure of Milton. Such sudden flowerings can never be wholly accounted for. History cannot assemble all the facts or establish exhaustively their relation to the event. All it can do is to take soundings, and to recognize that whatever is true in other areas, in poetry at least everything depends at last on the existence of individual genius. If Donne had become one of the pseudo-martyrs he derided, or if he had pursued his long-held worldly course; if George Herbert had died before those last years at Bemerton; if Crashaw had not read George Herbert's *The Temple* or, alternatively, had not been drawn, in spite of it, to Rome; if Vaughan had fallen on the field of battle, and Traherne's work had been permanently lost—if all these things had happened, where would the golden age have been? They did not happen. And we may ask ourselves the less unprofitable question: what were the conditions in English religion and English poetry that provided the soil in which their religious poetry could grow?

First, then, the state of religion. Since four of the five poets I have named were convinced Anglicans, while only one was a convert to Rome, balancing Donne's conversion from Rome, and since none of them showed any sign of the leaven of Puritanism, we should at this point look to the state of the Church. In the seventeenth century the Church of England was in the process of finding its center of gravity or (to vary the metaphor) was discovering the potentialities of the *via media*. The middle way had been established by law in the Elizabethan Settlement, and its basic philosophy had been luminously expounded by Hooker; but it had not succeeded in welding its Catholic and Protestant elements into a distinctive and harmonious whole. While the more militant form of Protestantism was frowned on and curbed by the queen, Elizabethan Anglicanism was strongly Protestant in character, so that one thinks of Spenser, for all his medieval inheritance, and for all his loyalty to Elizabeth and her Settlement, as predominantly a Protestant poet. One does not so think of Donne, Herbert, and Vaughan: they are distinctively Anglican in outlook.

To say that the process of adjustment in the seventeenth century entailed a new emphasis on the Catholic inheritance is true, and significant, to a point. It was this aspect of Laud's policy which most impressed and exasperated the Puritans and, ever after, those who would emphasize the Catholic character of the Church (as, for example, did the Tractarians) would look back to the seventeenth century for their authority. But the new emphasis on Catholic doctrine in that century was, in a larger view, part—and a necessary part—of the shaping of the *via media*, and was compatible with strong opposition to Rome, as Laud himself (despite Puritan libels) plainly demonstrates; and it was against the whole philosophy of the *via media*, not against this part of it only, that the Puritans rebelled.

It is ironic, though understandable, that the shaping of the distinctive Anglican position should have been the prelude to the temporary ruin of the Church. The blame may be divided between the stubborn recalcitrance of the Puritans and the stubborn political unwisdom of Laud. So powerful a force was religion in the seventeenth century that religion and politics could not be kept apart, and the combination was fraught with danger. But before Caroline politics, of which the ecclesiastical policy of Laud was a part, brought matters to a crisis, the Church had undergone a rich and varied development, of which its religious poetry was a fruit. None of the poets was politically minded (in the sense that the Puritan Milton, under the stress of events, was to become), though Donne no doubt could grasp and approve some of the political implications of the *via media*. What he and the others most valued was the rich and varied inheritance which it put at their disposal, and the protection and freedom— yes, freedom—which it offered for the individual's pursuit of the religious life. For tolerance is an essential attribute of the *via media*, as even Laud partly understood: if we can get behind his insistence on outward conformity, we find a liberal theologian, a patron of learning, and even an administrator who knew that belief, as distinct from outward action, could not be compelled. One of the surest testimonies to this aspect of the Anglican position is the richness and variety of the poetry which it permitted and nourished, in which we may include the verse of such markedly Protestant Anglicans as the Fletchers, and even (by a slight relaxation of our terms of reference) the early poetry of Milton, and notably, of course (by a relaxation of another sort), the prose of Sir Thomas Browne (who "took not his religion from Rome or Geneva"), of Jeremy Taylor, and of that "dear, fine, silly old angel" (as Lamb called him) Thomas Fuller.

44

Donne, we may believe, found in the Church of the middle way something that satisfied his free-ranging, inquiring mind, and perhaps valued it as anchor and safeguard for a turbulent spirit much prone to extremes. Herbert, we know, added to his other sources of attachment an aesthetic response to the *via media* with its ritual, simple, solemn, and purified, but ritual still.

> I joy, dear Mother, when I view
> Thy perfect lineaments, and hue
>   Both sweet and bright:
> Beauty in thee takes up her place,
> And dates her letters from thy face,
>   When she doth write. . . .

Then, after contrasting her "fine aspect in fit array, / Neither too mean, nor yet too gay" with the extremes of dress and undress in other churches:

> But, dearest Mother, what those miss,
> The mean thy praise and glory is
>   And long may be.
> Blessed be God whose love it was
> To double-moat thee with His grace,
>   And none but thee.

This in the days of the Church's prosperity. Had Herbert lived to see her plight twenty years later, he would have echoed the cry of the Church in Vaughan's poem, also with a memory of Herbert's called *The Brittish Church*.

> And while these here their mists and shadows hatch,
>   My glorious Head
> Doth on those hills of myrrh and incense watch.
>   Haste, haste, my dear!
>   The soldiers here
> Cast in their lots again,
>   The seamless coat
>   The Jews touch'd not,
> These dare divide, and stain.

The range of seventeenth-century literature as it bears on or takes its origin in religion is remarkable—the range in content and in style. There is no decline in vigor from the spacious days, and there is on the whole a notable increase in depth and sophistication. Periods, of course, have an awkward habit of overlapping; and in the first three decades of the new century, many writers who had commenced their careers under Elizabeth came to their full development—Bacon, Shakespeare, Jonson, Chapman, and Donne himself, to mention only a few. I will select three examples in religious poetry to which we shall not have occasion to revert.

John Davies of Hereford was a moderate Roman Catholic living peaceably enough under Elizabeth and in the increasing toleration of James's reign. He was at best a minor poet, but at that best could use the sonnet with fine effect and with an interesting extension in typology to a personal religious experience.

> As in the sacrifices of the Law
> There was an Altar, Priest, Host, Fire, and Wood:
> So this to that in likeness near doth draw,
> And wants but Holy Fire to make it good.
> The Altar is my Hope; the Host my Heart;
> The Priest my Faith; my Love the Fuel is:
> All these, O Lord, are ready, but the art
> To fire the Fuel wants: then do thou this!
> I am but passive in this holy Act,
> Thou the sole Agent: yet O make me fit
> To work with thee together in this Fact
> With all the forces of my Will and Wit!
> And sith, dear Lord, all things so ready be,
> Give Fire to sacrifice my Heart to thee.

The Anglican Sir Henry Wotton, the perfection of much that was best in the later phases of the Renaissance in England, starts with the commonplaces of natural religion, with the world as

46

evidence of God's power and glory, and man a little world in himself, but finds in this view of man less a foundation on which to build than an incentive to turn simply and wholly to Christ.

> Eternal Mover, whose diffusèd glory,
> To show our grovelling reason what Thou art,
> Unfolds itself in clouds of nature's story,
> Where man, thy proudest creature, acts his part;
> Whom yet, alas, I know not why we call
> The world's contracted sum, the little all;

For

> Are not brute beasts as strong, and birds as gay,—
> Trees longer lived, and creeping things as wise?
> Only our souls were left an inward light
> To feel our weakness and confess Thy might. . . .
>
> Let these poor notes ascend unto Thy throne,
> Where majesty doth sit with mercy crown'd,
> Where my Redeemer lives, in Whom alone
> The errors of my wandering life are drown'd:
> Where all the choir of Heaven resound the same,
> That only Thine, Thine is the saving Name. . . .
>
> Now have I done; now are my thoughts at peace;
> And now my joys are stronger than my grief:
> I feel those comforts, that shall never cease,
> Future in hope, but present in belief;
> Thy words are true, Thy promises are just,
> And Thou wilt find Thy dearly-bought in dust!

Fulke Greville was uncompromisingly Protestant, and also a figure of greater weight. No one can doubt the depth and intensity of a religious experience grounded in the philosophy of religion and life strongly colored by stern Calvinist theology.

> Thy power and mercy never comprehended,
> Rest lively imag'd in my conscience wounded;
> Mercy to grace, and power to fear extended,
> Both infinite, and I in both confounded;
>     "Lord I have sinn'd, and mine iniquity,
>         Deserves this hell; yet Lord deliver me."

47

> If from this depth of sin, this hellish grave,
> And fatal absence from my Saviour's glory,
> I could implore His mercy Who can save,
> And for my sins, not pains of sin, be sorry:
> Lord, from this horror of iniquity,
> And hellish grave, Thou wouldst deliver me.

The solemnity of the utterance raises the plain style to dignity, and the character of the experience gives it tension. We recognize in Greville (as we hardly do in Davies or Wotton) the tone of the new century.

In the seventeenth century there was much that was new and revolutionary in thought—it was the century of Bacon, Descartes, and Hobbes, and of the beginnings of Deism with George Herbert's older brother, Lord Herbert of Cherbury—but so far as religious poetry was concerned, the general effects were delayed and their consideration may be postponed. Donne complained that the new philosophy brought all in doubt. But it did not shake Donne's own firm religious convictions. Certainly the tensions in the religious poetry of the period spring from no visitings of doubt about God as Creator, Sovereign, and Saviour, but only (as in the example quoted from Greville) from the age-old doubt regarding the state and fate of the Christian's own soul. Despite the increased sophistication of seventeenth-century thought and literature, and despite the new and disruptive forces already receiving abstract formulation, there is room still for a quite simple and literal faith.

It is customary to think of the more significant seventeenth-century poets as falling under the influence of Donne or of Jonson, or sometimes (different as the two models are) of them both. One encounters also of course some lingering followers of Spenser. These last are not very important in themselves or for religious verse, save as we recognize in the young Milton a

Spenserian strain. The characteristic Spenserians are the Fletchers, with whom religious verse can rise no higher than Giles
Fletcher's florid *Christ's Victory and Triumph*, in which Scriptural poetry forsakes its usually rather dismal plainness—but
with scarcely more happy results. Nor did the school of Jonson
make much contribution to religious poetry. It was predominantly secular in spirit: Jonson's own heavily emphasized ethic
was humanistic rather than religious, and his more lighthearted
disciples, such as Herrick, tended to shed even the ethic.

Herrick indeed wrote his self-styled *Noble Numbers or, His
Pious Pieces*, but they fall in general far below his *Hesperides*.
They are at their best when Herrick is most himself and exhibits
a very mundane kind of piety, as in the familiar *A Thanksgiving
to God*.

> Lord thou hath given me a cell
>   Wherein to dwell;
> A little house, whose humble Roof
>   Is weather-proof;
> Under the sparres of which I lie
>   Both soft, and drie;
> Where thou my chamber for to ward
>   Hast set a Guard
> Of harmlesse thoughts, to watch and keep
>   Me, while I sleep.

Then, after a catalogue of many other creature comforts:

> All these, and better Thou dost send
>   Me, to this end,
> That I should render, for my part,
>   A thankful heart;
> Which, fir'd with incense, I resigne,
>   As wholly Thine;
> But the acceptance, that must be,
>   My Christ, by Thee.

When, on rare occasions, Herrick attempts a higher strain, as in *Good Friday: Rex Tragicus*, where the Crucifixion is presented as tragic drama, the Cross its stage, and Christ its Roscius, the effect seems somewhat forced and hollow. Perhaps the closest Herrick comes to genuine religious poetry is in such lines as

> I'le come, I'le creep, (though thou dost threat)
> Humbly unto Thy Mercy-seat:
> When I am there, this then I'le do,
> Give Thee a Dart and Dagger too;
> Next, when I have my faults confest,
> Naked I'le shew a sighing brest;
> Which if that can't Thy pitie wooe,
> Then let Thy Justice do the rest,
>     And strike it through.

In other hands the Jonsonian or plain style can achieve higher effects, as in this Christmas poem by young Sidney Godolphin, who fell on the field of battle fighting for Church and king.

> Lord when the wise men came from far
> Led to thy cradle by a star,
> Then did the shepherds too rejoice,
> Instructed by thy angel's voice,
> Blest were the wisemen in their skill,
> And shepherds in their harmless will.
>
> Wisemen in tracing nature's laws
> Ascend unto the highest cause,
> Shepherds with humble fearfulness
> Walk safely, though their light be less:
> Though wisemen better know the way,
> It seems no honest heart can stray.
>
> There is no merit in the wise
> But love, (the shepherd's sacrifice).
> Wisemen, all ways of knowledge past,
> To th' shepherds' wonder come at last;
> To know, can only wonder breed,
> And not to know, is wonder's seed.

A wiseman at the altar bows
And offers up his studied vows
And is received; may not the tears,
Which spring too from a shepherd's fears,
And sighs upon his frailty spent,
Though not distinct, be eloquent?

'Tis true, the object sanctifies
All passions which within us rise,
But since no creature comprehends
The cause of causes, end of ends,
He who himself vouchsafes to know
Best pleases his creator so.

When then our sorrows we apply
To our own wants and poverty,
When we look up in all distress
And our own misery confess,
Sending both thanks and prayers above,
Then though we do not know, we love.

It is not fanciful, I think, to see in the comprehensiveness, the
humility, and the very calm of such a poem a spiritual reflection
of the *via media*.

It is tempting not only to look back at Southwell's Christmas
pieces but also to place beside Godolphin's, for comparison, two
poems of his own century, in different styles, and illustrating
other kinds of religious and poetic sensibility. Inevitably one
thinks of *On the Morning of Christ's Nativity*. More than one
might at first glance suppose, its motive is also love; for Milton
called it his "birthday gift for Christ" and in the prelude to the
hymn he introduces an image which records this motive of love
and makes it the seal at once of his dedication and inspiration.

See how from far upon the Eastern road
The star-led Wizards haste with odours sweet:
O run, prevent them with thy humble ode,
And lay it lowly at his blessed feet;

> Have thou the honour first thy Lord to greet,
> And join thy voice unto the Angel Quire,
> From out his secret Altar touched with hallowed fire.

The image is from Isaiah, where the prophet is so touched by a seraph; in Christian symbolism, as Milton well knew, the seraphim stand for love of God. But when this is granted, the poem departs widely from Godolphin's. The intellectual humility of the latter is foreign to Milton; his is a learned poem, and for him religious experience issues less in an attitude than in an idea. Here the idea is that at the coming of Christ the pagan deities are put to flight: truth and purity banish falsehood and corruption.

> Peor and Baalim
> Forsake their temples dim,
> With that twice-battered god of Palestine;
> And moonéd Ashtaroth,
> Heaven's Queen and Mother both,
> Now sits not girt with tapers' holy shine;
> The Libyc Hammon shrinks his horn,
> In vain the Tyrean maids their wounded Thammuz mourn.

Then, after dealing faithfully with the "brutish gods of Nile,"

> Nor all the gods beside
> Longer dare abide,
> Not Typhon huge ending in snaky twine.
> Our Babe, to shew his Godhead true,
> Can in his swaddling bands control the damned crew—

and we realize that he is remembering his Pindar, and saying to us, Christ is our Hercules, as he has already called Christ Pan, the shepherds' god. Before he comes to the banishment of the pagan gods, Milton has sung of the angels' song, and reverting to a favorite image, Pythagorean and Platonic in origin, has called on the music of the spheres to "Make up full consort to the angelic symphony," and, further, has placed his poem in the tradition of Virgil's Messianic Eclogue by associating with the birth of a child the return of the golden age. All this is characteristic, and premonitory—as if Milton were trying over the notes to be sounded later when he becomes the one great Puritan poet, but a Christian humanist still.

Very different is the hymn with which the Roman Catholic Crashaw greets the *The Nativity*: there all is tenderness and that play of theological wit, that exploiting of paradox, already adumbrated in Southwell.

> We saw Thee in Thy balmy nest,
>     Young dawn of our eternal day!
> We saw thine eyes break from their East
>     And chase the trembling shades away.
> We saw thee, and we blest the sight,
> We saw thee, by thine own sweet light. . . .
>
> Welcome, all wonders in one sight!
>     Eternity shut in a span.
> Summer in winter; day in night.
>     Heaven in earth, and God in man.
> Great little one! whose all-embracing birth
> Lifts earth to heaven, stoops heav'n to earth. . . .
>
> Welcome, though not to those gay flies,
>     Gilded i' th' beams of earthly kings;
> Slippery souls in smiling eyes;
>     But to poor shepherds, homespun things:
> Whose wealth's their flock; whose wit, to be
>     Well read in their simplicity.
> Yet when young April's husband-show'rs
>     Shall bless the fruitful Maya's bed
> We'll bring the first-born of her flow'rs
>     To kiss thy feet and crown thy head.
> To thee, dread lamb! whose love must keep
>     The shepherds, more than they the sheep;
> To thee, meek majesty! soft king
>     Of simple graces and sweet loves.

Each of us his lamb will bring
Each his pair of silver doves;
Till burnt at last in fire of thy fair eyes,
Our selves become our own best sacrifice.

Though theological wit is peculiarly the province of Crashaw, and the combined note of tenderness and almost mystical fervor is his own, we recognize here a member of the school of Donne: the school which (apart from Milton) made, as we have already hinted, by far the greatest contribution to religious poetry in the seventeenth century—here is one of the celebrated Metaphysicals.

We can hardly escape, I suppose, saying a word about this term. It was fastened on the group of poets by Dr. Johnson, though anticipated by Dryden, and even (in a long-unpublished letter) by William Drummond of Hawthornden, who complains that "some men of late, transformers of everything [have] consulted upon [poetry's] reformation, and endeavoured to abstract her to metaphysical ideas and scholastic quiddities." Johnson quite rightly finds the essence of their wit in "a kind of *discordia concors*, a combination of dissimilar images or discovery of occult resemblances in things apparently dissimilar." Two of his other judgments have been left to the sometimes excessive admiration of our own century to correct. First, that, abandoning altogether the idea of poetry as an imitative (that is, a representational) art, they did not even depict the inward "operations of the intellect." (In fact, the direct reverse is true: one is repeatedly startled by the vividness of physical representation, and for the mental, one is even inclined to think that "psychological" would be a more adequate term than "metaphysical" to describe them.) And so with Johnson's second complaint, that, given over wholly to intellectual ingenuity and its surprises,

54

these poets "were not successful in representing or moving the affections" (a misconception corrected by T. S. Eliot's insistence on their astonishing success in uniting thought and feeling, which can be easily accepted even by those who have some misgivings about his dogma of "unified sensibility").

This brief comment on the term "metaphysical" is designed as much to clear the ground as to be of direct service in what I have to say about the religious poetry of the century. Dryden's glancing allusion, it is worth remembering, refers only to Donne's love poetry, and almost without exception Johnson's examples (with as many from Cowley as from Donne) come from their secular verse. Metaphysical imagery, so called, still figures to a considerable degree in Donne's religious poetry, and in a reduced and modified form in George Herbert's; it is even, on occasion, pushed to an extremity in Crashaw's; in Vaughan's (when present at all) it coalesces with his occultism; while in Traherne's it virtually disappears. Again, the content of metaphor and simile differs much from poet to poet. It is principally Donne who would come under Drummond's censure for introducing "metaphysical ideas and scholastic quiddities," while George Herbert and, in their different ways, the others achieve whatever effect of *discordia concors* they attempt by simpler comparisons. In other words, the importance of Metaphysical imagery as a single uniform element in religious poetry can be easily exaggerated, and will be unless we remember that each of the poets has his individual style, responding indeed to the subject on which he is writing, but corresponding to his own religious and aesthetic sensibility and experience.

There is room for a fuller study of Donne's religious experience than has yet been attempted. Here we can do no more than remind ourselves of some of the facts of his outward and inward experiences, as testified in his own writings, and set aside the problem of their precise relation and the part each played in the patent transformation of his life and poetry which was their final outcome. His earliest interest in religion, as seen in his Satyre III, is primarily intellectual and turns in large part on the question where true authority in religion lies, as is natural enough if Donne has not yet determined between his family's Roman Catholicism and the Anglicanism which his worldly ambitions made almost imperative. For the time being he is equally critical, indeed contemptuous, of those who too easily accept Rome, Geneva, or the Establishment, of everything indeed save the quest for truth.

> . . . doubt wisely; in strange way
> To stand inquiring right, is not to stray;
> To sleepe or runne wrong, is. On a huge hill,
> Cragged and steep, Truth stands, and hee that will
> Reach her, about must, and about must goe;
> And what the hills suddennes resists, winne so.

That Donne at last satisfied himself upon this issue, and accepted with full intellectual conviction the Anglican position, admits of no doubt: he became a loyal son of the Church of England long before he was fitted to become one of her ornaments. Markedly different in temperament from the gentle, judicious Hooker, he is still a churchman after Hooker's pattern, but with an added note of spiritual fervor which is his own. He insists on an underlying unity in the diversity of the contemporary Christian Church. The one essential is faith in Christ and in salvation through Christ; and whatever church preserves it Donne will not reject as a branch of the true Church—whether, like Rome, it erects on this foundation a superstructure that runs some danger of obscuring (though from no will to abandon) the foundation, or whether, like some reformed churches, it needlessly sacrifices things comely in themselves and of proved advantage to the Church's life and mission. He prefers the pure and effective order of the *via media* and could wish for reunion on its basis, but still he declares that the one foundation is Christ and salvation through Christ. Having found his haven, he did not cease to think about the true Church. There is no necessity to read doubt or dissatisfaction into the Holy Sonnet XVIII, "Show me, deare Christ, thy spouse, so bright and clear"; it should, surely, be understood in an ecumenical sense: the spouse is the true Church Universal, which must still be sought in and through Christ.

To the side of Donne's mind which welcomed the philosophy of the *via media*, his *Litany* (amid its deeper notes) bears testimony: repeatedly on different counts he prays to keep his position in the mean. Of the doctors, the great theologians, of the historic Church: "Lord, let us run / Meanways, and call them stars, but not the sun"; on an excess of other-worldliness: "From thinking us all soul, neglecting thus / Our mutual duties, Lord deliver us"; on a joyless asceticism (as also a thoughtless gaiety):

> From being anxious, or secure,
> Dead clods of sadnesse, or light squibs of mirth,
> From thinking, that great courts immure
> All, or no happinesse, or that this earth
> Is only for our prison fram'd . . .
>     or that they are maim'd
> From reaching this world's sweet, who seek thee thus,
> With all their might, good Lord deliver us;

and finally

> That our affections kill us not, nor die,
> Hear us weak echoes, O Thou Ear and Eye.

57

The mean of Aristotle, and of Anglicanism, appealed to Donne's intellect and to his practical sense, but also perhaps it was an attraction of opposites: here was a corrective for that impulse to extremity in thought and feeling which was natural to his daring, probing mind and strongly passionate nature.

To intellectual conviction, sufficient for acceptance of the English Church, was gradually added a depth of personal religion through faith in Christ. Its first beginnings Donne traces to his marriage (so disastrous in a worldly view), but the effect seems to have been produced slowly, and in the later phases a Platonic friendship with the Countess of Bedford played its part, to whom he addresses poems of high-flown idealized devotion. The final outcome of it all was a transformation of his life and poetry —first, the bringing of a proud and turbulent spirit to its knees, and then, the dedication of large intellectual, and larger emotional, resources to the service of God in poetry and in the Church. It is no necessary reproach that Donne, the converted sinner, like the saintly George Herbert after him, entered the ministry only when the hopes of worldly success were abandoned. Both were fully prepared for the sacred office, and Donne delayed till he felt that he could assume it with benefit to the Church and not disgrace. Their ministries are the best vindication of their genuine calling. Donne's exercise of his is written in the great sermons, and its dependence on his own spiritual life is plain from the *Devotions upon Emergent Occasions* and the Divine Poems, while we have his own testimony that his ministering to others cleared and fortified his personal faith.

For a full account of Donne's religion one would have to examine not the Divine Poems only but the sermons, in which he ranges over a vast area of human and Christian experience. Highly as Donne valued the liturgy and the sacraments, he put

preaching, which has been called the new sacrament of Protestantism, on a parity with them. "There is no salvation but by
faith," he declares,

nor faith but by hearing, nor hearing but by preaching; and they
that think meanliest of the Keys of the Church and speak faintliest
of the Absolution of the Church, will yet allow that those keys lock
and unlock in preaching, that absolution is conferred or withheld in
preaching, that the proposing of the promises of the Gospel in
preaching is that binding and loosing on earth which binds and
looses in heaven.

For, as he says in another sermon,

Let no man think that God has given him so much ease here, as to
save him by believing he knoweth not what or why. Knowledge cannot save us, but we cannot be saved without knowledge; faith is not
on this side knowledge, but beyond it. We must necessarily come to
knowledge first, though we must not stay at it. . . . For a regenerate
Christian, being a new creature, hath also a new faculty of reason,
and so believeth the mysteries of religion out of another reason than
as a mere natural man he believed natural and moral things: he
believeth them for their own sake by faith, though he take knowledge of them before by that common reason, and by those human
arguments, which work upon other men in natural or moral things.

By Donne, the intellectual, knowledge is always to be valued,
reason never to be despised. For, as he says in his *Elegie upon
. . . Prince Henry*, "reason, put to' her best extension, / Almost
meetes faith and makes both centres one." But if in the sermons
Donne gives the reason of the faith that is in him, he also draws
on the depth (not breadth) of his own religious experience: his
sense of sin, his repentance, but also his relapses, his depression
of spirit, his recurrent doubts and fears, and at last in spite of
everything his assurance of salvation in Christ; and it is on these
personal experiences that the Divine Poems dwell.

The chronology of Donne's poems is beset with difficulties,

but two things seem clear: that there is a transitional phase in his poetry in which religion appears coupled with, and sometimes overshadowed by, Platonic idealism (as in the poems to the Countess of Bedford and in the *Anniversaries* in memory of Elizabeth Drury), but that accompanying these, and long before his taking orders, the more purely religious poetry begins. An early example is *The Crosse*, in which Donne expresses his devotion to the symbol (one of the aids to devotion which the *via media* allowed him to retain from earlier days), but goes on:

> Material crosses then, good physic be,
> But yet spiritual have chief dignity.

And these latter he enumerates, with three remarks that seem specially significant, as glancing at his own weaknesses: the danger that "self-despising" may "get self-love," with spiritual pride issuing from humility—"therefore cross / Your joy in crosses"; the danger attendant on all departures from the mean, even in religious meditation: "Cross those dejections, when it [the heart] downward tends, / And when it to forbidden heights pretends"; and, finally, the danger inherent in Donne's own mode of expression and his delight in its ingenuity:

> So when thy brain works, ere thou utter it
> Cross and correct concupiscence of wit—

a thought echoed in his *Litany:* "When we are mov'd to seem religious / Only to vent wit, Lord deliver us."

We are carried deeper into Donne's religious experience by his first series of Divine Poems, *La Corona*, the crown woven of meditations on Christ's earthly course, with the last line of each sonnet repeated as the first line of the next, and with the first line of the first sonnet, "Deign at my hands this crown of prayer and praise," repeated as the last line of the final sonnet, on the Ascension, thus completing the circle:

> O strong Ramme, which hath batter'd heaven for mee,
> Mild Lambe, which with thy blood, hast mark'd the path;
> Bright Torch, which shin'st that I the way may see,
> Oh, with thine own blood quench thine own just wrath,
> And if thy Holy Spirit, my Muse did raise,
> *Deign at my hands this crown of prayer and praise.*

The desire to center his life in Christ is emphatic in his later verse, and with it a sense of his own unworthiness and utter dependence. Forced to journey on Good Friday, and riding westward, he reflects on the anomaly, only to conclude:

> O Saviour, as thou hang'st upon the tree,
> I turne my backe to thee, but to receive
> Corrections, till thy mercies bid thee leave.
> O think me worth thine anger, punish mee,
> Burne off my rusts, and my deformity,
> Restore thine Image, so much by thy grace,
> That thou may'st know mee, and I'll turne my face.

So, in the first of the Holy Sonnets:

> I runne to death, and death meets me as fast,
> And all my pleasures are like yesterday;
> I dare not move my dimme eyes any way,
> Despaire behind, and death before doth cast
> Such terrour, and my feeble flesh doth waste
> By sinne in it, which it t'wards hell doth weigh;
> Onely thou art above, and when t'wards thee
> By thy leave I can looke, I rise againe;
> But our old subtle foe so tempteth me,
> That not one houre my self I can sustaine;
> Thy Grace may wing me to prevent his art,
> And then like Adamant draw mine iron heart.

"I runne to death": the phrase is significant of Donne's recurrent preoccupation with the subject up to and including the last of his sermons, *Death's Duel,* and that episode, hardly to be cleared of morbidity, of Donne's standing for his portrait in his shroud. Indeed one must face the fact of a strain of morbidity

61

in Donne's powerful imagination, which comes out strongly in his protracted image, in *Of the Progresse of the Soule—The Second Anniversary*, of the womb as a grave, and of life a passage from death to death. The terror of death, but also of life, is vividly before him, and the corruptions of the grave, but not of the grave alone, are presented with an effect almost physical. There is something of the medieval ascetic in the later Donne, and his *contemptus mundi* clothes itself in images of disgust. Extremity, and not the mean, seems to be the natural habitat of his mind. But the end of these meditations is always renewed faith in Christ. *Death's Duel* finishes with a consideration of Christ's last days as the perfect preparation for death, and his death as the perfect death: and there, says Donne, "we leave you in that blessed dependency, to hang upon him that hangs upon the Cross."

Among the most extreme expressions of the *contemptus mundi* are Donne's two *Anniversaries*, the *First Anniversary* dwelling on the decay of the world and all that it contains, the *Second Anniversary* on the progress of the soul. Their occasion was the death of a young girl, Elizabeth Drury, the daughter of Donne's patron, who is treated not only as an example of beauty, purity, and devotion but as the very Platonic idea of these qualities and the cause of their existence here on earth, so that her death means their removal and the leaving of life in this world, and the world itself, to their natural decay and corruption. There is a more precise condemnation than is sometimes recognized in Ben Jonson's comment that if *An Anatomie of the World—The First Anniversary* "had been written of the Virgin Mary, it had been something," for it has been shown that, at some points, Donne is actually echoing meditations on that subject, but with application not to the Mother of Christ but, with an extremity of hyperbole, to the young girl whose death he is commemorating. How far Donne's answer, "that he described the idea of a woman, and not as she was" (if correctly reported), is satisfactory, the reader must be left to decide. It will hardly alter our judgment that these are not in their essence religious poems, though they are poems in which Donne's religious feeling finds expression—and sometimes eloquent and moving expression. (But, indeed, eloquence and energy never fail him in the *tours de force* which are the two *Anniversaries*.) The energy, the eloquence, and their origin here in genuine religious feeling, can be illustrated by the famous lines on the approach of death:

> Thinke then, my soule, that Death is but a Groome,
> Which brings a Taper to the outward roome,
> Whence thou spiest first a little, glimmering light,
> And after brings it nearer to thy sight:
> For such approaches doth heaven make in death.
> Thinke thy selfe labouring now with broken breath,
> And thinke those broken and soft notes to bee
> Division, and thy happiest Harmonie.
> Thinke thee laid on thy death-bed, loose and slacke;
> And thinke that, but unbinding of a packe,
> To take one precious thing, thy soul from thence.
> Thinke thy selfe parch'd with fever's violence,
> Anger thine ague more, by calling it
> Thy Physicke; chide the slacknesse of the fit.
> Thinke that thou hear'st thy knell, and think no more,
> But that, as Bels call'd thee to Church before,
> So this, to the Triumphant Church, calls thee.
> Thinke Satans Sergeants round about thee bee,
> And thinke that but for Legacies they thrust;
> Give one thy Pride, t'another give thy Lust:
> Give them those sinnes which they gave thee before,
> And trust th' immaculate blood to wash thy score.
> Thinke thy friends weeping round, and thinke that they
> Weepe but because they goe not yet thy way.
> Thinke that they close thine eyes, and think in this,

That they confesse much in the world amisse,
Who dare not trust a dead mans eye with that,
Which they from God, and Angels cover not.
Thinke that they shroud thee up, and think from thence
They reinvest thee in white innocence. . . .
Thinke that they bury thee, and thinke that right
Laies thee to sleepe but a Saint Lucies night.
Thinke these things cheerefully. . . .

Indeed, all Donne's contemplations of chance and change, danger, death, decay, and corruption conclude, and find their resolution, in an act of faith in Christ. For danger, and departure from home and friends, hear him on setting out for Germany.

In what torne ship soever I embarke,
That ship shall be my embleme of thy Arke;
What sea soever swallow mee, that flood
Shall be to mee an embleme of thy blood;
Though thou with clouds of anger do disguise
Thy face; yet through that mask I know those eyes,
   Which, though they turn away sometimes,
     They never will despise.

I sacrifice this Iland unto thee,
And all whom I lov'd there, and who lov'd mee;
When I have put our seas 'twixt them and mee,
Put thou thy sea betwixt my sinnes and thee.
As the trees sap doth seek the root below
In winter, in my winter now I goe,
   Where none but the, th' Eternall root
     Of true Love I may know.

Nor thou nor thy religion dost controule,
The amorousnesse of a harmonious Soule,
But thou wouldst have that love thy selfe: As thou
Art jealous, Lord, so am I jealous now,
Thou lov'st not, till from loving more, thou free
My soul: Who ever gives, takes libertie.
   O, if thou car'st not whom I love
     Alas, thou lov'st not mee.

Seale then this bill of my Divorce to All,
On whom those fainter beames of love did fall;
Marry those loves, which in youth scatter'd bee
On Fame, Wit, Hopes (false mistresses) to thee.
Churches are best for Prayer, that have least light:
To see God only, I goe out of sight:
    And to 'scape stormy dayes, I chuse
    An Everlasting night.

As he makes ready for the final voyage from which no traveler returns, a sense of the multitude of past offenses afflicts him, and in imagination he re-presents them to God for his forgiveness, with the warning, "When thou hast done, thou has not done / For I have more." But in the last of the three brief stanzas, fear is confronted by an inward assurance drawn from the deaths of an essentially personal religious experience—and is vanquished.

I have a sin of fear, that when I've spun
My last thread, I shall perish on the shore;
But sweare by thy selfe, that at my death thy sonne
Shall shine as he shines now, and heretofore;
    And, having done that, Thou hast done,
    I feare no more.

And it is in this blessed assurance that, though motionless, he runs to death.

Since I am comming to that Holy roome,
    Where, with thy Quire of Saints for evermore,
I shall be made thy Musique; As I come
    I tune the Instrument here at the dore,
    And what I must doe then, thinke here before. . . .

I joy, that in these straits, I see my West;
    For, though theire currants yield return to none,
What shall my West hurt me? As West and East
    In all flatt maps (and I am one) are one,
    So death doth touch the Resurrection. . . .

We thinke that *Paradise* and *Calvarie*,
  *Christs* Crosse, and *Adams* tree, stood in one place;
Looke Lord, and finde both *Adams* met in me;
  As the first *Adams* sweat surrounds my face,
  May the last *Adams* blood my soul embrace.

So, in his purple wrapp'd receive me Lord,
  By these his thornes give me his other crowne;
And as to others soules I preach'd thy word,
  Be this my Text, my Sermon to mine owne,
  Therefore that he may raise the Lord throws down.

Donne's is a complex and passionate nature prone to extremities of thought, feeling, and imagination, and these receive full expression in his religious as in his secular verse. But the mark of his religious poems is that they end with the resolution of tension, which, if it is the outcome of his faith, is also the achievement of his poetry. For in such poetry the religious and the aesthetic experience unite and afford each other mutual support. It is the fashion to contrast Donne and Milton (and the differences are obvious and great), but I can think of no better phrase to describe what happens in the religious poetry of both of them than Milton's about a "new acquist of true experience," issuing in "Calm of Mind, all passion spent."

The contrasts in temper between Donne and his friend and poetic disciple George Herbert are apparent at a glance. Herbert has nothing of Donne's strong animal nature, a source of that abounding and sometimes self-perplexing energy that marks Donne's verse. It is perhaps a deficiency in such energy as much as anything else that prevent's Herbert's poetry from rising to sustained flights. In their marriages, the contrast is complete. Donne's runaway love match with Anne More wrecks his worldly prospects, fills his life with anxieties (which he comes to regard as concealed blessings), and is crucial in bringing order to his affections and in turning his thoughts to God: love has its role in leading him to the love of God. On the contrary, it is only after his long-delayed entry into holy orders that George Herbert is united with Jane Danvers, who (in Walton's phrase) was "so much of a platonic as to fall in love with Mr. Herbert unseen." They dwell, no doubt harmoniously, together for the few remaining years at Bemerton, with Herbert's three nieces as inmates of a household which, we imagine, reflects something of the monastic quiet and piety of Little Gidding; but there is no indication whatsoever of influence from Jane Danvers on Herbert's life or poetry.

In their entry into holy orders, the experiences of Donne and Herbert do, indeed, run more nearly parallel, but here too there are differences. Herbert was spared the intellectual problem of Donne's choice of a Church. He was born and brought up in the Church of England, found her *via media* wholly acceptable to his mind and temper, loved her beauty (as we have seen), and gave her the unreserved devotion of a naturally religious heart. If he held back from giving her also his active service in the ministry, it was from no reproach of conscience regarding his own life, no fear of bringing scandal upon her, but by clinging to the worldly but hardly culpable ambition natural to one of his family and standing—the ambition of making a figure in secular life; the world alone was the adversary, not, as with Donne, the world, the flesh, and the devil of doubt and cynicism. But we should not understimate the power of this adversary or the struggle that it cost George Herbert to subdue it. He has left us, in the poem *Affliction*, an epitome of that struggle, and of God's dealing with him to break his pride and draw him to himself. When from his deathbed Herbert sent the manuscript of *The Temple* to Ferrar of Little Gidding, it was (as Walton tells us) with these words: "Sir, I pray [you] deliver this little book to my dear brother Ferrar, and tell him he shall find in it a picture of the many spiritual conflicts that have passed betwixt God and my soul before I could subject mine to the will of Jesus, my Master, in whose service I have now found perfect freedom."

It is significant that we catch in this last phrase an echo from the Book of Common Prayer ("O God, whose service is perfect freedom"), and the significance deepens as we place beside it the best-known and best-loved, perhaps, of all George Herbert's poems:

I struck the board, and cry'd, No more.
                    I will abroad.
What? shall I ever sigh and pine?
My lines and life are free; free as the road,
Loose as the winde, as large as store.
                    Shall I be still in suit?
        Have I no harvest but a thorn
        To let me bloud, and not restore
What I have lost with cordial fruit?
                    Sure there was wine
        Before me sighs did drie it: there was corn
                    Before my tears did drown it.
        Is the yeare only lost to me?
                    Have I no bayes to crown it?
No flowers, no garlands gay? all blasted?
                    All wasted?
        Not so, my heart: but there is fruit,
                    And thou hast hands.
        Recover all thy sigh-blown age
On double pleasures: leave thy cold dispute
Of what is fit, and not. Forsake thy cage,
                    Thy rope of sands,
Which pettie thoughts have made, and made to thee
        Good cable, to enforce and draw,
                    And by thy law,
        While thou didst wink and wouldst not see.

Away; take heed:
I will abroad.
Call in thy deaths head there: tie up thy fears.
He that forbears
To suit and serve his need,
Deserves his load.
But as I rav'd and grew more fierce and wild
At every word,
Me thoughts I heard one calling, *Child!*
And I reply'd, *My Lord.*

This is the record of a genuine struggle between religion and the world, between a false liberty and a true; and if the victory is wrought in a single word, it is a word from God and for Herbert all-sufficient. The simple evangelical conception that he is God's, that Christ purchased him, recurs in other moods less intense than this in *The Collar*; for example, renunciation takes on in *The Quip* a note lighthearted and almost gay, till it deepens in the still unembarrassed affirmation of the final stanza.

The merrie world did on a day
With his train-bands and mates agree
To meet together, where I lay,
And all in sport to geere at me.

First, Beauty crept into a rose,
Which when I pluckt not, Sir, said she,
Tell me, I pray, whose hands are those?
*But Thou shalt answer, Lord, for me.*

Then Money came, and chinking still,
What tune is this, poore man? said he:
I heard in Musick you had skill:
*But Thou shalt answer, Lord, for me.*

Then came brave Glorie puffing by
In silks that whistled, who but he?
He scarce allow'd me half an eie.
*But Thou shalt answer, Lord, for me.*

Then came quick Wit and Conversation,
And he would needs a comfort be,
And, to be short, make an Oration.
*But Thou shalt answer, Lord, for me.*

Yet when the houre of thy designe
To answer these fine things shall come;
Speak not at large; say, I am thine:
And then they have their answer home.

Since we have no certain chronology of the poems, and their arrangement furnishes no consistent clue, it is impossible to trace in *The Temple* the course of the struggle "betwixt God and his soul" or to isolate the moment of victory, but only to detect, as they appear with different emphasis in different moods, the elements operative in both. Nor is it probable that the struggle or the fluctuations of mood ceased even in the years of his ministry at Bemerton, but rather that the grounds of the internal debate shifted: the world had lost its attraction, but the counterforce was not always operative or its presence immediately felt. This is the subject of many of the poems, and the poems are the means of re-creating or revivifying the intense religious experience.

My stock lies dead, and no increase
Doth my dull husbandrie improve:
O let thy graces without cease
        Drop from above! . . .

The dew doth ev'ry morning fall;
And shall the dew out-strip thy Dove?
The dew, for which grass cannot call,
        Drop from above.

Death is still working like a mole,
And digs my grave at each remove:
Let grace work too, and on my soul
        Drop from above.

Sinne is still hammering my heart
Unto a hardnesse, void of love:
Let suppling grace, to crosse his art,
    Drop from above.

O come! for thou dost know the way:
Or if to me thou wilt not move,
Remove me, where I need not say,
    Drop from above.

Or again:

How should I praise thee, Lord! how should my rymes
    Gladly engrave thy love in steel,
If what my soul doth feel sometimes,
    My soul might ever feel!

Although there were some forty heav'ns, or more,
    Sometimes I peere above them all;
Sometimes I hardly reach a score,
    Sometimes to hell I fall.

O rack me not to such a vast extent;
    Those distances belong to thee:
The world's too little for thy tent,
    A grave too big for me. . . .

Yet take thy way; for sure thy way is best:
    Stretch or contract me thy poor debter:
This is but tuning of my breast,
    To make the music better.

Whether I flie with angels, fall with dust,
    Thy hands made both, and I am there:
Thy power and love, my love and trust
    Make one place ev'ry where.

Like Donne, Herbert had as the background for his personal religious life the public duties of an active ministry; but in circumstances how different! Not for him the brilliant career of the great preacher at St. Paul's, at the court, and before the most challenging auditory of all at Lincoln's Inn, but instead the

humble duties of a country parish. To these the accomplished
scholar and courtier, who "knew the ways of learning" and the
pleasures and refinements of the great world, applied himself
with steady devotion, and set down as "a mark to shoot at" his
*Priest to the Temple, or the Country Parson His Character and
Rule of Holy Life*. His parson is to be the father of his flock,
their guide, philosopher, and friend: he is to be all things to all
men, and to preach and to exemplify (as we cannot fail to see)
the doctrine of the mean. He is to inculcate piety, but on the
way to this, prudence, virtue, and reverence; this is the whole
burden of *The Church Porch*, the long poem which introduces
*The Temple*; and he will not despise simple and homely teaching of the sort one finds in his own collection of proverbs, in
his gnomic verses, and indeed in the images from common life
that abound in his more personal poems. All this is implicit in
the well-known poem *Virtue*, turning, as it does, on the most
palpable images of transient beauty, the images usually associated with the *carpe diem* motif, but here more deeply felt and
directed to a simple moral issue, which (when it appears) takes
form in an image startling only in its simplicity.

> Sweet day, so cool, so calm, so bright,
> The bridall of the earth and skie:
> The dew shall weep thy fall to night;
>          For thou must die.
>
> Sweet rose, whose hue angrie and brave
> Bids the rash gazer wipe his eye:
> Thy root is ever in its grave,
>          And thou must die.
>
> Sweet spring, full of sweet dayes and roses,
> A box where sweets compacted lie;
> My musick shows ye have your closes,
>          And all must die.

Only a sweet and virtuous soul,
Like season'd timber, never gives;
But though the whole world turn to coal,
    Then chiefly lives.

But the ultimate ground and motive of all Herbert's utterance is religious, and central for him in the religious life is the Church whose priest he is. It is significant how often Herbert suggests in temper and attitude a later figure in Anglican history, John Keble. Though not systematically ordered, and much less closely and constantly related to the corporate life of the Church, The Temple, too, is a manual of devotion: it is the seventeenth century's Christian Year. Both are characteristic of the Anglican tradition, and not least in including a note of evangelical experience and piety, which was the quality that gave The Temple its appeal to the Puritan Richard Baxter, to John Wesley, and to William Cowper, as it was to give the Christian Year its vogue beyond, as well as within, the Anglican communion.

Among those on whom the effect of The Temple was immediate were two strongly contrasting poets, the Anglican layman Henry Vaughan and the convert to Roman Catholicism Richard Crashaw.

So little indeed has Crashaw's poetry or his religious sensibility in common with Herbert's that we should hardly have suspected any dependence upon The Temple were it not for his hyperbolical praise of the book and his naming of his own Steps to the Temple. The son of an ultra-Protestant scholar and divine, Crashaw came under the influence of Anglo-Catholic teaching at Cambridge, to which he responded with eagerness. He also became a frequent visitor at Little Gidding, where Herbert's friend Nicholas Ferrar lived with his family a life of semi-monastic order and seclusion, and it was perhaps by Ferrar that Crashaw was led to his admiration of The Temple. Until the time of the Civil War he lived contentedly enough within the Anglican fold, following such Catholic practices as it freely allowed. Some have suggested that, but for the Puritan ascendancy and the outbreak of the Civil War, he might have continued to do so to the end. But this seems doubtful; for if circumstances forced him into exile from Cambridge and sent him to join the court of Henrietta Maria at Paris, it was a deep temperamental attraction that drew him to Italy and the Roman Church. He seems to have felt no intellectual difficulty about the Church of England's position, or in quitting it: he simply hastened to what he felt to be his true home. Alone among English poets of his day, he had an affinity plainly with Continental Catholicism and the type of religious sentiment and poetic utterance fostered by the Counter Reformation. Others might draw to a limited extent on Catholic manuals of meditation, but there is no mistaking them for anything but English poets and formulators of the Anglican tradition.

The difference was at bottom one of temperament and personal endowment. In Crashaw we miss altogether the tough intellectuality of Donne and the strong animal nature. There is nothing in his secular verse that requires to be disciplined, brought under control, renounced, or repented: it is all idealized passion, and can be and is readily transferred to his religious poetry. There is no evidence of protracted inward struggle such as it cost George Herbert to renounce the world for God; nothing of the fluctuating sense of God's so ardently desired presence: nothing then of the attendant humility and hard-won assurance. Instead, there is an ardor of devotion to Christ, the Virgin, and, among the saints, to Mary Magdalene and the Spanish mystic Saint Teresa, expressed in poems fraught with sensuous and erotic imagery and marked by a constant play of

wit. These things appear at their best and most chastened in
*The Nativity* (already quoted in part); and at their most notori-
ously extravagant in *The Weeper*, on the tears of Saint Mary
Magdalene.

> Not in Evening's eyes
> When they red with weeping are
> For the Sun that dyes,
> Sits sorrow with a face so faire:
> No where but here did ever meete
> Sweetnesse so sadd, sadnesse so sweete.
>
> When Sorrow would be seene,
> In her brightest Majestie,
> (For she is a Queene)
> Then is she drest by none but thee.
> Then, and onley then, she weares
> Her proudest Pearls, I mean thy tears. . . .
>
> Well does the *May* that lyes
> Smiling in thy cheekes, confesse
> The *Aprill* in thine eyes;
> Mutuall sweetnesse they expresse:
> No *Aprill* e'er lent kinder showers,
> Nor *May* return'd more faithfull flowers. . . .
>
> But can these fair flouds bee
> Friends with the bosom fires that fill thee? . . .
> O floods, O fires, O suns, O showers!
> Mix'd and made friends by Love's sweet powers.
>
> 'Twas his well pointed dart
> That dig'd these wells, and drest this Vine,
> And taught that wounded heart,
> The way into these weeping Eyne.
> Vaine loves avant! Bold hands forbeare,
> The Lamb hath dipt his white foote here.
>
> And now where e're he strayes
> Among the Galilaean mountains,
> Or more unwelcome wayes,
> Hee's follow'd by two faithfull fountaines,
> Two walking baths, two weeping motions;
> Portable and compendious Oceans. . . .

And so on, in a riot of images, till at last the tears themselves speak and declare their destination.

> Much lesse meane we to trace,
> The fortune of inferior gems,
> Prefer'd to some proud face,
> Or perch't upon fear'd diadems:
> Crown'd heads are Toyes; We go to meete,
> A worthy object: Our Lord's Feet.

Still more characteristic of Crashaw's religious sensibility and his mode of utterance are his *Hymn to St. Teresa* and his poem *The Flaming Heart*, descriptive of the saint's picture with a seraph beside her; here (with more concentrated effect) the poet couples images of love, of wounding, and of death to suggest the ardor and ecstasy of her mystical experience and of his own response to it. Yet it would be unjust not to recognize in Crashaw the existence, on rare occasions, of a simpler and less florid note, as in the *Hymn for the Blessed Sacrament*:

> Lo, the full, final sacrifice,
> On which all figures fix'd their eyes;
> The ransom'd Isaac and his ram,
> The manna, and the Pascal Lamb!
> Jesu, Master just and true!
> Our Food and faithful Shepherd too!
> O by thyself vouchsafe to keep
> As with thyself thou feed'st thy sheep.
>
> O let that love which now makes thee
> Mix with our low mortality
> Lift our lean souls and set us up
> Convictors of thine own full cup,
> Coheirs with Saints: that so all may
> Drink the same wine and the same way;
> Nor change the pasture, but the place,
> To feed of thee in thine own face.

This reflects an experience much closer to the kind we meet in Herbert; and we may notice, further, that the idea and almost the very words are echoed by Henry Vaughan's poem *The Holy Communion*: "Become both food and shepherd to thy sheep." The dependence of Vaughan on Herbert is much closer than is Crashaw's. He credits Herbert with having by his "holy life and verse gained many pious converts," of whom, he says, "I am the least." There is no mistaking Vaughan's genuine piety or his devoted loyalty to the Church of England, now fallen on evil days. Much of the spirit of Herbert lives on in his poetry, and extends even to the prose; for it seems more than coincidence that Herbert translated a treatise on "Temperance and Sobriety," and Vaughan one on "Temperance and Patience"; and while the solitary devotions of the country layman, *The Mount of Olives*, find no parallel in Herbert's prose, many of them are associated with the Church and her services, and all are such as the Country Parson must have approved. But there are elements in Vaughan's experience and in his poetry that go beyond Herbert's. There is in him more of the mystic and much more of the poet of nature (though, like Herbert, he refuses to "rest in nature, not in nature's God"), and there is some element (how much has been debated) of Hermetic philosophy, which, like his twin brother Thomas (who was deeper in such studies), he seems to find quite compatible with his Christian and Anglican piety.

The rich variety of elements, appearing and reappearing in different contexts, makes it difficult to arrive at any general statement about Vaughan's religious and poetic experience. He has been regarded, on the one hand, as essentially the poet-recorder of religious experience, and, on the other (to put the matter a little too baldly), as simply the poet, and one whose wide knowledge of various traditions put at his disposal an abundant supply of images and of pseudo-statements with and around which to construct his poems. Faced with such an alternative, we can only remind ourselves that the relation of aesthetic to extra-aesthetic experience (be it religious or of any other kind) is not so simple as each of the two alternatives would seem in their different ways to assume; that where a poem takes its rise in some extra-aesthetic experience, it does not simply record the experience—it builds upon it, realizing a new experience attainable only through the poem itself; and, finally, that Vaughan states categorically the dependence of his poems on his religious experience.

> My God! thou that didst dye for me,
> These thy death's fruits I offer thee;
> Death that to me was life and light . . .
> Some drops of thy all-quickning blood
> Fell on my heart; those made it bud
> And put forth thus, though Lord, before
> The ground was curst and void of store. . . .

It is one thing to emphasize Vaughan's possession of a large body of knowledge and imagery available for poetry; quite another to assert, with a modern critic, that this only awaited an external stimulus to call it into creative action, and that the whole process was purely poetic and had nothing to do with religion. Such an assertion is not borne out by the poems: there is no reason to limit the stimulus to some external happening (often it is administered by some inward reflection on Scripture or some memory of past feeling), and no ground for separating the religious and the poetic motive. Always, whether at the starting point or emerging fully articulated as the poem proceeds, there is a clearly recognizable religious experience.

We may note in passing an objection, coming this time from

those who would concentrate on the religious to the depression of the poetic element: namely, that the religious experiences are fragmentary and fail to achieve finality of vision, expressing indeed yearning rather than attainment. This is in effect to limit religious experience to the ordered and controlled system of meditation prescribed by the manuals, whose influence on the Anglican poets can be detected (and has been perhaps exaggerated), but which does not supply the only criterion for judging their experience. It is also to ignore the nature and limits of the lyric, their poetic vehicle.

To express (that is, to realize) a vital inner experience Vaughan can draw (as occasion warrants) on a variety of traditions, but the foundation on which the experience rests is, almost without exception, some central Christian dogma or some recognized Christian attitude. Thus in his poem on *Christ's Nativity*, the experience is plainly grounded on the Incarnation, apprehended as fact, not metaphor. The little poem commences indeed as a hymn of rejoicing at the birth of the Redeemer, extends to involve the tradition of all nature's sharing in this joy and swelling the note of praise, is stayed by the poet's yearning that he might be as constant as God's lower creatures, descends into the contemplation of his own inconstancy and unworthiness, but rises once more in the final assurance that Christ can make him both worthy and constant by being born anew in his heart.

> Awake, glad heart! get up, and Sing,
> It is the Birth-day of thy King,
>     Awake! awake!
>     The Sun doth shake
> Light from his locks, and all the way
> Breathing Perfumes, doth spice the day.

Awak, awak! heark, how th' wood rings,
Winds whisper, and the busy springs
    A Consort make;
    Awake, awake!
Man is their high-priest, and should rise
To offer up the sacrifice.

I would I were some Bird, or Star,
Flutt'ring in woods, or lifted far
    Above this Inne
    And Rode of sin!
Then either Star, or Bird, should be
Shining, or singing still to thee.

I would I had in my best part
Fit Roomes for thee! or that my heart
    Were so clean as
    Thy manger was!
But I am all filth, and obscene,
Yet if thou wilt, thou canst make clean.

Sweet Jesu! will then; let no more
This Leper haunt, and soyl thy door!
    Cure him, Ease him
    O release him!
And let once more, by mystick birth
The Lord of life be borne in Earth.

The progression is from an external fact, the Incarnation, to a fact of inward experience, felt as equally real though only to be expressed in a time-honored metaphor, but it is the fact embodied in the metaphor that is important. This progression, then, is the essential experience which the poem realizes.

On the way from outward fact to inward experience, Vaughan invokes an idea which appeals strongly to him: the constancy of the whole Creation in its unconscious glorifying of God; and to the idea he recurs.

I would I were a stone or tree,
    Or flower by pedigree,

Or some poor highway herb, or spring
　　To flow, or bird to sing!
Then should I, tied to one sure state,
　　All day expect my date;
But I am sadly loose and stray,
　　A giddy blast each way;
　　O let me not thus range:
　　Thou canst not change.

It is an idea of course familiar to Vaughan in the *Benedicite omnia opera* ("All ye works of the Lord bless ye the Lord: praise him and magnify him for ever"). But it is not held with the same degree of commitment as are the two fundamental facts on which the poem turns: God's immutability and his own addiction to change; and in another context and mood, the yearning for constancy can take an entirely different, an other-worldly direction.

My Soul, there is a Countrie
　　Far beyond the stars,
Where stands a wingèd Centrie
　　All skilfull in the wars,
There above noise, and danger
　　Sweet peace sits crown'd with smiles,
And one born in a Manger
　　Commands the Beauteous files,
He is thy gracious friend,
　　And (O my soul awake!)
Did in pure love descend
　　To die here for thy sake,
If thou canst get but thither,
　　There grows the flower of peace,
The Rose that cannot wither,
　　Thy fortress, and thy ease;
Leave then thy foolish ranges;
　　For none can thee secure,
But one, who never changes,
　　Thy God, thy life, thy Cure.

The two attitudes can be easily reconciled under the dogma to which the poet is fully committed, "Thou canst not change," so that examples of constancy in a changing world are but reflections of the constancy of God and the heavenly order and are (precisely as Vaughan applies them) for our admonition.

To understand the poetry of Vaughan, as of the other poets of his school and age, it is necessary to recognize his whole-hearted commitment to the great dogmas of the Christian religion. On and around these the essential experiences realized in his poems turn. Only when we have apprehended this fact shall we be able to determine what is primary and what secondary in the poems themselves. Indeed, this is true of the reading of all poets who (in accordance with, or in defiance of, the current of their age) retain a firm hold on these dogmas. The gradual relaxing of that hold is a crucial fact of later history which has (as we shall see) momentous results for religious poetry. It also entails (as we no doubt already experience) the need for imaginative readjustment by the modern reader when confronted with the poetry we have been considering.

If we can achieve this adjustment, it is not in most instances very difficult to distinguish what is primary in the poet's experience and what is subsidiary, useful in its context, but not involving any final commitment. In one of his best-known poems, Vaughan reflects on the common farmyard sound of the crowing cock—Shakespeare's bird of dawning—and here indeed the starting point is an external happening.

> Father of lights! what Sunnie seed,
> What glance of day hast Thou confin'd
> Into this bird? To all the breed
> This busy Ray thou hast assign'd;
>     Their magnetisme works all night,
>     And dreams of Paradise and light.

Their eyes watch for the morning hue,
Their little grain expelling night,
So shines and sings, as if it knew
The path unto the house of light.
    It seems their candle, howe'r done,
      Was tinn'd and lighted at the sunne.

If such a tincture, such a touch,
So firm a longing can impowre
Shall thy own image think it much
To watch for thy appearing hour?
    If a mere blast so fill the sail,
      Shall not the breath of God prevail?

O thou immortall light and heat!
Whose hand so shines through all this frame,
That by the beauty of the seat,
We plainly see who made the same.
    Seeing thy seed abides in me,
      Dwell thou in it, and I in thee! . . .

Here—though by critics much has been made of the Hermetic imagery—it is evident that it involves no such commitment as does the single phrase "thy own image"; and in any case, it is Christian thought and feeling that control the whole experience. Again the dialogue of the Body and the Soul in *The Evening Watch* is a tender fantasy, but it is grounded in the full acceptance of the Resurrection.

### Body

Farewell! I goe to sleep; but when
The day-star springs, I'le wake agen.

### Soul

Goe, sleep in peace; and when thou lyest
Unnumber'd in thy dust, when all this frame
Is but one dramme, and what thou now descriest
    In sev'rall parts shall want a name,
Then may his peace be with thee, and each dust
Writ in his book, who ne'r betray'd mans trust!

*Body*

Amen! but hark, e'r we two stray,
How many hours do'st think 'till day?

*Soul*

Ah! go; th'art weak, and sleepie. Heav'n
Is a plain watch, and without figures winds
All ages up. Who drew this Circle even

He fils it; Dayes, and hours are *Blinds*.
Yet, this take with thee; The last gasp of time
Is thy first breath, and mans *eternall Prime*.

A good deal more difficult to determine is the exact status, in *The Retreate*, of Origen's doctrine of the pre-existence of the soul and Plato's theory of reminiscence (itself an extended metaphor).

Happy those early dayes! when I
Shin'd in my Angell-infancy.
Before I understood this place
Appointed for my second race,
Or taught my soul to fancy ought
But a white, Celestiall thought,
When yet I had not walkt above
A mile, or two, from my first love,
And looking back (at the short space,)
Could see a glimpse of his bright face;
When on some *gilded Cloud*, or flowre,
My gazing soul would dwell an houre,
And in those weaker glories spy
Some shadows of eternity;
Before I taught my tongue to wound
My Conscience with a sinful sound,
Or had the black art to dispense
A sev'rall sin to ev'ry sence,
But felt through all this fleshly dresse
Bright *shootes* of everlastingnesse.
O how I long to travell back
And tread again that ancient track!

That I might once more reach that plaine,
Where first I left my glorious traine,
From whence th' enlightened spirit sees
That shaded City of Palme trees;
But (ah!) my soul with too much stay
Is drunk, and staggers in the way.
Some men a forward motion love,
But I by backward steps would move,
And when this dust falls to the urn
In that state I came return.

Is this belief or merely an elaborate metaphoric embodiment of Vaughan's nostalgic craving for innocence? I do not know. Perhaps Vaughan himself did not. In any event, The Retreate is a link with seventeenth-century Platonism, and suggests some common ground with the religious sensibility of Thomas Traherne, whose voluminous Poems and prose Centuries of Meditation remained in manuscript till our own century.

As documents these are sufficiently remarkable. If we had no other knowledge of Traherne, we should hardly suspect them of being the work of a divine who gladly conformed to the Church of England at the Restoration, wrote a telling criticism of the Roman Church, and produced a valuable treatise on Christian Ethicks. The Poems seem more akin to the thought and temper of some Puritan mystic or even one of the sect of Quakers.

With the other poets, Traherne presents a striking contrast; and with Vaughan himself, there is more to contrast than to compare. Traherne never tires of dwelling on the happy innocence of childhood, which seems to depend not on what the soul of the child brings with it but simply on his own sentient life on what his innocent eyes behold in the world around him. He is another Adam, and the world his Eden. If Vaughan's Retreate seems in measure to anticipate Wordsworth's Intimations of Immortality, Traherne's poems, as they revert repeatedly to this condition, which was that of his own childhood, stand, despite the religious reference, a good deal closer to Wordsworth's early naturalism. That the condition of innocence was subsequently lost Traherne admits, but less through sin, original or actual, than through gradual succumbing to the world and its false values: the shades of the prison house close in, and here we are reminded of Wordsworth's ode. But neither of this gradual loss nor of the conversion which restored to the poet something of the lost state, is much account given: it is on the initial or the restored innocence that all the emphasis falls. We may recognize in the three stages some parallel to Christian experience, but hardly more than a parallel, since the dogmatic basis so evidently present in Vaughan's poems is here almost entirely lacking. Its absence is of course not in itself fatal. That the reminiscence of childhood innocence is for Traherne a genuine experience which helps to restore something like the lost state, we must believe. The deficiency lies elsewhere. It is that this experience is never more than fitfully united to a poetic experience of equal power: it is not that Traherne eschews metaphor and substitutes assertion for image (as he does), but that there is hardly a poem which does not run out into diffuseness or lapse into the prosaic. One is tempted to say that his best poem is the *Serious and Pathetical Contemplation of the Mercies of God*, in the tradition of the *Benedicite omnia opera*.

As with the Elizabethans, rigorous selection has here been necessary, the only disadvantage of which is that it conceals the extent and variety of religious writing, a disadvantage somewhat mitigated by our earlier soundings in the poetry of the period. Many names might be added: William Drummond, a substantial part of whose verse is on religious themes; Henry More, the

Cambridge Platonist, with disquisitions in Spenserian verse on the soul, including its pre-existence and its sleep between death and Resurrection; Joseph Beaumont, the Anglo-Catholic friend of Crashaw (who, however, did not accompany him to Rome), with *Psyche*, a long allegorical poem on the soul's pilgrimage, but also such religious lyrics as his *Morning Hymn* to Christ

> Shine, my only Day-Star, shine:
> So mine eyes shall wake by Thine;
> So the dreams I grope in now
> To clear visions all shall grow;
> So my day shall measured be
> By Thy Grace's clarity . . . [;]

Edward Benlowes, a convert from the Roman to the English Church, with his *Theophila*, another progress or ascent of the soul, whose structure follows closely the manuals of meditation; Francis Quarles (Anglican, but with something of Puritan severity), who added to Scriptural paraphrases such penitential verses as

> Thou art my God, by thee I fall or stand;
> Thy grace hath given me courage to withstand
> All tortures, but my conscience and thy hand.
>
> I know thy justice is thyself; I know,
> Just God, thy very self is mercy too;
> If not to thee, where, wither shall I go?
>
> Then work thy will; if passion bid me flee,
> My reason shall obey; my wings shall be
> Stretch'd out no further than from thee to thee[;]

and the more Puritan George Wither, whose reliance on inspiration rather than art seems to have been on the whole ill founded. These in addition to other writers who on occasion composed religious verses—but whom we must pass over in silence.

Finally, there is one name, more famous in its day than any

we have mentioned, which cannot be so lightly dismissed. Abraham Cowley assembled in his own person many of the leading interests of his age, literary, philosophic, religious, and even (though this was not his talent) political. Later it will be necessary to mention his interest in science, in its patron Bacon, and its offspring, the Royal Society, whose first historian, Bishop Sprat, was also Cowley's first biographer, while his closest friend was William Harvey. Nor did his interests stop there, but extended to the philosophy of Thomas Hobbes. Cowley was withal devoutly religious, and a son of the national Church, who served Henrietta Maria in exile, but, unlike his friend Crashaw, did not forsake his Anglican principles. It was with sincerely religious intent that he undertook his Biblical epic the *Davideis*. In the open invocation he addresses the Saviour:

> Thou, who didst *Davids* royal stem adorn,
> And gav'st him *birth* from whom thyself was't *born*.
> Who didst in *Triumph* at *Deaths Court* appear,
> And slew'st with thy *Nails*, thy *Cross* and *Spear*. . . .
> Who, heav'ns *glad burden* now, and justest pride,
> Sit'st high enthron'd next thy great *Fathers* side,
> (Where hallowed Flames help to adorn that Head
> Which once the *blushing* Thorns environed . . . )
> Ev'en *Thou* my breast with such blest rage inspire,
> As mov'd the tuneful strings of *Davids Lyre*,
> Guid my bold steps with thy old *trav'elling Flame*
> In these untrodden paths to Sacred Fame;
> Lo, with *pure hands* thy heavenly *Fires* to take,
> My well-chang'd *Muse* I a chaste *Vestal* make!
> From earths vain joys, and loves soft witchcraft free,
> I consecrate my *Magdalene* to Thee!

In the preface, Cowley denied the superiority of fiction to truth in poetry, and made an eloquent plea for the poetic worth of Scriptural subjects, as compared with "those mad stories of the gods and heroes" enshrined in the classics, which for the pagans

were "the whole body (or rather chaos) of [their] theology"
and better than no religion at all, but for us "ought to appear
no better arguments for verse than those of their worthy succes-
sors the knights errant." His purpose, completed to the end of
the fourth book, was a twelve-book epic on the adventures of
David before he became king, drawing the story from Scripture,
the epic structure from Virgil, and the embellishments not from
classic myth (from which Cowley would cut completely free)
but from his own invention and interests—a notable example in
Book I being a college (after the model of Bacon's New Atlantis) devoted to religion and science which the poet bestows upon
Samuel and the Prophets. Cowley's design is not only to champion Scriptural poetry but to rescue it from the dead level of
paraphrase as illustrated, he says, by Quarles (and, he might
have added, by Drayton and others). Its importance lies in the
degree (and it is not very great) in which it anticipates the effort
of John Milton.

# ᵴ IV ᵴ

## MILTON

I<small>F MILTON STANDS APART</small> from the other religious poets of the
seventeenth century it is first of all as the great figure stands
apart from the lesser eminences in any age, as Dante stands
apart from his contemporaries, or for that matter as Shakespeare
does from his: he stands apart by sheer power, by depth of insight and sustained significance of utterance. But in Milton's
case there are other and added reasons. It has been said that
English poetry spoke one language in his youth (the language
of the poets we have been considering) and another in his old
age (the language of Dryden and emerging neoclassicism), and
that Milton spoke neither of them. This is in large measure true.
And the reason is that in poetic style Milton inherits more fully
than his contemporaries the fruits of the classical renaissance:
he goes back directly for his models to Greece and Rome (as in
*Paradise Lost* and *Samson Agonistes*), or takes his place in a
continuous tradition developed from these sources (as in *Lycidas*). There is a sense, then, in which Milton seems to belong
rather to European than to English literature; and if he loses
some of the beauties, he escapes the local and temporary pecu-
liarities which mark English poetry in his day. Modern criticism
attempts to find some common ground with his contemporaries

under the terms "mannerism" and "baroque"; but the stubborn fact remains that to the unprejudiced the effect of his poetry is strikingly different from that of Crashaw's or of Donne's. His style differs with his subjects, but its most characteristic form is reached in the grand style of *Paradise Lost*, that poem which "has pleased many and pleased long." A second reason for Milton's isolated position is his relation not to the classical renaissance alone but to the Reformation, or in what is commonly called (though not always with complete understanding) his Puritanism. The religious poetry of his age is predominantly Anglican, and from the Anglicanism of Donne and Herbert, Vaughan and even Traherne (much more from the Roman Catholicism of Crashaw), Milton is progressively alienated. And finally, what is most important of all, there is Milton's own strongly individual personality which, with his life experience, leads him into uncharted ways of thought and feeling.

One of the features of Milton's mind and art which have disquieted even some of his admirers is the note of deliberation, of conscious planning, which marks alike his career and his poetry. It is already apparent in his student days, when he determines not merely to be a poet, or a poet giving some part of his effort to religious verse, but rather one who will dedicate his whole life and energy to the service of God in poetry. No doubt the resolve was influenced, in some degree, by those changes in the English Church which rendered service in its ministry impossible to the young Puritan; but there were deeper causes, and the process was less simple than this bare statement would suggest. His Latin verses written at Cambridge, and especially the superb Elegy V, *On the Coming of Spring*, show how wholeheartedly he could respond to the pagan naturalism of the secular renaissance and its classical models: in its frank acceptance, and even in its imagery, the elegy inevitably suggests Swinburne's "When the hounds of spring are on winter's traces." But very soon after this a change is seen. In the Elegy VI (a verse epistle to his friend and confidant, Charles Diodati) Milton repudiates the pagan attitude to life and poetry, suggests his ideal of what the true poet should be—one void of offense, a priest washed with lustral waters for his religious sacrifice, a dedicated spirit and truly inspired: "from his lips and breast he breathes forth Jove." The terms are classical (in the manner of the Christian humanist), but the meaning is plain to read. For (by a sudden transition) Milton continues, "You would know what I am doing: I am hymning the infant Saviour: this poem is my birthday gift for Christ: the first light of Christmas morning brought me the theme." The poem, of course, was *On the Morning of Christ's Nativity*, at which we have already glanced, and we can see it now in its true significance as the first pledge of the sort of poet Milton hopes to be.

But the way was not as easy as at first it seemed. The next three years give evidence of hesitation, even of some retreat. It is signalized by the only unqualified and acknowledged failure in the whole canon: *The Passion*, a poem on the Crucifixion, breaks off at the eighth stanza.

> Or should I thence hurried on viewles wing,
> Take up a weeping on the Mountains wilde,
> The gentle neighbourhood of grove and spring
> Would soon unbloosom all their Echoes milde,
> And I (for grief is easily beguiled)
> Might think th' infection of my sorrows loud,
> Had got a race of mourners on som pregnant cloud.

How beautiful the lines are—and how exquisitely inappropriate! Clearly, the religious subject can no longer capture the poet's imagination, no longer achieve the union of religious and aesthetic experience found in *On the Morning of Christ's Nativity*, but, on the contrary, leaves his mind open to every wayward fancy that crosses it. Milton's grief is indeed too easily beguiled, and the poem falters and stops. Why did Milton preserve this fragment and print it among his *Poems* with a note of apology? Surely because it had a profound personal significance for him: one might almost call the printing an act of penance. All the rest of his verse till he leaves Cambridge is secular in subject; but in one of his Petrarchan sonnets, written in Italian, where he owns the absolute sway of love (for "Oft-times Love has shown / That what he wills, he never wills in vain"), the young poet unexpectedly adds:

> O that this hard and sterile breast might be
> To him who plants from Heaven a soil as free.

But for the most part these Cambridge poems hold, as it were, Milton's deeper experiences at arm's length—even the beautiful *Arcades* and *L'Allegro* and *Il Penseroso*, though in the last-named there are overtones, not to be lightly dismissed, as in the invocation to Melancholy.

> And joyn with thee calm Peace, and Quiet,
> Spare Fast, that oft with gods doth diet,
> And hears the Muses in a ring
> Ay round about *Joves* Altar sing . . .

(where the ascetic note of Elegy VI is blended with a memory of Hesiod's dream of the Muses); and yet more in the lines

> But first, and chiefest, with thee bring,
> Him that yon soars on golden wing,
> Guiding the fiery-wheeled throne,
> The Cherub Contemplation.

Here the images combined are of different origin—the symbolic hierarchy of the angels, and Ezekiel's vision of the moving throne of God. Contemplation is called a cherub, because in the hierarchy the Cherubim symbolized the rational contemplation of the Creator's perfection, just as the Seraphim symbolized the love of that perfection when known, and the third group of angels—the Thrones (for there is a double meaning in the "fiery-wheeled throne")—symbolized action for God, the execution of his judgments. The Christian Platonist Pico della Mirandola had written:

Thus if musing upon the Creator in his creation we are busy with the leisure of contemplation, we shall flash on every side with cherubic light. If by love we burn for the Creator alone with that devouring fire of his, we shall suddenly burst into flame in the likeness of a Seraph. But how can we either love or judge things unknown? Therefore with his own light the Cherub makes us ready for the seraphic fire and also illuminates us for the judgment of the Thrones. Let us make ourselves one with him and be caught up into the heights.

What is implied is that Platonic scale of ascent already met in Spenser's *An Hymne of Heavenly Love* and *An Hymne of Heavenly Beautie*, and it is this that gives direction to the studies of *Il Penseroso* and issues in the final hope that "old experience" (that is, systematic experimental study) may at last "attain / To something of prophetic strain," that patient thought may mature to inspiration. *Il Pensoroso* is not primarily a religious poem, but we shall miss part of its meaning, and most of its significance in Milton's development, if we ignore these overtones.

For it is in them that we get a hint of the next stage in Milton's self-dedication, and of the ensuing years of study (to equip himself with knowledge for his task), and not of study only but of self-discipline that he may become (in his own words) "a true poem, that is, a composition and pattern of the best and honourablest things." In Cicero's ideal conception, the orator must combine the ready command of all knowledge with a character of known and approved integrity. This conception the Renaissance incorporated in its ideal of the poet; and Milton reads it in a religious light. The true poem that Milton would become is a Christian poem—the image adopted is aesthetic, but the meaning is moral and religious—and it points the way (whether so intended or not) to that union of aesthetic and religious experience which (as we have said) is the essence of religious poetry. But before Milton dare choose poetry as his mode of service, he must be sure that his powers are equal to the task; and the outcome of his reappraisal is Sonnet VII, "How soon hath time."

The starting point is an unaccustomed mood of self-distrust, and the burden of the octave is the small achievement of his late-maturing powers: "my late spring no bud nor blossom sheweth." This is the problem. But now for the first time the pattern that is to be characteristic of Milton asserts itself: the problem is not so much solved as transcended; it is raised to a level where self-regarding thoughts are irrelevant; the power is as God wills; only the resolve to use it in his service is Milton's responsibility. And so the sestet proceeds to its conclusion: "All is"—all that matters is—"if I have grace to use it so / As ever in my great Task-master's eye." This time there will be no hesitation or retreat; the lines might furnish an epigraph for all the rest of Milton's poetry. And so he can go forward to that renewed preparation for his lifework whose character we have described.

The immediate outcome of the experience realized in Sonnet VII is three religious poems whose relation to what has gone before is significant: one (*On Time*) celebrates the triumph of the

Christian over time; another (*On the Circumcision*) is plainly designed to make good the failure of *The Passion*, for it treats the event as the first wounding of Christ and the type of his Crucifixion; and the third and best of the poems (*At a Solemn Musick*) returns to a theme in *On the Morning of Christ's Nativity*, the reunion of earth and heaven symbolized by the music of men and angels, but with a deeper sense of how

> . . . disproportion'd sin
> Jarr'd against natures chime, and with harsh din
> Broke the fair musick that all creatures made
> To their great Lord, whose love their motion sway'd
> In perfect Diapason, whilst they stood
> In first obedience, and their state of good.
> O may we soon again renew that Song,
> And keep in tune with Heav'n till God ere long
> To his celestial consort us unite,
> To live with him, and sing in endless morn of light.

And so we return to the Christian's promised triumph over time and change. These poems are, as it were, a renewed pledge of Milton's resolve. But for the next five years the task is preparation, not performance; and he writes but two poems, *Comus* and *Lycidas*, both by request.

By request! But to an astonishing degree Milton turns them to his own purpose, and that purpose the further realization of his religious experience. He is asked to furnish a masque for the installation of the Earl of Bridgewater as Lord President of Wales, and what he responds with is *Comus*, which fulfills every requirement, but whose theme is the trial and triumph of chastity. This poem, in its depth, has not always been well understood, and a whole lecture would hardly suffice to clear away the mistaken or partial interpretations and securely establish its meaning. First, one must recognize that it is indeed a masque (or at least an entertainment that adapts to its use the various elements of the masque), but that it is also allegorical poetry in the general tradition of Spenser's *Faerie Queene*, where (in Milton's phrase) "more is meant than meets the ear." The form of its simple action is the journey of the Lady Alice Egerton and her two brothers to Ludlow, there to greet their parents, the earl and countess. In a wild wood, the Lady is separated from her brothers, and (deceived by his disguise as a rustic swain and his offer of shelter) she is led by Comus (the son of Bacchus and Circe, and a seducer with magical powers) to his palace. The brothers are joined by the Attendant Spirit, who leads them to their sister's rescue. Meanwhile we have seen her successfully resistant to all the wiles of her captor. This point most critics, friendly or the reverse, have taken to be the climax of the action, but quite wrongly as I believe. For when, on the entrance of the Attendant Spirit with the brothers, Comus flees, the Lady is found safe indeed, but utterly paralyzed by the enchanter's spell, unable to proceed on their journey to Ludlow, which is the dynamic of the action. To effect her release, the Attendant Spirit must summon a second and superior power, Sabrina, the goddess of the Severn, who performs the feat through the agency of water. This surely is the climax of the action, the point where movement is restored; and they hasten on to Ludlow, there to join the waiting parents. On its literal level this is simple folktale: with the beautiful lady and the evil magician, the beneficent fairy (two in fact) and magic and counter-magic. It is folktale as Book I of *The Faerie Queene* is chivalric romance: but "more is meant than meets the ear."

Each of the three settings has its symbolic value: the wild wood is the world, where good and evil grow up together; the palace of Comus is one of those concentrations of evil encountered therein, a place of special danger and temptation, and so of testing; and Ludlow, the goal of endeavor, is at once the paternal dwelling and the heavenly city: it stands for what another poet is to call "the kindred points of heaven and home." Assumed in the whole theme is the traditional framework of nature and grace. The Attendant Spirit is the agent of God's providence in the natural order; but it is Sabrina, with her significant symbol of water, those "drops of precious cure," who represents saving grace. By her natural virtue the Lady has withstood all temptation; and in suggesting that this is not the climax of the action, I would not for a moment deny its great importance in Milton's view (you may call it the first of two crises if you will). But it leaves the Lady immobilized, unable to press forward to the appointed goal, and beyond the aid of the Attendant Spirit: only Sabrina can rescue her, only the grace of God can save; and lest the reader should miss the point, the Attendant Spirit underlines it:

> Come, Lady; while Heaven lends us grace
> Let us fly this cursed place. . . .
> I shall be your faithful guide
> Through this gloomy covert wide;
> And not many furlongs thence
> Is your Father's residence. . . .

I have said that the whole theme assumes the traditional framework of nature and grace, that is, the progression from nature to grace; and it is from the standing ground of grace that the Attendant Spirit utters his Epilogue: the key to the whole deeper meaning of the masque. For in a series of symbolic images—the crown of all the superb poetry which has gone before—he retraces the ascent through the natural order up to the point where it is transcended in the Christian vision of freedom through virtue achieved by the grace of God. From the standing ground of grace the whole natural order is transfigured: everything falls into place, and (as when God looked upon it in the Creation) it is seen to be good. First come symbols of natural beauty, and with them the note of freedom and joy (the golden fruit of the Hesperides is no longer dragon-guarded); next, the generative principle, figured in the love of Venus and Adonis (as in Spenser's allegory of the Garden of Adonis); then, far above them, the intellectual or heavenly love, figured by the celestial Cupid and Psyche his betrothed, whose destined offspring is not Pleasure (as in the old legend) but a twin birth whose names are Youth and Joy, and these (if we know our Milton) we shall recognize as the Platonic twins, offspring of love in its higher manifestation—namely, Knowledge and Virtue—now transformed in the light of grace to Youth eternal and Joy ineffable. And finally, in the last six lines we come to the light of grace itself—the light that has illuminated all the preceding images. By grace, virtue is free and not constrained (this is the doctrine of Christian liberty); by grace, it can ascend beyond the music of the spheres (that favorite symbol of ordered harmony) and reach the heaven of heavens (and the higher harmony of the angelic choir); and if Virtue feeble were, there is still the grace of God which Virtue can invoke—that grace symbolized by Sabrina's intervention. First, then, the images of natural beauty, freedom, and joy:

> All amidst the gardens fair
> Of Hesperus, and his daughters three
> That sing about the golden tree:
> Along the crispèd shades and bowers
> Revels the spruce and jocund Spring;
> The Graces and the rosy-bosomed Hours
> Thither all their bounties bring. . . .

Iris there with humid bow
Waters the odorous banks, that blow. . . .
And drenches with Elysian dew
(List, mortals, if your ears be true)
Beds of hyacinth and roses,
Where young Adonis oft reposes,
Waxing well of his deep wound,
In slumber soft, and on the ground
Sadly sits th' Assyrian queen.
But far above, in spangled sheen,
Celestial Cupid, her famed son, advanced
Holds his dear Psyche, sweet entranced
After her wandering labours long,
Till free consent the gods among
Make her his eternal bride,
And from her fair unspotted side
Two blissful twins are to be born,
Youth and Joy. . . .
    Mortals that would follow me,
Love virtue; she alone is free.
She can teach ye how to climb
Higher than the sphery chime;
Or, if Virtue feeble were,
Heaven itself would stoop to her.

This is surely not the merely negative and ascetic doctrine that too many of the critics have found in *Comus*. Rather, it betokens the realization of a genuine religious experience by the poet—a sense of dependence on the grace of God, of the liberating effect of grace bestowed, and of nature transfigured when viewed from the vantage ground of this experience. And the experience was realized, and could be realized, only through the poem, only by the fusion of aesthetic and religious experience which the poem effects. That (as I see it) is the true meaning of Milton's *Comus*.

*Lycidas* is no less remarkable. Its occasion—that is, its starting point—is the death by drowning of Edward King, a former fellow student at Christ's College, Cambridge, perhaps little more than an acquaintance. The form chosen is the pastoral elegy as it comes down from Theocritis, enriched by many accessions on the way, including the power to carry a weight of allegorical meaning, and long since given a decisive new direction by the Christian hope of immortality, so that the poem no longer ends on a note of mourning, but of consolation—indeed, of triumph which subsumes consolation. This is the pattern which Milton is to employ again in the *Epitaphium Damonis*, the moving Latin elegy for his friend Diodati. But in *Lycidas* he puts the form to special and peculiar use. Unlike Diodati, Edward King is viewed throughout more as a type than as an individual; and though Milton is careful never to make the equation specific or obtrusive, he plainly sees in King's promise and his fate something potentially applicable to himself. King's death becomes a type of the cutting short of a life of virtue and high promise by what looks like the hand of chance. But death is not the only way in which a life of dedication may be thwarted; there is also the state of society in which the individual finds himself, exemplified appropriately enough for Edward King (who was destined to the ministry) and for Milton (the religious poet, whose present hope was to write a national Christian epic) by the festering sore of corruption in the Church. Before these thoughts of the harsh realities of life and chance, change and death, the Arcadian fancies of the pastoral tradition fade and their note is shattered. Twice there is a measure of reassurance through a partial appeal to an overruling Providence, and the pastoral note is deliberately restored. But not till these are gathered up in the final assurance of faith, as in the traditional pattern of Christian elegy, do they become fully effective, and then in retrospect even the pastoral images can release their secondary suggestion of hope. We are told that as the sun sinks beneath the watery floor to rise again, so Lycidas "sunk low, but mounted high / Through the dear might of him who walked the waves," is at once received among the saints and assigned his office here below.

> Now *Lycidas* the Shepherds weep no more;
> Henceforth thou art the Genius of the shore,
> In thy large recompense, and shalt be good
> To all that wander in that perilous flood.

The "perilous flood" is this world of chance and change, and Lycidas has already commenced to exercise his beneficent influence on those who travel through it. Of that influence (as the Epilogue makes clear), the poet himself is the first recipient. For his poetic contemplation of Lycidas and his fate has wrought in him a transformation. With faith fortified and vision cleared, and with a mind at peace, he again takes up his lifework: "Tomorrow to fresh woods and pastures new." This bare account can give no impression of the complex pattern and the poetic beauty of *Lycidas*; but at least it lets us see how once more Milton has turned an occasional poem to the realization of a genuine religious experience.

Milton's hopes and exertions, struggles and defeats, public and private, during the twenty years in which he postponed his poetry to his labors in the cause of the Puritan revolution—the cause of liberty and religion as he conceived it to be—left their abiding mark on his mind and on his later poetry. It is a sterner Milton that confronts us in the three great poems published and largely written after the collapse of all his hopes for England with the Restoration of the monarchy and the Established Church. For his subject matter he turns now directly to the Bible, and in his hands Scriptural verse at last achieves the poetic level of which it is worthy. For his poetic form he goes back to the great original sources: *Paradise Lost* is a classical epic on a Scriptural theme (the only classical epic that can make good its claim to stand beside Homer and Virgil), and *Samson Agonistes* is the most perfect example of the Greek tragic form ever achieved in a modern language. Only *Paradise Regained* looks to a Scriptural source for form as well as content; for, following a tradition that goes back to Saint Jerome, Milton regarded the Book of Job as the model of a brief epic, which he was content to follow. In form and content alike, the great Puritan becomes the great purist. If he is more Scriptural, he is also more strictly classical than ever before.

It is sometimes said that Milton's Puritanism has triumphed over his Christian humanism, but this does insufficient justice to the complexity of the change. His confidence in average human nature has sustained a series of shocks, and more and more his only hope is fixed on a remnant, saved and saving. There is no more thought of a national Christian epic, no more talk of "God's Englishmen" or of a nation rising with united fervor to cast aside its chains; instead he writes of the Fall of Man and of Christ's redemption of those whose will it is to be saved. Certainly his Christian humanism has changed its direction and emphasis. This is reflected in his attitude to classical image, myth, and story. Whatever there was in his earlier attitude of the syncretism dear to the heart of his humanist predecessors, this has disappeared. The figures of classic story belong to the kingdom of darkness, or if they are employed in a neutral sense, it is with some epithet that marks them as mere figments of the imagination: thus, of the Heavenly Muse when compared with Calliope, "For thou art heavenly, she an empty dream." Only the "antique symmetry" of the poems themselves is there to remind us of Milton's still ardent discipleship of the classics.

More significant is the fading of his early Christian Platonism, a link, as it were, between nature and grace and an invitation to mysticism. With it goes that element of dualism, and attendant asceticism, which the neo-Platonists had made some effort to transcend but had succeeded only in concealing. In the later Milton, Platonism is largely replaced by a sort of Christian Stoicism, whose temper is quite different. It is rationalistic in a narrower sense, and anti-mystical. However austere its ethic, it will have nothing to do with the Platonic dualism—nothing to do with a transcendent world of ideas or with spirit and matter as diverse and opposing entities; what we call matter and spirit are simply different degrees of the same, the one underlying substance. Milton's thought is now securely monistic in basis, and on its monistic base he erects a hierarchy of ethical values, essentially rationalistic in structure. His monism brings him into line with the tradition which commences with the earliest of the Stoics and reaches its culmination with Spinoza, the outlines of whose system Milton may have known through their common friend Henry Oldenburg. But he is faced with a problem not met by Spinoza: he must accommodate his basic position to Christianity and the Bible, in which he ardently believes—his effort to do so is written in the pages of his *De Doctrina Christiana* and of *Paradise Lost*; and he must of course retain the Christian conception of the Fall and of Redemption.

All this he does by an extreme development of two Protestant principles: first, that Scripture is the sole source of doctrine (the Church and tradition have in themselves no authority, and their elaborate superstructures are mere "metaphysical theology"), and, secondly, that final responsibility for interpretation lies with the individual believer, who has, after all, the gift of the Spirit for his guide. Extreme as is Milton's position, there is nothing arbitrary in his applying of his principles. His appeal is to reason on two levels: first, his literal reading of Scripture must conform to all the known facts and submit to criticism by the canons of logic; secondly, for him the gift of the Spirit means essentially the clearing of the intellectual faculties and the progressive restoration of that intuitive perception of the law of nature which was obscured but not obliterated by the Fall, and which, when restored, constitutes a second and (in case of seeming conflict) a superior scripture. The outcome is startling enough, for it includes a number of "heresies," any one of which would technically have rendered Milton liable to the death penalty by a statute of the Long Parliament. He denies Creation *ex nihilo* (on the ground that "create" in Genesis does not mean to create from nothing, but to give form to an already existent substance), and asserts instead what amounts to something like creation *de Deo* (for God, who is infinite and omnipotent, is the source of every substance, and includes in himself the one primal substance). This is the point essential to Milton's monism and ultimately to his view of man, as created in God's image, and "a living being . . . one and indivisible . . . not made up and framed of two distinct and different natures as of soul and body, but a being individual, animated, sensitive, and rational." Again, Milton reacts strongly against the Calvinist dogma of election and reprobation and the denial to man of all freedom of the will: he cannot on such an assumption write his great theodicy (for *Paradise Lost* is theodicy as well as Scriptural epic) and "justify the ways of God to men."

Once more, Milton's reliance on the words of Scripture alone leads him to an Arian (but not a Socinian) position on the Trinity: the Son is not co-eternal or in his nature equal with the Father; he is the first and highest of all created beings ("the first

born of every creature") raised to divinity, and even to an equality of honor, by the Father; for though a created being, he is the
true image of the Father, and his office is, by word and act, to
make manifest the otherwise inapprehensible God. This is the
position argued in the *De Doctrina* and vividly present in *Paradise Lost*, where we witness the Son proclaimed as "throned /
Equal with God, and equally enjoying Godlike fruition," and in
*Paradise Regained*, where the angels hail him:

> True Image of the Father, whether thron'd
> In the bosom of bliss, and light of light
> Conceiving, or remote from Heaven, enshrin'd
> In fleshly Tabernacle, and human form—

always and everywhere the Son is the true image of the Father.
It is necessary to make this clear, because Milton's departures
from orthodoxy, and notably his view of the Trinity, are among
the grounds on which by some critics he is denied the title of a
Christian poet. It must suffice here to reply that his heterodoxy
leaves the impulse of worship unimpaired.

The treatment of God in *Paradise Lost*, to which better objection has been taken, also depends on Milton's theology, and on
his refusal of that recourse to mystical symbol which served
Dante so well. His conception of God as the infinite, omnipotent, omnipresent cause of all things—of a God who before the
Creation can say:

> Boundless the Deep, because I am who fill
> Infinitude, nor vacuous the space.
> Though I uncircumscrib'd my self retire,
> And put not forth my goodness, which is free
> To act or not, Necessity and Chance
> Approach not mee, and what I will is Fate—

that conception is evidently highly abstract and philosophic in
nature. Of God, as he actually is, we can form no precise concep-

tion, save as he is revealed in Christ; any account which the Bible gives is one accommodated to the finite human mind, but it is after all God's own accommodation; and so Milton adopts (in every passage save the one just quoted) the anthropomorphic image supplied by the Old Testament. He makes clear (in the *De Doctrina*) the grounds of his choice, though we can hardly perhaps approve it.

One other aspect of Milton's theology is so important that it must not pass unnoticed here—namely, his radical development of the doctrine of Christian liberty. Not content with the common view that in fulfilling the Law, Christ abrogated it only in its ceremonial and judicial aspects. Milton, like Luther, insists that the Gospel replaces the whole Law, ceremonial, judicial, and moral, substituting for a compulsive and prescriptive rule to be obeyed to the letter, a principle of faith and love, voluntarily accepted, and depending not on the letter but on the spirit. Thus the outward Law is replaced by an inward, written (as Milton says) by the Spirit in the heart and mind of the believer. Here evidently we are back at the idea of the inward and superior Scripture already mentioned. Further, we are at the very heart of Milton's conception of liberty, which demands the abolition of outward restraints only that an inward control may take their place. Ideally there is no conflict between order and liberty thus conceived; for liberty is none other than order self-imposed from within. True liberty (as Michael tells Adam) always "with right Reason dwells / Twinned, and from her hath no dividual being." Virtue is its foundation and its end; and God's service (as Abdiel tells the incredulous Satan) is indeed perfect freedom.

We have described *Paradise Lost* as a classical epic on a Christian theme, and as the poem in which Scriptural poetry at last comes into its own. The poem's action is too familiar to require summary. Indeed, so deep an impression has it made upon the English mind that only with an effort can one remember what is in the Bible and what in Milton. But in the Bible, we reflect, the story of the Fall is folktale in which events just happen: we are hardly concerned with the personality of the actors or the motives of their action. But Milton has undertaken to humanize the story and motivate the action by casting it in the quasi-dramatic form of epic narrative—a formidable task. He has paralleled with the Fall of Man (and at the same time contrasted) the Fall of the Angels, and this too he has motivated and humanized, creating the unforgettable figure of Satan. He has added to the threefold setting adumbrated in Homer (Heaven, Earth, and the nether world) a fourth—the Chaos—and to each he has given its special significance not as an external locality merely but as a state of mind: Heaven is perfect order, symbolized by the song and dance of the unfallen angels about the throne of God—angels who hourly prove, as Abdiel says, that God's service is perfect freedom; unfallen Earth and the life of our first parents there are a reflection of the heavenly order but translated from angelic to human terms, and from the heroic to the idyllic mood; Hell is the very reverse of Heaven (as though it were a reflection seen in a distorting mirror)—not disorder, but something much worse, perverted order, where the fallen angels surround the throne of Satan, whose pride has aspired to a false freedom, and whose service is perfect slavery; and lastly there is the Chaos, whose note is unorder, but which holds the potentiality of order, being in substance good, but lacking as yet the good of form. This is supplied when Milton gives his account of the Creation, drawing on the tradition of the hexaemeron and giving it final expression; but for another reason also Milton dwells on the Creation: goodness is ever constructive; evil, the reverse (Satan can exclaim, "For only in destroying I find ease / To my relentless thoughts"). Creation then is the manifestation of God's constructive goodness, and redemption (which is the poem's secondary theme) is the parallel manifestation of his reconstructive goodness.

Enough has perhaps been said to remind us of the vast and complex structural pattern of *Paradise Lost*, where every detail is significant. It is fascinating to compare the poem with Virgil's (its only rival) simply as an example of epic structure. Virgil, it is often said, has compressed into the *Aeneid* an *Odyssey* and an *Iliad*, making skillful use of the epic device of retrospective narrative and placing at the point of juncture Aeneas' visit to the nether world and his vision of the Rome that is to be. Milton shows the same or greater architectonic power. His retrospective narrative, presented by the archangel Raphael, is (like Aeneas' narrative to Dido) an epic within the epic; it provides, in the parallel action of the Fall of the Angels, the Homeric battles which the primary subject will not afford, and it further permits that account of the Creation whose significance we have noticed. The purpose of Raphael's visit is to orient our first parents in their state of innocence. It is balanced in the two final books of the poem by the visit of the archangel Michael, to reorient them to a fallen world, and this entails the vision of a future fraught indeed with woe, but lightened by the promise of salvation. Thus does Milton accommodate—it is one illustration among a hundred—epic structure and Christian theme not by reducing the former but by elaborating its pattern beyond that of any of his predecessors. Nor is this surprising; for, like all great systems of thought, the Christian scheme is itself a vast pattern of events, ideas, and values, on which Milton can confidently draw.

The pattern of the Christian scheme is that of a divine

comedy, which abounds in tragic episodes, but whose final outcome is not in doubt; and it should be observed that, thus stated
in abstract terms, it fits well enough the pattern of the Virgilian
(though not of the Homeric) epic. *Paradise Lost* centers on one
of the great tragic episodes, the Fall of Man, which conditions
indeed the rest of the Christian pattern: first, as it is the source
of all conflict and all suffering, but, second, as it necessitates divine redemption. All this is implied in the very first lines of
*Paradise Lost*.

> Of Man's First Disobedience, and the Fruit
> Of that Forbidd'n Tree, whose mortal tast
> Brought Death into the World, and all our woe,
> With loss of *Eden*, till one greater Man
> Restore us, and regain the blissful Seat,
> Sing Heav'nly Muse. . . .

Here, then, are the primary and secondary themes, or rather
say, here is the primary tragic episode seen against the larger pattern of divine comedy in which it holds its place. And here too
is a new element of pattern supplied by the Christian scheme—
namely, the conception of Christ as the Second Adam, who by
his obedience will win all, and more than all, that Adam's dis-
obedience lost, exchanging for an earthly paradise, not only the
new heaven and the new earth promised by Saint Paul and to be
echoed in Michael's pointing to the final outcome, but, here and
now, the paradisal mind of the true believer, that "paradise within thee happier far," which, says Michael, Adam may also reach.

Further, the conception of Christ as the Second Adam gives
us our clue to the vexed question of who is the hero of the poem.
Much romantic criticism to the contrary notwithstanding, it is
not Satan, who is heroic no doubt, but with a purely pagan, indeed a perverted, heroism. It is Christ, the model of the Christian heroic, who defeats Satan in the war in heaven and (as

Michael makes clear to Adam) will defeat him again and forever. In the larger scope of the divine comedy, Christ is the hero
and victorious protagonist, Satan the defeated antagonist. In
the segment of the story on which Milton centers, Adam is that
paradoxical figure, the defeated protagonist who has to be rescued, a figure new to epic (though there is perhaps a hint of it in
the Redcrosse Knight rescued by Prince Arthur); but in Christ,
the Second Adam, the paradox is resolved.

Since the action of *Paradise Lost* centers in Satan's temporary
triumph, it is not surprising that to critics out of sympathy with
Milton's religious beliefs, and prone to ignore the larger context
of the Christian scheme, Satan should seem to dominate the
poem, to be in fact protagonist and hero. That this is not Milton's intention, however, is plain enough from the text: first,
from the relentless self-revelation of Satan's great soliloquy at the
beginning of Book IV, where all his pretensions are stripped
away; secondly, from the comments which accompany all the
manifestations of his courage and indomitable will, of his tragic
grandeur or pathos; and, finally, from the steady deterioration of
the character till he is bereft of the last vestige of pagan heroism,
his courage, and becomes the serpent whose form he has voluntarily assumed. What Milton could not foresee was the impair-
ment of that Christian belief on which he relied in the reader,
and the general fragmentation of values, classical as well as
Christian, which allows us to admire courage and indomitable
will irrespective of the ends to which they are directed, to adopt
a thoroughly uncritical attitude to every plea for liberty and
equality, and to confuse overweening pride with legitimate self-
respect. Here poetry and history come into a new relation, and it
becomes the duty of historical criticism to restore the assumptions on which the poet worked.

This is something quite different from the mere reaction of neo-orthodoxy. If Satan is not the unqualified hero whom critics from Shelley to Walter Raleigh exalted, neither is he the fool, the comic character, that Charles Williams and C. S. Lewis would make him. Their comparison of him to Meredith's Sir Willoughby is completely inept; his egoism has much more in common with that of Homer's Achilles; and so far from being comic, Satan remains a tragic figure, both because of and in spite of his crimes, much as does Shakespeare's Macbeth.

Critics who admire Satan, as well as some who dislike both him and Milton, have sought to trace in the lineaments of the archrebel the likeness of the poet himself. Saurat, who has done much for the understanding of Milton—if more for the misunderstanding—seems at this point to be on the right track. He recognizes, as everyone must, the deep psychological insight of the portrayal, but also, as many have failed to do, Milton's utter condemnation of the Satanic figure, and he infers that in Satan, Milton depicts elements in his own life and temper which he has learned to recognize and condemn. We need not go on to Saurat's fantasy of Milton himself as the hero of *Paradise Lost*, engaged in a life-and-death struggle with his own creation. Let us say rather that Milton manifests the kind of imaginative sympathy that enables him to apprehend and present with extraordinary vividness the satanic point of view, that such sympathy, though it has its basis in Milton's own experience, has nothing to do with approbation, and that the vital experience, the one realized in and through the poem, involves in equal measure insight and judgment.

The very success of Milton's portrayal of Satan in human terms has tended to dwarf the poem's other characters: it has made us forget that epic does not demand the degree of individuation required in drama (though it may yield us an Achilles or a Satan), and that actually Milton scores a second triumph in his treatment of Adam and Eve.

We have said that the recasting of the sacred folktale of the Fall in epic terms presented a formidable problem. This was enhanced rather than diminished by the view which orthodoxy took of the state of innocence and the fall therefrom. The state of innocence seemed at once to eliminate all those elements of human experience requisite for characterization and to leave the Fall itself unexplained, indeed inexplicable. This latter fact Saint Augustine recognized, observing that our first parents could not have fallen had not their will already been corrupted before the dread event. But this predating of the Fall does nothing really to resolve the enigma: how and why did the will become corrupted? Tillyard has raised the question anew in connection with Milton's epic, but has made the mistake, I think, of assuming that Saint Augustine's view of the state of innocence was also Milton's, and clearly it was not.

As Milton conceives and presents it, the state of innocence permits a wide scope of human experience—everything indeed except (confessedly a large exception) the experiential knowledge of evil: evil is known only inferentially as contrary to the good experienced. But within these limits all the impulses of human nature come into play: impulses of wonder and admiration, of erotic emotion and mutual affection, of sensuous pleasure, and of religious awe, gratitude, and worship. And innocence is lost, and evil known experientially, only when two of these impulses—the one self-regarding though innocent, the other of love and obedience to God—come into conflict, and the will makes and approves what is palpably the wrong choice, preferring the lower impulse to the higher. That is what is implied in the lines which Saurat so disastrously misinterprets:

> Evil into the mind of God [that is, of angel] or Man
> May come and go, so unapprov'd, and leave
> No spot or blame behind. . . .

The words are spoken to Eve in connection with her dream of temptation, to reassure her, and us, that there has been no loss of innocence here; and they are equally applicable to other experiences recorded in the poem before the Fall, which betoken potential danger indeed, but as yet no corruption of the will. And this, we may be sure, is no mere literary device, but corresponds to Milton's reasoned conviction and to his whole mature conception of the nature of man.

On such a view of the state of innocence, the task of casting the story into epic form, though difficult, is not impossible, as it would be on the common view; for it leaves some scope for character and motivation. But Milton was wise to present his first picture of Adam and Eve in pastoral rather than in more dramatic terms, and only gradually to bring their characters into sharper focus and nearer to humanity as we know it. To say, however, as is often said, that this is, and of necessity, postponed till they have fallen and become thereby creatures like ourselves, is to have read the poem without care or perception.

There is indeed a heightening of dramatic interest as the crisis is approached and reached in Book IX; and Tillyard has rightly insisted that this interest is maintained at the highest pitch through Book X, through what he describes as the second crisis, when the fatal choice is reversed and the first faltering steps are taken on the long, painful road back. We may be grateful for this insight, and need not quarrel with his phase "the second crisis" or with his emphasis on an essentially human situation, but only with the entire substitution of psychology for religion in his exposition. What Milton actually presents in poignant human terms is no mere account of readjustment, but a profound study in the initial stages of repentance.

Of the Fall itself, the cause had been pride, and, essentially, pride means being self-centered, instead of God-centered. But the forms which the sin takes in Satan, Eve, and Adam differ; and in Adam (as Milton and Saint Augustine agree), it is uxoriousness (a form, by the way, much more intelligible on Milton's view of the preceding state of innocence than on Saint Augustine's). With eyes fully open, Adam deliberately chooses to share Eve's fate.

> . . . for with thee
> Certain my resolution is to Die;
> How could I live without thee, how forgoe
> Thy sweet Converse and Love so dearly joind,
> To live again in these wilde Woods forlorn? . . .
>     no, no, I feel
> The Link of Nature draw me: Flesh of Flesh,
> Bone of my Bone thou art, and from thy State
> Mine never shall be parted, bliss or woe. . . .
>     if Death
> Consort with thee, Death is to me as Life;
> So forcible within my heart I feel
> The Bond of Nature draw me to my owne.

But this motive (so eloquent of Adam's predicament and compelling of admiration though criminal in its outcome, as Milton well knows it to be) is soon forgotten in the horror and indignity of mutual recrimination. And when at last, after Adam's soliloquy, "O miserable of happy! Is this the end / Of this new glorious World, and me so late / The glory of that glory?"—a soliloquy whose echoes of Satan's suddenly crystallize in "To Satan only like, both crime and doom"—Eve makes the first tentative move toward reconciliation, Adam spurns her. "Out of my sight, thou Serpent, that name best / Befits thee with him leagued, thyself as false / And hateful." But Eve, persistent as ever, will not be rebuffed. "Forsake me not thus, Adam," she implores, acknowledges her offense to be not against God only, like his, but against God and him, and offers to return to the place of judgment, to confess her fault, and to pray that all the punishment may be borne by her alone. And Adam (how could he not?) relents. Once more he feels the bond of nature draw him to his own, and from Eve's contrition, perhaps too from his own spontaneous forgiveness of her, takes heart to catch the suggestion she has given.

> What better can we do, than to the place
> Repairing where he judg'd us, prostrate fall
> Before him reverent, and there confess
> Humbly our faults, and pardon beg, with tears. . . .

What Milton is telling us is that the very bond of nature which gave the impulse to Adam's sin now plays its part in leading Adam and Eve to take the first step in repentance. It is not that the poet has forgotten religion and substituted psychology for theology, but that he has united religious principle with human experience and made both of them more real and significant thereby.

The process is completed when, repentant, forgiven, and promised the opportunity of salvation, our first parents, once more fully united, quit their earthly paradise and face the harsh but challenging world we know.

> Som natural tears they dropd, but wiped them soon;
> The World was all before them, where to choose
> Their place of rest, and Providence their guide:
> They hand in hand with wandering steps and slow,
> Through Eden took their solitarie way—

but not before Adam has learned his lesson, the lesson of true obedience and Christian heroism.

> Henceforth I learne, that to obey is best,
> And love with feare the onely God, to walk
> As in his presence, ever to observe
> His providence, and on him sole depend . . .
>     that suffering for Truths sake
> Is fortitude to highest victorie. . . .
> Taught this by his example whom I now
> Acknowledge my Redeemer ever blest.

It is this that draws from Michael the promise of "a paradise within thee happier far."

Viewing the whole cycle, seeing the tragic event in the light of the divine comedy, Adam for a moment invokes the paradox of the fortunate Fall: the sin is indeed to be repented, but how can the outcome be regretted since God "all this good of evil shall produce"?

In *Samson Agonistes*, Milton attempts what has sometimes been thought to be impossible: the writing of a Christian tragedy—that is, a drama which, giving full weight to God's providential order, yet manages to achieve a tragic effect as complete and satisfying in itself as any in Sophocles or Shakespeare; and in this he succeeds: it is perhaps his greatest poetic triumph and the manifestation of his deepest religious insight. He adopts the strictest of classical forms, with unity of action, time, and place; and, as does Sophocles in *Oedipus at Colonus*, the closest analogue, he centers all our attention on the hero and his state of mind, but whereas Oedipus has already reached his decision and has only to repel whatever attempts to turn him aside, Samson must be brought to his decision all the way from a state of despair in which it could not conceivably have been taken.

We see him first the defeated champion, powerless in the hands of his enemies.

> Ask for this great Deliverer now, and find him
> Eyeless in Gaza at the Mill with slaves. . . .

As Samson is the first to acknowledge, it is all his own fault. His response is not yet repentance, but bitter self-reproach.

> [I,] like a foolish pilot, have shipwrackt
> My Vessel trusted to me from above. . . .
> Am I not sung and proverbd for a Fool
> In every street, do they not say, how well
> Are come upon him his deserts?

His state is unrelieved despair. To the Chorus he seems "As one past hope, abandoned / And by himself given over." Superficially viewed, the series of encounters (with the Chorus, and with Manoa, Dalila, and Harapha) seem to advance the action not at all. More adequately weighed, they are seen to effect the change in Samson's state of mind, on which the whole action must hinge. Samson is brought, first, to acknowledge that the primary offense has been not to himself but to God, and to acquiesce in the complete justice of his punishment; then, to implore forgiveness, but with no hope of restoration to God's service—for himself no hope of any kind, left simply to "Death's benumbing opium as his only cure"; next, to the dawning conviction that God in his own way will deal with Dagon. Then comes the encounter with Dalila: it is the trial of Samson's repentance, and he sustains it—no more yielding. The result is seen in the next encounter: Samson can now declare his hope of ultimate forgiveness; it is the first word of hope in all his utterance, and it is significantly phrased: he "despairs not," he says, of God's "final pardon / Whose ear is ever open, and his eye / Gracious to readmit the suppliant." And then, stung by Harapha's taunts, he suddenly challenges him, assuming almost unawares the role of God's champion once more; it is the perfectly natural outcome of repentance, returning confidence—and exasperation. This is typical of Milton's method throughout: we may assume the operation of God's grace—indeed, in the light of the outcome, we must do so—but Milton will make every change intelligible in human terms, as he does in the Fall and repentance of Adam and Eve. The stage is now set for the final scene, and here at last divine direction becomes evident. Samson had lamented as his chief affliction a "sense of Heaven's desertion," but at last the inner and mysterious voice speaks to him once more, and prompts him to obey (though why he cannot tell) his captors' summons. He goes, as God's instrument indeed but also as human individual and tragic hero; he goes (as the Chorus significantly sees) doubly armed with "celestial vigour" and "plain heroic magnitude of mind."

In this double view lies the secret of Milton's success. For in the first comment of Manoa and the Chorus on Samson's death, the focus is all on the tragic hero, and it culminates in the words:

> Nothing is here for tears, nothing to wail
> Or knock the breast, no weakness, no contempt,
> Dispraise, or blame, nothing but well and fair,
> And what may quiet us in a death so noble.

This is plainly Milton's version of the celebrated Aristotelian katharsis. And only then is the Chorus permitted to raise its eyes to the unfolding pattern of the divine comedy and the place of Samson's sacrifice in God's providential plan.

> All is best, though we oft doubt,
> What th' unsearchable dispose
> Of highest wisdom brings about,
> And ever best found in the close.

Oft he seems to hide his face,
But unexpectedly returns,
And to his faithful Champion hath in place
Bore witness gloriously; whence Gaza mourns
And all that band them to resist
His uncontrollable intent;
His servants hee with new acquist
Of true experience from this great event,
With peace and consolation hath dismist,
And calm of mind all passion spent.

Since God's ways are mysterious—acceptable by faith, but often baffling to reason—the result is rather to confirm and strengthen than to negate the effect realized on a lower level; and that is why Milton can conclude these lines also with his second formulation (the most famous indeed in all literature) of the Aristotelian katharsis: "calm of mind, all passion spent."

No poem, perhaps, could illustrate better than *Samson Agonistes* the potential of Scriptural poetry or the successful union of religious principle and human experience. Nor can one doubt that its composition meant for Milton the realization of an experience at once religious and aesthetic—even if we ignore the inescapable parallels between the poet and his hero.

The relation between Milton's later poems, dramatic or quasi-dramatic in form, and his own inner life is far too complex a question to be more than glanced at here. But glanced at it may be with *Paradise Regained* as the example.

The poem's subject is Christ's Temptation in the Wilderness, paralleling as it does the temptation in Eden, and permitting the elaboration of the pattern of Christ as the Second Adam, and the model of Christian heroism which he presents. The temptations follow the order of Saint Luke, and are (as Milton interprets them): the temptation of Christ to distrust God's provision and, taking matters into his own hands, satisfy his hunger by turning stones to bread; the temptation of the kingdoms, their power and glory, speciously offered by Milton's Satan as aids to Christ in attaining his Messianic kingdom; and the temptation to try God's providence by casting himself from the pinnacle of the Temple; and Christ, in his perfect faith and obedience, resists them all. This is the poem's primary theme. Satan's motive is to betray Christ if he can, or at least to discover whether he is indeed the promised Messiah and what it means to be called the Son of God. This is plainly stated. What is not stated but is borne in upon the reader is that by his resistance Christ is perfecting his knowledge of his own mission and nature and also finding out what it means to be the Son of God. The full realization comes to both at the same moment. Satan bids Christ cast himself down, for God will give the angels charge concerning him, or if he prefers—and this is pure irony, for it seems impossible—let him stand where he is. But Christ and the event can be also ironic: " 'Tempt not the Lord thy God,' he said [with evident double meaning] and stood. / But Satan smitten with amazement fell."

As Milton develops the temptations of the kingdoms, it is likewise borne in on us that these are the temptations of secular glory experienced by the Renaissance man—the glory of beauty, of fame, of power, and of knowledge; and we know that for Milton each of these had held a special attraction. It is as though in retrospect Milton were evaluating them anew and, through the medium of Christ, rejecting them. Especially insidious (as Milton must have discovered in the days of his action for the Puritan revolution) was the will to power concealing itself as zeal for God's service—for the establishment of his Kingdom on earth. And as for the secondary theme, of the office and nature of Christ, no question had given Milton more concern than this, the subject of the longest and most anxious chapter in his *De Doctrina*. And now under the aspect of Christ's earthly ministry, as in *Paradise Lost*, under the aspect of his place in Heaven, Milton returns to the subject and confirms by poetry and to his imagination the faith that he has established by an appeal to Scripture and reason: once more, and always, Christ is, as the angels sing, "True Image of the Father."

In Milton's religious poetry, as patently in Donne's, there is always a starting point in the poet's extra-aesthetic experience. Sometimes (as we have already seen in the sonnet on his blindness) the starting point is plainly stated, and with it the problem which it is the function of the poem to solve or transcend, thus effecting a release of emotional tension. More often the starting point must be inferred, for the mode of the poem is no longer that of direct statement, but of imaginative projection. Not less surely the problem is isolated for contemplation and the forces of understanding and faith are marshaled to confront it, so that the problem is solved or transcended, and the release of emotional tension achieved. And all this is accomplished more effectively because the full resources of the poet's imagination are brought into play, and the theme is supported and carried forward by an aesthetic pattern (with a strong structural basis) which has its own power of arousing and directing the emotions. In its total effect, springing from the coalescence of a religious and an aesthetic experience, resides the essence of the poem as an autonomous, but not isolated, work of art.

# ⇥ V ⇤

## RELIGION AND POETRY, 1660–1780

Though Donne was certainly aware of possibly disruptive forces at work in the science and philosophy of his day, these had no perceptible effect on his own religious life as revealed in the Divine Poems. While we may detect in Milton what look like affinities with Spinoza and one or two other contemporary thinkers, they do nothing to disturb his adherence to Scripture and the Christian scheme of salvation. As for the minor poets, it is evident that Cowley's welcome to the philosophy of Bacon, and even of Hobbes, leaves his Christian and Anglican piety untouched; that Vaughan's Hermetic studies and Traherne's quietism belong to quite different traditions, wholly opposed to the "new philosophy," and anyway were subordinated to their Christian faith; and that Herbert and Crashaw show no awareness whatever of new and disturbing currents of thought. Though these currents were all flowing before 1660, we are justified in having postponed our brief consideration of them to this point, after which their influence can be seen amid other cultural changes ushered in by the Restoration. "When Charles II entered Whitehall," said J. R. Green, "modern England was born." There is enough truth in the statement to invite us to take our bearings anew.

One of the marks of modern England (as of most other countries since the seventeenth century) has been the steady growth of secularism. After 1660, religion, without retiring from the political scene, exercised a less commanding influence than it had done in and preceding the days of Puritan rule. With the monarchy the Church was restored; it was not, however, the Church of Laud, but something cooler and less inflexible; and the Latitudinarians, as they were called, pious but moderate divines, and Christian rationalists, many of whom had weathered out the storm of the Puritan revolution at home, made their influence felt. (Burnet's *History of My Own Time* recognizes the strong influence of the Cambridge Platonists on the restored Church, and, in the light of later history, we may add the emergence of a tradition of liberal thought which, under the name of the Broad Church party, as distinguished from both High and Low, has continued to this day, with such famous names as Thomas Arnold and Benjamin Jowett in the nineteenth century and Dean Inge in our own.) At the Restoration a new golden age of the Anglican pulpit set in; but now the great preacher was not a Donne or an Andrewes, but a Tillotson or a Stillingfleet—cogent, simple, direct, and almost conversational in style. Samuel Pepys heard "the famous young Stillingfleet [preach] a most plain, honest, good, grave sermon in the most unconcerned and easy, yet substantial, manner that ever I heard in my life," and reports that the primate and the bishop of London held him to be "the ablest young man to preach the Gospel of any since the Apostles"—though an unconcerned manner is hardly the first quality one would think of as apostolic.

Not unnaturally, there was a reaction against Puritan "enthusiasm," as it was called (that is, the belief that one was directly and personally inspired) or what Hobbes called the "private spirit," as leading only to distraction and disturbance, if not, as in the past, to civil war and anarchy. Describing his burlesque hero Hudibras, Samuel Butler wrote:

> For his religion, it was fit
> To match his learning and his wit:
> 'Twas Presbyterian, true blue,
> For he was of that stubborn crew
> Of errant saints, whom all men grant
> To be the true church militant:
> Such as do build their faith upon
> The holy text of pike and gun;
> Decide all controversies by
> Infallible artillery;
> And prove their doctrine orthodox
> By apostolic blows, and knocks;
> Call fire and sword and desolation
> A godly-thorough Reformation,
> Which always must be carry'd on,
> And still be doing, never done:
> As if Religion were intended
> For nothing else but to be mended.

And, voicing the reaction, Dryden wrote:

> And after hearing what our Church can say,
> If still our Reason run another way,
> That private Reason 'tis more just to curb,
> Than by disputes the public peace disturb.
> For points obscure are of small use to learn;
> But common quiet is mankind's concern.

The great protector of common quiet was the Church of the *via media*; and it was a power to be reckoned with. In the panic days of the Popish Plot, it held loyally to the king and saved his throne; but when, after infinite patience, the Church saw its very existence menaced by his successor, it withdrew its support, and James II lost his kingdom. The *via media* indeed came to be expressed and valued as much in political as in religious terms, as is seen in Swift's allegory of the three brothers, Peter, Martin, and Jack (the Papist, the Anglican, and the Puritan); and under the Hanoverians the Church was too commonly thought of as the "Establishment" and as social and political rather than religious in its function, and too easily acquiesced in this role. It was Bishop Warburton, one of its luminaries, who prompted the witticism (with special reference no doubt to his book *The Divine Legation of Moses*): "There is but one God, and the Bishop of Gloucester is his Attorney General." But it is easy to exaggerate the supineness of the eighteenth-century Church and to minimize its contributions to religion and culture, forgetting that it gave rise to two religious revivals—the Methodist and the Evangelical—and could shelter a great philosopher like Bishop Berkeley, a great philosophical theologian like Bishop Butler, a great satirist like Swift, a great publicist like Addison, a great moralist like Dr. Johnson, and a great political thinker like Burke, in all of whom Anglicanism was a vital force; but of poets, in any effective sense (save for such minor figures as Bishop Ken, John Byrom, and Charles Wesley) perhaps only three—Christopher Smart, Cowper, and Crabbe—show at all the impress of the Church until, that is, one passes out of the eighteenth century and comes to the Romantic movement and to Wordsworth and Coleridge. But to return now to the beginning of our period, the last four decades of the seventeenth century, and the secularization of English life and thought.

In thought, the new secularism is most clearly seen in the partly divergent philosophies of Bacon and Hobbes, both of which are formulated before 1660 but become fully operative as forces only after the Restoration.

Bacon set as the goal of philosophy the investigation of all natural phenomena by the inductive process of observation and classification, with, as its end, the attainment of true knowledge and the application of that knowledge to the well-being of man, or, as it is phrased in Bacon's utopia, *The New Atlantis*, "The end of our foundation is the knowledge of causes . . . and the enlargement of the bounds of human empire, to the effecting of all things possible." Bacon was no enemy of religion, but he adopted a principle which, in effect, isolated it from the rest of life and invited exclusive concentration on the secular. He divided all philosophy into divine (whose truths were the subject of revelation) and human (whose truths were only to be attained by scientific investigation). He did not set them at odds; he conceded that while "a little philosophy inclineth man's mind to atheism . . . depth in philosophy bringeth men's minds about to religion; for while the mind of man looketh upon second causes scattered, it may sometimes rest in them, and go no further, but when it beholdeth the chain of them confederate and linked together, it must needs fly to Providence and Deity" —or, in other words, to some form of natural religion. The purpose of Bacon's principle of segregation was to prevent religion from impeding the quest for scientific truth—the knowledge of second causes—and perhaps (though in lesser degree) to safeguard organized and revealed religion from damage by science. It was accepted as a basic principle by the Royal Society, whose founding Cowley hailed as, in effect, Bacon's dream of the New Atlantis come true—Bacon the Moses of the new science, who had been granted a sight of the Promised Land but had not lived to enter it. Though not without a measure of qualification, then, Bacon banished religion and directed attention to secular knowledge and temporal well-being.

If Bacon's philosophy made for the secularizing of human thought by isolating it from religion, the philosophy of Hobbes was yet more drastic in its treatment of the issue. Abandoning all belief in spiritual causes, he sought to explain every phenomenon, physical or mental, only by reference to matter and motion. And, having thus shorn away all the traditional supports of morality and social order, he sought in the *Leviathan* to replace them by a principle of authority and a theory of moral and political obligation consonant with his basic materialism. To a much greater extent than Bacon's, Hobbes's philosophy provoked the active opposition of religion. The Church refused the provision made for it by Hobbes as the support and instrument of political power, and attacked his whole system as fundamentally anti-religious; and those philosophical divines, the Cambridge Platonists, who were not unwilling to accept Bacon's plea for a science confined to second causes, were determined opponents of Hobbes.

A third force, more difficult to measure, came into England in the philosophy of Descartes. He recognized the existence of both mind and matter (or thought and extension), proved that mind must exist since it was only by an act of mind that its existence could be doubted, and, on the basis of the mind's existence thus proved, proceeded to demonstrate from its innate idea of a perfect being the further existence of God. Thus Descartes was at first welcomed by the Cambridge Platonists as a valuable support for religion, and it was only as they discovered the fatal flaw in his system that they rejected him. This flaw was his failure to provide any adequate connection between thought and extension—and hence between God and the material world—which resulted in a dichotomy more fatal than Bacon's, since it was one of fact and not of convenience, a dichotomy which left the proof of God's existence intact in and to mind, but at the same time left the material world without dependence upon him and so to be explained in its essence and operation (if explained at all) in purely material terms.

So much, then, for the bearing on religion, wholly, or almost wholly, negative, of the secular and secularizing philosophies of Bacon, Hobbes, and Descartes. It follows that they could have no bearing on religious poetry save to direct the attention of poets and readers away from it, and to invite them to consider themselves and their world in terms other than religious—and this quite apart from the fact that both Bacon and Hobbes had (as we shall see) important and influential statements to make on poetry itself as a form of discourse.

But we are not yet done with currents of thought bearing on religion. About the time of the Restoration there emerged the new force of Deism—a more extreme form of rationalism than that represented by the Cambridge Platonists and the Latitudinarians, who called in natural religion as a basis or support for the Christian revelation. In essence Deism meant the rejection of revealed in favor of natural religion, and of faith in favor of reason. Deism or its forerunner (as formulated by Lord Herbert of Cherbury, the brother of the poet, in his Latin work on the *Religion of the Gentiles*) listed five points as the essentials of religion: the existence of a Supreme Being or God; the duty of worshiping him; recognition that his worship consists in virtue or the proper use of our faculties; the necessity of repentance; and a belief in punishments and rewards here and hereafter. These essentials were indeed present in all the revealed religions, but stood in no need of special revelation, since they were among the "common notions" imprinted in the minds of men by virtue of their humanity. Deism, thus conceived, was an elaboration of that natural religion assumed by theologians as offering a basis on which revelation could build, and often, called in to witness against atheism. There can be no doubt that Deistic modes of thought permeated much of the rational theology of those whom Dryden attacked as our "philosophizing divines"; and the narrow line dividing orthodoxy and Deism is seen in the indignation of Locke, the author of *The Reasonableness of Christianity*, when he found that the Deist John Toland had dedicated to him *Christianity Not Mysterious*. That Deism became increasingly skeptical as time went on, and increasingly hostile to Christianity, becomes apparent if we compare with Lord Herbert's such later writings as the *Philosophical Fragments* of Lord Bolingbroke, though Pope remained a conservative Deist, attacking no form of religion but turning his thought to syncretism as seen in his *Universal Prayer*.

It is often said that the God of Deism was an absentee god, who, having set the universe in motion, left it to run on by its own resistless and essentially mechanical laws. It is true that Deism did in measure follow the trend toward mechanism in eighteenth-century thought and seek to preserve its belief in a deity by separating Him from the machine he had created; but as a general statement of the Deist position, it overlooks the whole wing of the movement which eschewed mechanism in favor of a form of vitalism and preferred to push the idea of God's immanence up to or over the borders of pantheism. Neither wing succeeded in achieving the delicate Christian balance of God's transcendence and his omnipresence. But so far as poetry was concerned, the only contribution came from those Deists who emphasized immanence—that is, from Lord Shaftesbury and his followers, who, like the Cambridge Platonists, thought of causes as seminal and vital rather than mechanical. But more of this when we come to touch directly on Shaftesbury and his followers in poetry.

Meanwhile, the drift toward mechanism can be plainly seen in the shifting interpretation put upon the findings of the devoutly religious (if also Arian) Isaac Newton. "The main business of natural philosophy," Newton wrote, "is to argue from phenomena without feigning hypotheses, and to deduce causes from effects till we come to the very first cause, which is certainly not mechanical. . . ." The "very first cause" is none other than God, and he is necessary to account for the origin of a universe, bearing, as a study of the phenomena indicates, every mark of order and design, in the motions, for example, of the planets, which "could not spring from any natural cause alone, but were impressed by an intelligent agent." Nor was it the origin of this order only that required a reference to God, but its continuance and operation likewise depended on his concourse. "For does it not appear from [the] phenomena that there is a being incorporeal, living, intelligent, omnipresent, who in infinite space, as it were in his *sensorium*, sees the things themselves . . . and comprehends them wholly by their immediate presence to himself? This Being governs all things, not as the soul of the world but [immediately] as Lord over all." The reference here to the soul of the world is interesting: it was a hypothetical being revived from Plato by the pious Cambridge Platonists, and interjected between God, the first cause, and the operation of second causes. It was rejected by Newton, first, as superfluous, since one could and must argue directly to God's concurrence and intervention, and, secondly, because, as his phrasing shows, he sensed the danger that the soul of the world, or spirit of nature, might be identified with God, and result in the deifying of nature—that is, in pantheism—a danger clearly manifested in later thought. But our concern now is with an opposite tendency—the tendency to regard Newton's view of the world as purely mechanistic. Newton refused to decide whether or not gravity was a property of matter, but insisted that if it were, the argument for God's concourse and intervention was unimpaired. But it was precisely such assumptions of the sufficiency of matter and motion to explain all operations on mechanical principles, without reference to God, that led to an increasingly mechanistic interpretation of the Newtonian universe, which, in turn, encouraged Blake to bracket Newton, Bacon, and Locke (though Hobbes might have been a better choice) as the great proponents of mechanism and enemies of spiritualism, and, what is much more significant, caused even the better-informed Coleridge on occasion to identify Newtonianism with what he called the "mechanic philosophy." From physics the mechanical principle spread to psychology, and the genuinely religious David Hartley applied it to the operations of the mind, fondly supposing that he was imitating Newton, when in reality he was instead falling into the current of Hobbes. It is necessary to make this clear if we are to understand the reaction against the whole mechanistic philosophy which finally set in with Coleridge and the Romantics.

In the meantime, however, it is even more necessary to recognize that religious poetry survived this trend toward mechanistic materialism. It did so in two ways. First, there were poets who continued, like their predecessors in earlier periods, to rely simply on revealed religion and on personal or corporate religious experience; these poets extended from the Roman Catholic Dryden to the Evangelical Cowper, and beyond to Wordsworth and the Tractarians. Secondly, the poets who turned to natural religion, as either a support or a substitute for revelation, eschewed mere mechanism as incompatible alike with religion and with poetry, and saw in the ordered realm of nature full evidence of the working of a transcendent or an immanent deity; these poets extend from Pope and Thomson through Wordsworth.

Nor was this clinging to the idea of God as revealed in his works confined to the poets. Throughout the period, orthodox apologists continued to appeal confidently and often learnedly (as in the Boyle Lecture Sermons) to the argument from design. The Deists, so long as they remained Deists and did not deteriorate into mere skeptics, had every motive to cling to a revelation in or through nature, since they had abandoned any other. It was their clinging to a supposedly perfect and universally accessible system of nature, while rejecting revelation as full of anomalies and capriciously restricted to a minority of mankind, that prompted the most effective counterattack, Bishop Butler's *Analogy of Religion*, which undertook to produce as many apparent anomalies in the treasured system of nature (considered apart from revelation) as the Deists found in the Christian revelation, and posed this dilemma: would they then go on farther and on the very same grounds reject natural religion as well, or would they, on second thought, accept both nature and revelation and find in the higher all apparent anomalies resolved? Effective in its own day, Butler's great book was destined to a renewed fame and influence in the nineteenth century.

So much for the state of religion and the emergence of forces favorable or hostile to it in the period between the writers of the Restoration and the Romantic poets.

With the Restoration a marked change had also commenced in the theory and practice of poetry, which had its inevitable effect on religious verse. Commencing in Dryden, perfected in Pope, and defended in a rear-guard action by Dr. Johnson, the principles of Neoclassicism dominated the poetry of the period from 1660 to a date not easy to specify in the eighteenth century, when the oncoming forces which were to culminate in the Romantic movement made the description no longer fully applicable. The Neoclassical reform of poetry insisted on rationality in content, and combined lucidity in ease in expression. It assumed the classical principle of art as an imitation of nature, emphasized conscious artistry as opposed to inspiration, fostered argument, and eschewed enthusiasm and uncontrolled flights of imagination; its most characteristic vehicle was the heroic couplet. The style of course varied with the subject: Dryden, in *Religio Laici*, arguing coolly against both Puritans and Deists and in defense of the Established Church, selected, he said, a style "fittest for discourse and nearest prose"; but that the heroic couplet could rise to eloquence and express a degree of emotion is clear from *The Hind and the Panther*, written after his conversion to Rome, as from much of Pope's poetry, including his quasi-religious *Essay on Man*. But the neatly turned couplet did not permanently hold the field unchallenged. With Thomson's *Seasons*, Miltonic blank verse recommences its long career and becomes a principal vehicle for religious and philosophic poetry from Thomson to Wordsworth, and the ode was always in some degree exempted from the more rigorous restrictions of neoclassical rule. Immediately significant as these facts are for religious verse, there are others bearing on the nature of poetry which are yet more so, and must not pass unnoticed.

Bacon and Hobbes had something influential to say on this subject; and since Hobbes's impact was immediate, and Bacon's delayed, we may speak of them in reverse order. Just as Hobbes, having divested the state of all traditional moral and religious sanctions, sought to ground a theory of political obligation on what he took to be solid facts, so he brought poetry down to

earth and attempted to give the principles of Neoclassicism a
similar basis. "Time and education," he writes, "beget experience; experience begets memory; memory begets judgment and
fancy; judgment begets the strength and structure, and fancy begets the ornaments of a poem." Poetry is then a representation
of reality, but of such reality as is accessible to observation and
conformable to reason. "Beyond the actual works of nature a
poet may go, but beyond the conceived possibility of nature,
never." There is no place for the miraculous or for what runs
counter to, or transcends, human reason and experience. Nor
will Hobbes have anything to do with the idea of the poet as
one inspired. Invocation either of God or of the muses is "a
foolish custom, by which a man enabled to speak wisely, from
the principles of nature and his own meditation, loves rather to
be thought to speak by inspiration, like a bagpipe." Obviously
such views are not friendly to the idea of the poet as prophet
or perhaps to religious poetry of any kind.

But if it restricted the range of poetry, Hobbes's theory left
it in contact with reality (as he conceived reality) and did not
seek to depress it to the level of mere fiction indulged in for the
sake of entertainment alone. But precisely this was the effect of
Bacon's theory. He assigns history to the faculty of memory,
which stores up the knowledge of particulars; and philosophy
to the understanding, which operates inductively with these
particulars and arrives at truths of general application; but poetry,
he relegates to the imagination alone. This faculty, not being
tied to reality (as are memory and understanding) or assigned
a particular function in the advancement of knowledge, is free
to play at will and constructs its own fabric of fictions, which
Bacon calls "feigned history." He sums up:

History is referred to memory; poesy to the imagination; philosophy to the reason. And by poesy here I mean nothing else but feigned history. History is properly concerned with individuals [i.e., with particular facts], the impressions whereof are the first and most ancient guests of the human mind and are as the primary materials of knowledge. With . . . this material the human mind perpetually exercises itself, and sometimes sports. For as all knowledge is the exercise and work of the mind, so poesy may be regarded as its sport. In philosophy the mind is bound to [the nature of] things. In poesy it is released from that bond and wanders forth and feigns what it pleases.

A number of points deserve notice. The assignment of poetry to the imagination alone contrasts strongly with the Hobbesian and Neoclassical view, and we see in Bacon the shape of things to come, for this is a premonition of one Romantic theory of poetry which regards it as play. In Bacon, the assignment of poetry to the imagination is accompanied by the divorce of poetry from reality: fiction is not the means adopted by poetry but its essential nature. This will provoke a reaction in Blake, Wordsworth, and Coleridge, who will assert that the substance of poetry is truth and the imagination an organ—the supreme organ—of truth. Meanwhile, we may recognize in Bacon a fresh phase of the conflict between philosophy and poetry which is as old as Plato, but which now takes a new and highly significant form with truth the prerogative of science, and poetry dealing exclusively in pseudo-statements, a premonition of the modern theory of poetry glanced at in our preliminary definitions: Richards is in fact the distant descendant of Bacon. There is, however, one reservation which must be made: Bacon allows that in spite of (or should we say, rather, by virtue of?) its imaginative and fictitious character, poetry can on occasion be used for the presentation of doctrine in what he calls "poesy parabolical"; and here indeed we encounter a somewhat ominous linking of poetry and imagination with religion. Imagination, Bacon writes,

> is either invested with or usurps no small authority in itself. . . . For we see that in matters of faith and religion our imagination raises itself above our reason, not that divine illumination resides in the imagination, its seat being rather in the very citadel of the mind and understanding, but that the divine grace uses the motions of the imagination as an instrument of illumination, . . . which is the reason why religion always sought access to the mind by similitudes, types, parables, visions, dreams. . . . Nevertheless I see no cause to alter the former division; for imagination hardly produces sciences [i.e., forms of true knowledge], poesy . . . being to be accounted rather a pleasure or play of wit than a science.

On the poetry of the period from 1660 to 1740, including the more argumentative forms of religious verse, the Neoclassical theory in its Hobbesian and other forms exercised a considerable influence. From that time on to the great Romantics, the Baconian theory asserted its sway in secular if not in religious verse. Then, with Blake, Wordsworth, and Coleridge the reaction already mentioned set in: imagination was recognized as the supreme organ of truth, and poetry as its unrivaled vehicle. But there is good reason to infer that the Baconian doctrine was scotched, not killed, and that it has reasserted itself in our own day.

It may seem that our cursory, but still complicated, excursion into the history of thought as it bears on religion and poetry has merely postponed our arrival at the poetry itself; but without it we could hardly hope to see the poetry in its historical relations or against its contemporary background. No such detailed discussion was necessary for the religious poetry of the English Renaissance, because it proceeded on traditional religious lines, for the most part ignoring the ferment of thought and theory which was even then commencing to emerge. And of some religious poetry in our present period, this continues to be true. For different reasons, and in different ways, it is true perhaps of Dryden, in part of Addison, largely of Christopher Smart, and wholly of Cowper, but not at all of Pope or Thomson, or of the minor poets who can be associated with them.

Of Dryden, then, we may say that he was fully aware of the currents and cross-currents, secular and religious, in the thought of his day, and could judge of them in the light of other ages. "Every page," said Johnson, "discovers a mind very widely acquainted with art and nature and in full possession of great stores of intellectual wealth." We may add that they also discover a mind alert and active in extraordinary degree. Dryden delighted in the give and take, the thrust and parry, of debate, and startles the modern reader by his assertion: "He cannot be a good poet who cannot argue well." He tells us that the natural bent of his mind was skeptical. This at first led him to the philosophy of Hobbes, but further and more mature thinking seems to have brought the conviction that there were more things in heaven and earth than were dreamed of in that philosophy. Not more skeptical than conservative in temper, Dryden sought a principle of authority as in politics so also in religion.

In *Religio Laici* he writes:

> Dim as the borrow'd beams of moon and stars
> To lonely, weary, wand'ring travellers,
> Is Reason to the soul; and, as on high
> Those rolling fires discover but the sky,
> Not light us here, so Reason's glimmering ray
> Was lent, not to assure our doubtful way,
> But guide us upward to a better day.
> And as those nightly tapers disappear
> When day's bright lord ascends our hemisphere;
> So pale grows Reason at Religion's sight;

So dies, and so dissolves in supernatural light.
Some few, whose lamp shone brighter, have been led
From cause to cause, to nature's secret head;
And found that one first principle must be:
But what, or who that UNIVERSAL HE?
Whether some soul encompassing this ball,
Unmade, unmov'd; yet making, moving all;
Or various atoms' interfering dance
Leapt into form, (the noble work of chance;)
Or this great All was from eternity;
Not ev'n the Stagirite himself could see,
And Epicurus guess'd as well as he. . . .
Thus anxious thoughts in endless circles roll,
Without a centre where to fix the soul;
In this wild maze their vain endeavours end:
How can the less the greater comprehend?
Or finite reason reach Infinity?

Philosophy is impotent: religion must supply the principle of authority, of belief and action, if principle there be. So for the time being, Dryden defends revelation, liberally interpreted, against the attacks of the Deists, and in the name of "common quiet" he defends the Church against disturbing manifestations of the private spirit. But it seems unlikely that the quest will end here. Probably politics had as much to do as religion with Dryden's initial shift of allegiance to the Roman Catholic Church in the reign of James II, but it is impossible to doubt that, on a frankly fideist basis, he found there the philosophical and religious solution which he sought. This is clear from a directly personal passage of moving eloquence in *The Hind and the Panther*, that remarkable animal fable in which the milk-white Hind (the Church of Rome) and the Panther (the Church of England) carry on, with unflagging energy and interest, their protracted debate:

> What weight of ancient witness can prevail,
> If private reason hold the public scale?

But, gracious God, how well dost thou provide
For erring judgments an unerring guide!
Thy throne is darkness in the abyss of light,
A blaze of glory that forbids the sight.
O teach me to believe thee thus conceal'd,
And search no farther than thyself reveal'd;
But her alone for my director take,
Whom thou hast promised never to forsake!
My thoughtless youth was wing'd with vaine desires,
My manhood, long misled by wandering fires,
Follow'd false lights; and, when their glimpse was gone,
My pride struck out new sparkles of her own.
Such was I, such by nature still I am;
Be thine the glory, and be mine the shame!
Good life be now my task: my doubts are done:
(What more could fright my faith than three in one?)

Dryden, of the powerful, ranging mind, can find no secure support for religion in reason, and resorts simply to an act of faith—
a course foreshadowed in the relatively prosaic argument of
*Religio Laici.*

With the flight of James II, Dryden did not abandon the defeated cause; but specifically Roman Catholic poetry of any
significance disappears from English literature for the next century and a half.

No such desperate resort to faith as we find in Dryden marks
the quiet piety of Addison, a moderate Whig in politics (a
party not always marked by religion or by friendship for the
Church) and a tolerant but devoted Anglican. In his best-known
hymn, the Newtonian heavens "Their great original proclaim,"
he continues:

> What though in solemn silence all
> Move round the dark terrestrial ball?
> What though nor real voice nor sound
> Amid their radiant orbs be found?
> In reason's ear they all rejoice,

And utter forth a glorious voice,
Forever singing, as they shine,
"The hand that made us is divine."

But a more personal note is heard in such verses as,

When all thy mercies, O my God,
My rising soul surveys,
Transported with the view, I'm lost
In wonder, love, and praise.

O how shall words with equal warmth
The gratitude declare
That glows within my ravish'd heart!
But thou canst read it there.

Here we are not far from the Dissenter Isaac Watts at his all too rare best, as in one of the most famous of English hymns, "O God, Our Help in Ages Past," or even from Charles Wesley, or from William Cowper of the *Olney Hymns*. There is indeed a strain of simple personal piety running through the eighteenth century, and rising to a note of fervor in the Wesleyan and Evangelical revivals, which makes it a period of English hymn writing second only to the nineteenth century. The revivals made their great contribution in the hymns of Charles Wesley— festal hymns like that for Christmas, "Hark, the Herald Angels Sing," or the Easter hymn, "Jesus Christ Is Risen Today," as well as those for general and personal use like "Jesus, Lover of My Soul," and many more; in John Newton's "How Sweet the Name of Jesus Sounds," William Cowper's "O for a Closer Walk with God," and Augustus Toplady's "Rock of Ages, Cleft for Me." It is well to remember this strain of Christian and primarily Evangelical piety, untroubled by controversy, as we turn to the more philosophical poets—first to a group basically orthodox in their theology.

Edward Young's once famous *Night Thoughts* is known to

the literary historian as an early example of that romantic
melancholy which broods on death and the grave, a forerunner
of Gray's *Elegy* and kindred poems, and a fairly early example
of the revival of blank verse; but for us its interest lies in its
quality as religious poetry. A series of protracted meditations on
life, death, and immortality, running to nine books, the poem
springs, as the preface tells us, from the poet's own bereave-
ments and sorrows, and its form is dictated rather by what spon-
taneously rose in his mind from these sources than by any pre-
meditated design. It has, then, an experiential basis; and it
achieves some degree of structure and progression. Through
long contemplation of death and its controlling effect on life and
the joys of life, the poet reaches at the midway point the
Christian triumph, but only to experience, in the succeeding
book, a relapse under the renewed blow of fate.

> 'Tis vain to seek in men for more than man.
> Though proud in promise, big in previous thought,
> Experience damps our triumph. I, who late
> Emerging from the shadows of the grave,
> Where grief detain'd me prisoner, mounting high,
> Threw wide the gates of everlasting day,
> And call'd mankind to glory, shook off pain,
> Mortality shook off, in ether pure,
> And struck the stars, now feel my spirits fail . . .
> In sorrow drown'd—but not in sorrow lost
> (How wretched is the man who never mourn'd!)
> I dive for precious pearl in sorrow's stream.

And so the meditations recommence, reaching at last through a
vision of the Judgment (whose verdict our conscience anticipates) the conclusion that our very afflictions are our blessings if
they induce us to turn to God and virtue. Here the final meditation might—perhaps indeed should—have ended. But the poet,
firm in the conviction that devotion is the daughter of astrono-

my, turns to a contemplation of the Newtonian heavens, reaches back to Christian Platonism to bestow an angel on every star, and to the witness of the ages to teach "That nature is the glass reflecting God." Nor is that all (for this ninth Night—surely it must have been the longest of the year—runs to a generous 2,300 lines): he considers, in light of God's boundless power, the possible plurality of inhabited worlds, and though his only space vehicle is "Contemplation's rapid car," "from earth," he writes:

> . . . as from my barrier, I set out.
> How swift I mount! diminish'd earth recedes;
> I pass the moon; and from her farther side,
> Pierce heaven's blue curtain, strike into remote . . .
> I pause at every planet on my road,
> And ask for him who gives their orbs to roll. . . .

This and much more strike strangely on the ear two centuries later. It is the product of the state of knowledge in Young's period, as his questions addressed to "Ye searching, ye Newtonian angels" remind us; but the flights of fancy and the questions are not only inspired by piety, they all shape themselves within the framework of orthodoxy.

> Call'd here Elijah in his flaming car?
> Pass'd by you the good Enoch on his road. . . .

And are the inhabitants of other worlds also fallen, and are they by Christ redeemed? But natural religion, though read thus in the framework of revelation, gives way at the end to the revelation itself—the Trinity in Unity and the Incarnate Christ.

For all its prolixity, its exploiting of emotion for its own sake (as it often appears), and its not infrequent theatricality, the poem seems to realize and embody a genuine religious experience, and in its better moments to unite this with an adequate poetic experience, and so to qualify for inclusion, not as a document merely, but as an example of religious poetry.

Of documentary value mainly are the Seatonian poems, written at Cambridge year by year after 1750. The subjects were prescribed. Christopher Smart (the only name of note in the list) won five awards with poems on the Divine Attributes; other subjects were taken from Scripture (especially from the life of Christ), or dealt, in terms of orthodoxy, with such general subjects as Death, Heaven, Repentance, Charity, Humility, and Hope. Smart's and most of the others are in blank verse, though there were occasional excursions into other forms. Even in Smart there is little to suggest the energy and imagination of the later *Song to David*, though there are occasional premonitions, as in his description of the world beneath the waters and its inhabitants.

> While high above their heads Leviathan,
> The terror and the glory of the main,
> His pastime takes with transport, proud to see
> The Ocean's vast dominion all his own.

But the interval is emphasized if we compare the frigid invocation to David (whom the Gentiles called Orpheus) with the *Song* itself.

From the poetry of orthodoxy, we may turn back briefly to Pope—an avowed Roman Catholic and actually a moderate Deist. His *Essay on Man* is not primarily a religious poem (indeed it seems deliberately to refuse a religious theme).

> Know then thyself. Presume not God to scan;
> The proper study of Mankind is Man.
> Plac'd on this isthmus of a middle state,
> A Being darkly wise, and rudely great:
> With too much knowledge for the Sceptic's side,
> With too much weakness for the Stoic's pride,
> He hangs between; in doubt to act, or rest,
> In doubt to deem himself a God, or Beast;
> In doubt his Mind or Body to prefer;

> Born but to die, and reas'ning but to err. . . .
> Sole judge of Truth, in endless Error hurl'd:
> The glory, jest, and riddle of the world!

Yet there is an implicit religious reference throughout, which at times becomes explicit. The poem is a theodicy, drawing on such works as Archbishop King's *Origin of Evil*, and its purpose, in Pope's own phrase, to "vindicate the ways of God to man": it is thus a theodicy in terms of human experience and natural religion which deliberately challenges (in the line quoted) comparison with Milton's theodicy in terms of revelation, *Paradise Lost*.

In interpreting the poem, an initial problem must be faced. Responsive to the teaching of Locke, Pope is sensible of the limitations of the human mind.

> Say first, of God above, or Man below,
> What can we reason, but from what we know?

The method, then, must be empirical. But in Epistle I, the argument appears to proceed on *a priori* lines and to consist of a series of inferences from the idea of God as the all perfect Being. The contradiction disappears if we read these inferences as an extended hypothesis to be tested by experience in the remaining Epistles. Empiricism has discredited the older method. Pope will show that the truths which it sought to establish survive.

> Of Systems possible, if 'tis confest
> That Wisdom infinite must form the best,
> Where all must full or not coherent be,
> And all that rises rise in due degree;
> Then, in the scale of reas'ning life, 'tis plain,
> There must be, somewhere, such a rank as Man.

The necessary inference from the idea of God as Creator is that this is the best of possible worlds, in which "whatever is, is right"; and, confronted with the inescapable limitations and evils of human life, one can only answer that the good aimed at, and attained, is the good not of the individual or of the single species but of the Creation as a whole, and that the limitations of the human lot spring inevitably from man's place in the chain of being.

> Vast chain of Being! which from God began,
> Natures ethereal, human, angel, man,
> Beast, bird, fish, insect, what no eye can see,
> No glass can reach; from Infinite to thee,
> From thee to Nothing. . . .

The essential ideas contributing to the traditional notion of the Great Chain of Being (as Lovejoy has shown) are these: that existence is in itself a good (the common assumption of most Western thought and its predominantly "this-worldly" religion); that God's abounding beneficence bestowed this good as widely as possible by creating every conceivable grade of being, with no interval left unfilled, but that in every instance the differentiation of grades inevitably meant the bestowal of certain powers and the withholding of others. The result is a graduated scale marked in its total extent by plenitude—a conception comparable in its sweep and grandeur with Hooker's idea of universally prevailing law. To Pope the idea of plenitude, and its accompaniment, unending variety, makes its strong appeal, but even stronger to the artist of balanced and emphatic patterns is the appeal of the order and harmony that ultimately dominates the whole.

> All Nature is but Art, unknown to thee;
> All Chance, Direction which thou canst not see;
> All Discord, Harmony not understood;
> All partial Evil, Universal Good.

At the end of Epistle I, Pope's enthusiasm for the total scheme expresses itself not only in the conception of a transcendent Creator who is an artist, very much like Pope himself, but in the idea of God's immanence.

> All are but parts of one stupendous whole,
> Whose body Nature is, and God the soul;
> That, chang'd through all, and yet in all the same;
> Great in the earth, as in th' ethereal frame;
> Warms in the sun, refreshes in the breeze,
> Glows in the stars, and blossoms in the trees,
> Lives thro' all life, extends through all extent,
> Spreads undivided, operates unspent. . . .
> To Him no high, no low, no great, no small;
> He fills, he bounds, connects, and equals all.

Pope's friend and editor Bishop Warburton tried to rescue the poet from the imputation of pantheism. The idea of a world soul is found in the Cambridge Platonists, but there it is a created being, and not as here identified with the Deity. Partly by its very clarity, Pope's formulation seems much more categorically pantheistic than anything to be found in Wordsworth; but our concern is not with questions of orthodoxy but with the presence of a response at once religious and poetic.

The tendency to cross the line dividing omnipresence from immanence is also seen in the poetic prose of Anthony Ashley Cooper, third Earl of Shaftesbury, and in the poetry of James Thomson: both of them writers highly influential in their century, and the former, indeed, an influence upon both Pope and Thomson as well as on a number of lesser poets.

Shaftesbury is a transitional figure of great importance. In many ways a typical gentleman of the early eighteenth century, of the more contemplative sort, a moderate Whig, an Anglican with a cool but convinced attachment to the *via media*, the champion of free inquiry and the opponent of "enthusiasm" and superstition, the disciple at once of the ancient Stoics, the Cambridge Platonists, and the more moderate Deists, and a confirmed adherent of Neoclassical principles in art—he could still write such passages as the one quoted below, in which a new enthusiasm, for nature as a revelation of the divine, is expressed in prose that breaks through some of the restraint of Neoclassical art. It occurs in *The Moralists: A Rhapsody* (which is Shaftesbury's theodicy).

Hailing the fields and woods as his quiet sanctuary, ideal for the contemplation proper to man of his own and other natures and for meditation on the cause of things, he proceeds:

O glorious Nature, supremely fair, and sovereignly good! All-loving and all-lovely, all-divine! . . . whose sanctuary brings such wisdom, and whose contemplation such delight; whose single work affords an ampler scene and is a nobler spectacle than all which ever Art presented. O mighty Nature, wise substitute of Providence! impowered Creatress! or thou impowering Deity, thee I invoke and thee alone adore. To thee this solitude . . . , these rural meditations are sacred, whilst thus inspired with harmony of thought, . . . I sing of Nature's order in created beings, and celebrate the beauties which resolve in thee, the source and principle of all beauty and perfection.

Here we see the tradition of meditation divested of all penitential elements (since Shaftesbury assumes man's natural goodness) and confined to a contemplation of the works of the Creator, the world, and the mind of man. God, Shaftesbury continues, is at once the object and author of our thoughts. And thought is the one reality which it is impossible to doubt: all else may be imagined to be "dream and shadow," but in thought we are "in a manner conscious of that original and eternally existent Thought, whence we derive our own." For God has communicated himself to us "so as, in some manner, to inhabit within our souls," and God is "Original Soul, diffusive, vital in all, inspiring the whole," visible likewise in his works, and made apparent to us in the system of the world. Here, whatever its defects from a Christian or a humanistic standpoint, we must recognize a current of thought strongly opposed to mechanism, and able, in the not too exacting logic of Thomson's poetry, to unite with the original—the anti-mechanistic—current of Newtonianism.

With the spaciousness of the *Georgics* as precedent, James Thomson writes his poem on the seasons, mingling scenes from nature and rural life with philosophic reflections on nature and the God of nature. In these reflections the influence of Shaftesbury is dominant, but it is joined by that of Newton. Indeed, as McKillop has shown, all the major currents of religio-philosophic thought as applied to nature meet in *The Seasons*; and the reflections are supported by a more immediate response to the variety, grandeur, and beauty of nature than is found in the rather labored paragraphs of Shaftesbury. Though the subject is well worth pursuing in detail, we can afford here no more than a quotation from *A Hymn*, in which various currents of thought mingle and merge: a Shaftesburian sense of God's immanence, a Newtonian sense of his direction and control, the older traditions of God's power and goodness as revealed in the work of his hand, and of all his creatures as owing and paying him praise, and a sense of progression as the mark of nature's life, culminating in an apocalyptic note.

> These, as they change, Almighty Father! these
> Are but the varied God. The rolling year
> Is full of thee. Forth in the pleasing Spring
> Thy Beauty walks, thy Tenderness and Love. . . .
> Then comes thy Glory in the Summer months,

With light and heat refulgent. Then thy sun
Shoots full perfection through the swelling year,
And oft thy voice in dreadful thunder speaks. . . .
Thy Bounty shines in Autumn unconfin'd,
And spreads a common feast for all that lives.
In Winter, awful thou! with clouds and storms
Around thee thrown, tempest o'er tempest roll'd.
Majestic darkness! On the whirlwind's wing
Riding sublime, thou bidst the world adore. . . .
Mysterious round! what skill, what force divine,
Deep-felt in these appear! . . .
But wandering oft with brute unconscious gaze,
Man marks not thee, marks not the mighty hand
That, ever busy, wheels the silent spheres,
Works in the secret deep, shoots streaming thence
The fair profusion that o'erspreads the Spring,
Flings from the sun direct the flaming day,
Feeds every creature, hurls the tempest forth,
And, as on earth this grateful change revolves,
With transport touches all the springs of life.

Nature attend! join, every living soul
Beneath the spacious temple of the sky,
In adoration join, and ardent raise
One general song. . . .
Still sing the God of Seasons as they roll. . . .
Since God is ever present, ever felt
In the void waste as in the city full,
And where he vital spreads there must be joy.
When even at last the solemn hour shall come,
And wing my mystic flight to future worlds,
I cheerful will obey. . . .
                              I cannot go
Where universal love smiles not around,
Sustaining all yon orbs and all their sons
From seeming evil still educing good,
And better thence again, and better still,
In infinite progression. But I lose
Myself in him, in light ineffable!
Come then, expressive Silence, muse his praise.

Here natural religion has taken the place of revealed; nature is itself a sufficient revelation; and with revealed religion has disappeared that realistic—sometimes even excessive—sense of evil, which finds expression in the Christian dogma of man's Fall, accompanied by nature's dislocation, and of the imperative need of redemption by Christ. Fallen man can find in fallen nature, so runs the orthodox reply, only a snare and pitfall; what Shaftesbury, Thomson, and their fellows attribute to man in general can be truly experienced only by the redeemed: for the regenerate—and for them alone—nature itself is transfigured. This is the burden of William Cowper's criticism of such lines as I have quoted. It is significant, however, that Cowper writes under the influence of the Evangelical revival. More moderate Anglicans were less inclined to attack the excesses of Shaftesburian natural theology and natural ethics than tacitly to recognize allies in the struggle against materialism, mechanism, and the atheism (as they did not scruple to call it) of the tradition of Hobbes and Mandeville.

Thomson was but one of a series of poets who responded to the influence of Shaftesbury, but he will serve as sufficient example. In *The Seasons* he established the tradition of the long descriptive and reflective poem in blank verse which centered in nature and reached out from the individual scene to contemplate the scheme of things in its larger aspects: the tradition which culminates in Wordsworth's *Prelude*. A landmark on the way to that culmination is Cowper's poem *The Task*—at least in those parts (and they are many) devoted to nature. In detailed description Cowper (though of a more domestic landscape) takes a long step toward Wordsworth, but in philosophical outlook he is much more conservative than was Thomson. Cowper's philosophy of nature is bounded by the severe orthodoxy of the Evangelical revival: the poet who contemplated nature was the same who had joined John Newton in composing the *Olney Hymns*: who had written "There Is a Fountain Filled with Blood" (the redeeming blood of Christ), "O for a Closer Walk with God," "Sometimes a Light Surprises / The Christian as He Sings"— these and other familiar hymns.

> God moves in a mysterious way
>   His wonders to perform;
> He plants his footsteps in the sea
>   And rides upon the storm. . . .
>
> Judge not the Lord by feeble sense,
>   But trust him for his grace;
> Behind a frowning providence
>   He hides a smiling face. . . .
>
> Blind unbelief is sure to err,
>   And scan his works in vain:
> God is his own interpreter,
>   And He will make it plain.

This is Cowper's basic belief—the stern outlines of Calvinism in measure countervailed, but not rejected, by the natural gentleness of the man. The creed of Calvin has indeed two aspects: for the reprobate "a frowning providence," for the elect "a smiling face." Of the personal tragedy of Cowper, we need not speak— the returning delusion that he alone stood beyond the reach of grace. "I feel," he said, "unutterable despair"—yet despair which in the medium of poetry, in *The Castaway*, found its perfect utterance, though alas, no relief. For whatever his doubts—nay, convictions—regarding himself, Cowper never doubted the fundamentals of the creed he had adopted; and it is in the light of that creed that he approaches nature in its larger aspects, and repudiates the Shaftesburian, in favor of a Christian, view.

The more theoretic portions of *The Task* are not the most

highly valued; but they are essential for an understanding of Cowper. In his confutation of the philosophers, he couples, as they did, the appeal to nature and the source of liberty. He starts with the idea of Christian liberty, the doctrine which (though Cowper seems to forget this) had been central in Milton's thought.

> But there is yet a liberty unsung
> By poets and by senators unprais'd. . . .
> 'Tis liberty of heart deriv'd from heaven,
> Bought with his blood, who gave it to mankind,
> And seal'd with the same token. . . .
>            His other gifts
> All bear the royal stamp that speak them his. . . .
> But these are not his glory.

The natural Creation is of use indeed to confute the atheist, and for the Christian (as we shall hear) to yield him bounty and to point him home. But for all its seeming permanence, its day shall end—the order of nature is transient; only the order of grace is permanent. Philosophers like Shaftesbury (whose doctrine of a moral sense and whose aestheticism are plainly aimed at in the poet's phrases) are condemned to failure in their attempt to ground morality in nature and man's natural goodness.

> . . . [To] set him free,
> Charm the deaf serpent wisely; make him hear
> Of rectitude and fitness; moral truth
> How lovely, and the moral sense how sure
>           . . . to guide his steps
> Directly to THE FIRST AND ONLY FAIR.

Freedom can be achieved in one way and no other, by the grace of God.

> He is the free man whom the truth makes free,
> And all are slaves beside. . . .

> He looks abroad into the varied field
> Of nature, and . . .
> Calls the delightful scenery all his own:
> His are the mountains, and the valleys his,
> And the resplendent rivers; . . .

For he knows them as his Father's gift, and made for his behoof; and he sees

> A ray of heavenly light gilding all forms
> Terrestrial, in the vast and the minute,
> The unambiguous footsteps of the God.

Thus, for the regenerate, nature is also, as it were, born again, is restored to its primal innocence, becomes a possession, and no longer a pitfall and a snare. But even in nature so conceived, he finds no resting place. The stars (so prominent in eighteenth-century apologetics) have for Cowper another message.

> As one who long detain'd on foreign shores
> Pants to return, and when he sees afar
> His country's weather-bleach'd and batter'd rocks
> From the green wave emerging, darts an eye
> Radiant with joy towards the happy land,
> So I with animated hopes behold,
> And many an aching wish, your beamy fires,
> That show like beacons in the blue abyss,
> Ordain'd to guide th'embodied spirit home. . . .
>   So reads he nature whom the lamp of truth
> Illuminates—thy lamp, mysterious Word!

Nature is neither sufficient in itself nor a needed basis for revealed truth; rather, it is meaningless till interpreted by that truth.

> In vain thy creatures testify of thee
> Till thou proclaim thyself.

This is Cowper's more Evangelical way of stating a conclusion like that of Butler's *Analogy:* only in the light of revelation is the natural order comprehensible or (as we might almost say) tolerable; and it is essentially an elaboration of the position taken in the *Olney Hymns*.

> God is his own interpreter,
> And He will make it plain.

Before Cowper wrote his *Olney Hymns*, there was one magnificent and uncharacteristic outburst of lyric praise. Christopher Smart's madness took a form very different from Cowper's: it somehow released in him a flood of joy and an unguessed poetic power. We can see both in the *Song to David*, without looking beyond it to the fascinating but problematic *Rejoice in the Lamb*. The *Song to David* is, I suppose, a song in his honor, and at the same time one that embodies Smart's reading of David's attitude to God and his world. Running through its key words, "Adoration," "Strong," "Beauteous," "Precious," "Glorious," the *Song* mounts to a conclusion in Christ:

> For *Adoration* all the ranks
> Of angels yield eternal thanks,
>     And *David* in their midst;
> With God's good poor, which, last and least
> In man's esteem, thou to thy feast,
>     O blessed bridegroom, bidst. . . .
>
> Strong is the lion—like a coal
> His eyeball—like a bastion's mole
>     His chest against the foes:
> Strong the gier-eagle on his sail,
> Strong against tide, th' enormous whale
>     Emerges, as he goes.
>
> But stronger still, in earth and air,
> And in the sea, the man of pray'r;
>     And far beneath the tide;

And in the seat to faith assign'd,
Where ask is have, where seek is find,
   Where knock is open wide.

Beauteous the fleet before the gale;
Beauteous the multitudes in mail,
   Rank'd arms and crested heads. . . .

Beauteous, yea beauteous more than these,
The shepherd king upon his knees,
   For his momentous trust;
With wish of infinite conceit,
For man, beast, mute, the small and great,
   And prostrate dust to dust. . . .

Precious the penitential tear;
And precious is the sigh sincere,
   Acceptable to God:
And precious are the winning flow'rs,
In gladsome Israel's feast of bow'rs,
   Bound in the hallow'd sod.

More precious that diviner part
Of David, ev'n the Lord's own heart,
   Great, beautiful and new:
In all things where it was intent,
In all extremes, in each event,
   Proof—answ'ring true to true.

Glorious the sun in mid career;
Glorious th' assembled fires appear;
   Glorious the comet's train:
Glorious the trumpet and alarm,
Glorious th' almighty's stretch'd-out arm;
   Glorious th' enraptur'd main.

Glorious the northern lights astream;
Glorious the song, when God's the theme;
   Glorious the thunder's roar:
Glorious hosannahs from the den;
Glorious the catholic amen;
   Glorious the martyr's gore.

Glorious—more glorious is the crown
Of Him who brought salvation down
    By meekness, call'd thy Son;
Thou at stupendous truth believ'd,
And now the matchless deed's achiev'd,
    Determined, Dared, and Done.

We shall not hear this note again till we come to David's own song in Browning's *Saul*. The *Song to David* is the crowning achievement of Evangelical poetry. But it is in every respect untypical—of Evangelicalism, because it breaks through the bonds self-imposed by that creed; of its author, because, though inspired by piety, his earlier works, as Browning said,

    All showed the Golden Mean without a hint
    Of brave extravagance that breaks the rule[;]

and of its century, whose poetry in general is adequately described in Browning's phrase. Nor is it really premonitory of the poetry of the Romantic period, save as it betokens a release of emotional power and a resort to symbol.

Standing on the verge of the Romantic period (and in his later works moving well into it) is the figure of George Crabbe, a salutary reminder of basic conservatism in both the religion and the poetry of the eighteenth century. For our purpose his interest is mainly documentary, since in his mature works he eschews specifically religious themes, confining himself to narrative and description of contemporary life as observed from the vantage point of a parish clergyman. Impressed by the merit of Crabbe's early poetry, and satisfied that his basic piety fitted him for holy orders, Burke recommended him to the Bishop of Norwich for ordination, and to the Duke of Rutland as domestic chaplain, and both Burke and Rutland remained his constant patrons and friends. The fact is worth recording, because it is typical of many an episode in the history of the English Church which has enabled it to make a unique contribution to the national culture, to learning, and to letters. The Church gave him security and a modicum of leisure; it also fixed him in the firm position of orthodox Christianity from which to treat the range of secular subjects open to the close observation of a parish priest. This firm adherence to the *via media* is seen not only on the rare occasions when he comments (as in *The Borough*) on "Sects and Religious Professions" but in the sound criteria of good sense, rational religion, and morals, assumed in his realistic and frequently satirical portraits. Conservative in literary form and harking back to the Augustans in meter and diction, he has a deeper affinity with them, as seen in his realism: his imagination (though he would not lay claim to its possession) moves always in close contact with the actual and immediate life around him; but he is no mere imitator: he extends his observation to rural life and scenes and writes with his eye on the object. In this indeed he shows some affinity at least with Wordsworth among the Romantics, and it is significant that Crabbe won the esteem not only of Burke and Johnson but of Wordsworth and Scott as well.

The piety which Burke saw and approved finds direct utterance in some of Crabbe's early verses, and here the interest for us is more than documentary. In *The Sacrament* he writes:

> O! sacred gift of God to man,
>   A faith that looks above,
> And sees the deep amazing plan
>   Of sanctifying love. . . .
>
> I know thou did'st ordain for me,
>   Thy creature, bread and wine;
> The depth of grace I cannot see,
>   But worship the design.

But, despite the grimness of many of his landscapes, nature has also for him a religious message and admonition, as in the brief poem *Night*; and in *The Resurrection*, he finds in the return of spring the type and symbol of its promise.

> Yes!—wintry winds have ceased to blow,
>   And trembling leaves appear,
> And Nature has her types to show
>   Throughout the varying year.

What Keble and Newman will erect into a "sacramental" relation of nature to grace, and later critics identify as archetypal, Crabbe, with a simpler piety, accepts in the attitude of his own lines in *Night*.

> Vouchsafe to me that spirit, Lord!
>   Which points the sacred way,
> And let thy creatures here below
>   Instruct me how to pray.

# ⁘ VI ⁘

## THE ROMANTICS: 1780–1840

As we approach the Romantic period, we must pause to take our bearings once more. But on the threshold we are confronted by the portentous and in many ways untypical figure of William Blake. It is equally impossible to bypass him and to speak adequately of his purposes and achievements under the limitations of our rapid survey. A few generalizations—and those of the baldest—must suffice; and it seems wise to attempt them before considering the background of the great Romantics.

Where students recognize anticipations of his ideas, Blake does not. The ideas which he inherits he pushes so far as to leave all timid anticipators behind and subject to the condemnation heaped on the prevailing system. In poetry and art, he opposes the whole Neoclassical tradition (and with it in large measure the classics themselves, on which it purports to be grounded) as fostering imitation whether of nature or of models and utterly repressive of imagination and genius. In philosophy, he opposes the whole empirical tradition, which he regards as synonymous with materialism, and which is symbolized for him by three names, Bacon, Newton, and Locke. This philosophy restricts reality to nature, and thought to reason operating on material phenomena as reported by the senses, whereas Blake holds reality to be spiritual and to be reached only by the imagination, which he calls "spiritual sensation." He opposes the whole system of organized religion and ethics, partly as it has come to terms with the prevailing philosophy and art, but mainly because it is ascetic and repressive of individual energy, and hence productive of endless hypocrisy. Blake would claim that he rebelled against these traditions in the name of Christianity—but of Christianity as he understood it, not as it was officially conceived and taught.

Such an attitude was of course at utter variance with the idea of the *via media* (whatever form that idea might assume), and Blake has no dealings with the eighteenth-century Church save to condemn it. But with the tradition of Dissent, in which he was brought up, he has a tenuous connection (though in its main eighteenth-century forms he would condemn it too): the connection is with the Dissenting tradition at its leftward extremity, where individualism ran rampant, under the auspices of the doctrine of the Inner Light, and dogma collapsed, inviting alliance with every variety of opinion from millenarianism to the philosophy of Boehme, and the doctrine of Christian liberty turned toward Antinomianism. There is some counterpart of all these tendencies in Blake, together with much from Neoplatonic, Gnostic, and other sources. The result was a more or less complete and conscious inversion of orthodox Christianity and its doctrines: with humanity taking the place of deity (the incarnate Christ indeed God, because there is no other God than man), with the forgiveness of sins ending in a denial of sin, and of the Fall, and the need of regeneration, save perhaps as the Fall could be identified as succumbing to the false conceptions that Blake condemned, and finally with the casting of Jehovah, as author of the Law, in the role of villain, not to mention the substitution of energy for humility as the parent of the virtues. In the Prophetic Books, where Christian terminology is largely abandoned for one of Blake's own invention, something like a fall from primal innocence and unity is an essential element in a psychological process at once individual and universal; and this is, or can be, followed by a restoration to unity which is a counterpart of redemption and regeneration. If, in intention, Blake is reinterpreting Christianity, calling it back to its true self, he discards natural religion altogether: "There is no natural religion." This is because, so far from being the only knowable reality, nature in itself is not real at all: it is a mere shadow cast by the ultimate reality, which is not material but spiritual: it can thus convey no ultimate truth, is without religious significance, is a mere impediment: one must look not at it, but through it, by resorting to imagination, the only organ of truth. And for the natural man, Blake has inherited, but put his own interpretation upon, the most extreme Calvinist formulation: commenting on Wordsworth's phrase "natural piety," he writes, "There is no such thing as natural piety because the natural man is at enmity with God."

Though individual in their mode of expression, Blake's writings have their conspicuous place in the tide of human thought. His equation of humanity and deity looks on to the religion of humanity (so called) despite an enormous difference in philosophical basis, form, and tone from that desiccated creed. His sense of the inadequacies (he would use a stronger term) of the empirical tradition—its ignoring or destroying of spiritual values —looks on to the idealist reaction. His assertion of the imagination as the supreme organ of truth anticipates the claims made for it by Coleridge and Wordsworth, which eliminate, however, Blake's depression of nature in favor of imagination. That there is a real difference here is emphasized by Blake's marginal comment on Wordsworth's poem on the "Influence of Natural Objects in Calling Forth and Strengthening the Imagination": "Natural objects . . . weaken, deaden and obliterate Imagination in me. Wordsworth must know that what he writes valuable is not to be found in Nature." But such repudiation is qualified by other statements which suggest that for Blake nature when penetrated by the imagination is nature transfigured. To the French Revolution he responded with hope and pity, while repudiating the narrow philosophy which saw liberty merely as external enfranchisement and not, as he did, a liberation of the spirit; and he was one of the earliest critics of the emerging Industrial Revolution and its dehumanizing effects.

I am fully aware of the inadequacy of this staccato treatment, which to lovers of the *Songs of Innocence* and *Songs of Experience* may well seem to bear little relation to the Blake they know. It is arguable, indeed, that in these and in other short poems the essence of Blake's value as poet resides, and that in the Prophetic Books the poet is submerged by one struggling to elaborate into a system his basic intuitions about human life. Certainly in the *Songs of Innocence* we find a note of freshness and wonder almost wholly absent from English poetry since Vaughan and Traherne, and there and in the *Songs of Experience* a vividness and immediacy of perception and expression almost without parallel. We find too a spontaneous effusion of love and pity very different from the self-conscious—the calculated—emotion of the sentimentalists and an imaginative sympathy which led Blake straight to the human heart of more than one problem. Whether the impulse is to be described as religious or merely humanitarian, I will not attempt to decide. Perhaps

Blake, with his equation of deity and humanity, would admit little distinction between them.

Having said then what we can afford of Blake, we turn, still briefly, to the state of religion and poetry in the Romantic period —a not much easier task! We should observe at the outset that religion has not yet encountered the two new and formidable obstacles that it will meet in the Victorian period—namely, a view of nature, supported by a vast body of evidence, and (to all seeming) incompatible with a divine origin and government of living species, a severe blow to both natural and revealed religion; and, secondly, the critical examination of Scripture and Scriptural history which seems to impair the whole structure of Christian evidences.

Though Butler's warning of the anomalies apparent in nature if viewed without recourse to revelation had never been successfully challenged, and sensitive observers must have been conscious of the endless warfare in the animal world to be glimpsed by Keats in his *To J. H. Reynolds, Esq.*, there was as yet no general sense of nature as "red in tooth and claw." For the more orthodox, Paley's *Natural Theology* furnished a satisfactory summation of the argument from design; and those who preferred a more immanent form of deity could still find a resting place in the sentimentalized nature of Shaftesbury and Thomson. No doubt changes were at hand. Already, but almost imperceptibly, the static world picture of the earlier eighteenth century was giving way to a conception of temporal progression, of development, which was to be one of the master ideas of the new century, but with as yet no very drastic disturbance of general outlook. Erasmus Darwin was ready to propound his theory of evolution, but it required a great deal more evidence, and a much wider diffusion, before it could seriously disturb traditional modes of thought; nor did it, like the theory of his famous grandson, emphasize the aspects of nature most shocking to religious sensibilities of whatever cast. For the time being indeed, we need hardly take it into account.

Though with an increase of momentum, the forces opposed to religion were, then, largely what they had long been. First, there was the encroachment of mechanistic modes of explanation of both natural and human phenomena (the kind of explanation arrived at in the seventeenth century by Hobbes), which was fostered, for the most part inadvertently, by the negations of Empiricism, and illustrated in the steady transformation of Newtonianism, but was now reinforced by the bolder speculations of French materialists, who repaid with interest their initial debt to English thought. Secondly, there was the yet older tradition of skepticism, which had coalesced with Deism and given it an increasingly negative character. Nor was this all: in the middle of the century, skepticism had found a potent ally in David Hume, who had revealed the full possibilities of negation, and indeed nescience, latent in the Empirical philosophy.

To meet these converging (though not necessarily cohering) challenges, religion had, it seemed, no new resources on which to draw. The orthodox could only take their stand on what still appeared to be the (more or less) "impregnable rock of Scripture," fortified within themselves, in the case of Wesleyan and Evangelical, by a strong infusion of experiential religion, while the Church, though less impervious to philosophical thought, was content, for the most part, to cling to the argument from design and to preach practical morality and civic duty. The unorthodox who yet retained some feeling for natural religion, and recoiled from the crude inadequacies of materialism, could only look to the tradition of Shaftesbury and Thomson—perhaps as emotionally reinforced by the (at best ambiguous) influence of Rousseau. Meanwhile, the impasse to which the genius of Hume had conducted the Empirical philosophy, if it did not actually support the Materialists, at least played into their hands, by appearing to remove all metaphysical basis for supernatural explanation or religious belief. Nor was the not unskillful appeal to a (technically conceived) "Common Sense," by the only British school of philosophy bold enough to come to grips with the problem, found adequate to its solution.

Long before the period ended, however, Coleridge (as meditation on his reading and his own mental experience was brought to a focus by his study of Kant and Schelling) had concluded that if a solution were possible, it entailed an entirely different approach. He had launched his attack on the "mechanical philosophy" on a wide front, and had commenced to evolve the Transcendental system which, though uncompleted, was destined to influence subsequent religious thought. It is significant that this system was the work of a poet (though one who abandoned poetry for metaphysics), that it involved a new reliance on the imagination and a new theory of poetry, and that it drew some of its data from the observed experience of Wordsworth—all of which I must try to indicate in its proper place. Before the end of the period, also, a new religious revival within the Church had commenced. The Oxford Movement differed markedly in character and direction from the Evangelical, and not least in requiring some intellectual basis, which it found in the thought of Newman.

Movements of thought do not occur in a vacuum. We are dealing, after all, with the period of the French Revolution and its aftermath, as the names of Coleridge and Wordsworth are sufficient to remind us, and philosophical and religious issues cannot be isolated from social and political in these poets or more generally. Broadly speaking, the forces in thought hostile to religion, and especially to the Church, associate themselves with a degree of enthusiasm for the revolution, though the more radical forces of Dissent also manifest sympathy for it and the Unitarians Price and Priestley find themselves aligned on its side with Godwin and Tom Paine, and strongly opposed to and by the essentially Anglican Burke. With this form of radical Dissent, Coleridge is also associated in the days of his early sympathy with the revolution. Wordsworth, on the other hand, has no such association (or comparatively little), and points rather to another qualification: the possible union of political radicalism with a more or less vague adherence to a religion of nature. Rousseau was one of the progenitors of the revolution no less than Helvetius and d'Holbach, and the Rousseauist current is illustrated in Wordsworth's friend Michel Beaupuy. But when these qualifications are allowed, the initial generalization remains substantially true, and is confirmed in their reaction against the revolution when Coleridge and Wordsworth are carried toward the political conservativism of Burke and at the same time toward the Established Church.

Shelley, on the other hand (who was of course born too late to participate in these immediate responses), aligns himself passionately on the side of radicalism and his own version of materialism, and against all—and especially Christian—religion. Though Shelley divested himself of his materialism, and characteristically flew to an opposite extreme in his own brand of Platonism, he retained his radical sympathies and most of his antipathy to Christianity and its institutions.

It is clear that in the Romantic movement we must recognize two distinct currents. One is radical, and, with whatever extension of imaginative and emotional range, still traces its inheritance in considerable degree to the eighteenth century. The other is conservative, and reacts against that inheritance in two ways: first, by an appeal to history, not forgetting the contribution of the Middle Ages (indeed the attitude to the Middle Ages is a good touchstone by which to distinguish the two currents); and, secondly, by the demand for a new philosophical approach to the questions of evaluation and belief. The radical current is illustrated by the earlier Wordsworth and Coleridge, and by Shelley; the conservative, in an unphilosophical form, by Scott and, more profoundly, by the later Wordsworth and Coleridge and by Newman and the Oxford Movement. On the Continent, one of the forms taken by the reaction against the French Revolution was the Catholic revival; different as were its origins, and the types of radicalism and irreligion which it confronted, the Oxford Movement was a distant English counterpart of the Catholic revival.

Such parallels must always be handled with caution. Even when the celebrated "fog in the Channel" is absent, ideas crossing it suffer a sea change. As an influence in England, Continental radicalism lost whatever relevance it once had soon after the French Revolution, though its ghost still walked in Chartism. The force to be reckoned with in the years after the close of the Napoleonic Wars was one which had been mustering under the direction of Bentham and James Mill and assumed the name of Philosophical Radicalism. It was the heir of the Empirical tradition in philosophy and showed the same addiction to material and mechanistic explanations of phenomena; but it was strongly practical in bent, and owed as much to political economy as to philosophy of any school. Though it could on occasion co-operate with Dissent, its whole outlook was secular, and it was hostile to religion and especially to the Church. It provoked a strong reaction, which found expression in Coleridge in what might very well be called philosophical conservatism, and it contributed largely to that "liberalism" which Newman identified as the enemy.

Now back to the poets, and to the earliest phase of Coleridge's religious experience, as it blended with his revolutionary sympathies, in *Religious Musings*. When he wrote this "Desultory Poem . . . on the Christmas Eve of 1794," he was a Unitarian in religion, with a strong emotional attachment to the human Christ, "whose life was Love," and who more than the works of nature bore "the true impress" of the Creator. God, he declares, is

> . . . one Mind, one omnipresent Mind,
> Omnific. His most holy name is Love.
> Truth of subliming import! with the which
> Who feeds and saturates his constant soul,
> He from his small particular orbit flies
> With blest outstarting! From himself he flies,
> Stands in the sun, and with no partial gaze
> Views all creation; and he loves it all,
> And blesses it and calls it very good!
> This is indeed to dwell with the Most High!

Failure to recognize this truth and to live by the rule of love is the root of all evil and suffering: it leaves man centered only in self, ready to prey upon his fellows and, blinded by superstition, to make war, in the name of Christianity, on all who would be free. (Coleridge cites in a footnote arguments used in Parliament to support war on revolutionary France.) There is more in this vein, but optimism triumphs over the spectacle of rapine and oppression, superstition and war; for "God is diffused through all," and out of evil itself comes forth good. Knowledge and freedom will triumph in the end; and their prophets are

"Philosophers and Bards," and among them "he of mortal kind /
Wisest"—namely, David Hartley, whose unqualified disciple, in
this phase of his development, Coleridge is. Hartley's *Observations on Man* exercised a profound, if temporary, influence upon
him, and through him, a few years later, on Wordsworth. Tracing everything back to ideas of sensation, Hartley purported to
show how by the "association of ideas," operating under the impetus and consolidating power of pleasure and pain, there
emerged, from these, ideas of a higher order, effecting on the
way a transition from the self-regarding to the altruistic, and culminating in ideas of Deity and of the moral sense. Though purely mechanistic in character, and assigning no activity to the
mind itself, Hartley's scheme preserved a hierarchy of values, an
internal sanction for an altruistic ethic, a place for Deity, and a
note of optimistic determinism—all of which appealed strongly
to Coleridge and was united with his Unitarian beliefs and revolutionary sympathies. Thus the poem concludes with an apocalyptic vision:

> . . . The veiling clouds retire,
> And lo! the Throne of the redeeming God
> Forth flashing unimaginable day
> Wraps in one blaze earth, heaven, and deepest hell.

One need not deny, perhaps, that this congeries of loosely
connected ideas yielded to the young Coleridge a species of religious experience, but one may certainly question the success of
its fusion with an aesthetic experience in the "Desultory Poem."

No doubt through the influence of Coleridge, the first poem
of Wordsworth's to which we must direct our attention bears
the stamp of Hartley's scheme. It is the famous *Lines Composed
a Few Miles above Tintern Abbey*, when Wordsworth has recovered from the shock and disillusion administered by the

course of the French Revolution, but has not yet aligned himself with the forces of conservatism in Church and state. Here one must observe that Wordsworth's interest in speculative thought differs markedly from Coleridge's, depending always on its power to throw light on his own moral and aesthetic experience, and this for the time being Hartley's empirical account of the mind's operation appeared in measure to do. Thus in *Tintern Abbey*, after recognizing the three stages in his developing attitude toward nature—the unconscious response of his boyhood with its glad animal motions; the conscious and utter absorption of his youth, when the sounding cataract haunted him like a passion; and the present state of restored responsiveness, sobered now by hearing as part of the total symphony "the still, sad music of humanity"—he continues:

> . . . Therefore am I still
> A lover of the meadows and the woods,
> And mountains . . .
>                     of all that mighty world
> Of eye and ear,—both what they half create,
> And what perceive; well pleas'd to recognize
> In nature and the language of the sense
> The anchor of my purest thoughts, the nurse,
> The guide, the guardian of my heart, and soul
> Of all my moral being.

It is well to note one phrase which can be brought within the Hartleian scheme only by giving it a very much restricted meaning: what the senses perceive and what they "half create"; for here is implied an activity of the imagination in the very act of perception, for which Wordsworth will presently find his own phrase, "creative sensibility."

But before he reaches in *Tintern Abbey* his Hartleian formulation, he has struck another and a specifically religious note, which also outruns Hartley.

... And I have felt
A Presence that disturbs me with the joy
Of elevated thoughts; a sense sublime
Of something far more deeply interfused,
Whose dwelling is the light of setting suns,
And the round ocean, and the living air,
And the blue sky, and in the mind of man:
A motion and a spirit, that impels
All thinking things, all objects of all thought,
And rolls through all things.

The Presence was the being whom Wordsworth repeatedly recognized in the sights and sounds of the natural world, and in the operations of the human mind—the being whom he later addressed in *The Prelude* as

Wisdom and Spirit of the Universe!
Thou soul that art the Eternity of thought,
And givest to forms and images a breath
And everlasting motion, not in vain
By day or star-light thus from my first dawn
Of childhood didst thou intertwine for me
The passions which build up our human soul.

Though unrecognized at the time, his early experiences amid the scenes of nature were (as subsequent reflection taught him to see) manifestations of the Presence. The passages quoted are of the kind that Coleridge was later to condemn as savoring too much of pantheism, but there can be no doubt that for Wordsworth they realized an experience in which a religious and a poetic response were perfectly united. Nor may we omit one more example—and a famous one—the poet's emotion on journeying through the Simplon Pass, as "recollected in tranquillity" in *The Prelude*:

... The immeasurable height
Of woods decaying, never to be decayed,
The stationary blasts of water-falls,

And everywhere along the hollow rent
Winds thwarting winds, bewilder'd and forlorn,
The torrents shooting from the clear blue sky,
The rocks that mutter'd close upon our ears,
Black drizzling crags that spake by the way-side
As if a voice were in them, the sick sight
And giddy prospect of the raving stream,
The unfetter'd clouds, and region of the Heavens,
Tumult and peace, the darkness and the light
Were all the workings of one Mind . . .
Characters of the great Apocalypse,
The types and symbols of Eternity,
Of first and last, and midst, and without end.

The passage follows immediately upon reflections on the imagination "and all the might of its endowments," and is itself instinct with that power. As Wordsworth called up in memory such experiences, the *active* co-operation of the mind in them must have become ever more apparent to him and the insufficiency of the Hartleian mode of explanation.

Under a variety of influences, in which we may include his observation of the creative mind of Wordsworth at work, Coleridge too was drawn away from his earlier empiricism. The empirical account of the mind, even the revered Hartley's, viewed it, he came to see, as essentially the passive receiver of ideas of sensation, which then, on a purely mechanical principle, and with no active participation by mind or will, grouped themselves into fixed patterns of association. According to that school, he writes, "Mind . . . is always passive, a lazy looker-on at the external world. If the mind be not passive, if it be indeed made in God's image—and too in the sublimest sense of the image of the Creator—there is ground for suspicion that any system built on the passiveness of the mind must be false as a system." It is interesting to observe the religious cast of his argument—or at least of the terms chosen. Wordsworth came to a similar conclusion, but characteristically grounded it on his own intuition:

> We have had deepest feeling that the mind
> Is lord and master, and that outward sense
> Is but the obedient servant of her will.

Coleridge had long been a reader in traditions very remote from the empirical, and on these he drew in his search for a countervailing theory. A not too difficult transition seemed to be offered by Bishop Berkeley, empirical in method, but idealist in result, and assigning to the mind the stupendous act of creating its own world, whose *esse* was *percipi*. (Having named his first son Hartley, Coleridge called his second Berkeley; and if he had continued this useful practice, we should have had a valuable guide to his intellectual history—it would have required, however, an inordinately large family.) But Plato and the Platonist tradition left a more permanent mark on his thinking than did Berkeley, and from Coleridge some imprint upon Wordsworth, still in quest of theories that would help to explain his own experience. And so in the famous *On the Intimations of Immortality* it is not surprising to find the poet modifying the relatively simple account given in *Tintern Abbey*, and for that purpose adopting the Platonic idea of the pre-existence of the soul and its fading reminiscence of its earlier state. We are reminded, of course, of Vaughan's *Retreate*; which, however, it has been decided, Wordsworth probably did not know.

There is about the ode (greater poem though it be) something much more tentative than the affirmations of *Tintern Abbey* or those to be resumed in *The Prelude*. It is not the Platonic theory of the soul, or even the intimations of immortality, that are at the heart of the poem: it is Wordsworth's own experiences in the presence of nature and the changes that come

over them with the passage of the years—experiences which
these ideas serve perhaps to organize and illuminate. The first
four stanzas were written, he tells us, three years before the rest
were added; and these four present the essential situation from
which the poem takes its rise:

> There was a time when meadow, grove and stream,
>> The earth, and every common sight
>>> To me did seem
>> Apparelled in celestial light,
> The glory and the freshness of a dream.
> It is not now as it hath been of yore. . . .
> The things which I have seen I now can see no more.

He can apprehend and even bring himself to join in nature's
springtime festival, but

>> Whither is fled the visionary gleam?
>> Where is it now, the glory and the dream?

In *Tintern Abbey*, he had noticed a loss of his first rapturous joy
in the presence of nature, but had found full compensation in
the power to reflect on what he saw, to relate to it "the still sad
music of humanity," and to experience the "Presence that disturbs [him] with the joy / Of elevated thoughts." But now the
sense of loss is uppermost, and it is for this that (after the long
interval) he seeks an explanation in a reference to pre-existence
and reminiscence; and yet the final conclusion is not remote
from that reached in *Tintern Abbey*:

> And O, ye Fountains, Meadows, Hills, and Groves,
> Forebode not any severing of our loves!
> Yet in my heart of hearts I feel your might;
> I only have relinquished one delight
> To live beneath your more habitual sway. . . .
> The innocent brightness of a new-born Day
>> Is lovely yet;

The Clouds that gather round the setting sun
Do take a sober colouring from an eye
That hath kept watch o'er man's mortality. . . .
Thanks to the human heart by which we live,
Thanks to its tenderness, its joys and fears,
To me the meanest flower that blows can give
Thoughts that do often lie too deep for tears.

And in the fuller account in *The Prelude*, it is rather the pattern of *Tintern Abbey* than of *On the Intimations of Immortality* that is elaborated and modified, though other elements of Platonism are incorporated in the poem.

But to return to Coleridge and his movement away from Hartley and Empiricism and toward his new theory of imagination, which, if it was in part inspired by Wordsworth, was also appropriated by him. The degree of Coleridge's debt to German philosophy, also a reaction against the tendencies of the Empirical tradition as they culminated in Hume, need not concern us, or whether, on his visit to Germany with the Wordsworths, Coleridge lost himself (as Hazlitt said) in the mazes of the Harz forest and the Kantian philosophy. What finally emerged was a theory of the creative imagination which rescued it from the Baconian aspersion that it was the mere play of the mind and productive not of the truth but of fiction; which asserted, as against Hobbes and his fellows, that imagination was the power that furnished the strength and structure of the poem; and which, avoiding the Blakean dichotomy of imagination and the imitation of nature, attempted a synthesis of the two—the synthesis exemplified in the poetry of Wordsworth.

We can do little more here than quote a famous passage in the *Biographia Literaria*, and one other, less familiar, from the *Lay Sermons*, observing again the religious basis of Coleridge's argument.

Every act of perception is an act of the primary imagination, and it is creative and a reflection in the finite mind of God's creative act that produced, or rather continually produces, the world; and the secondary imagination, the creative activity of poet and artist, while differing in the mode of its operation, is one in kind with the primary, and thus partakes at once of its validity and its reflection of the divine act.

The primary imagination I hold to be the living power and prime agent of all human perception, and as a repetition in the finite mind of the eternal act of creation in the infinite I AM. The secondary imagination I consider as an echo of the former, co-existing with the conscious will, yet still as identical with the primary in the kind of its agency, and differing only in degree and in the mode of its operation. It dissolves, diffuses, dissipates in order to re-create; . . . it struggles to idealize and unify. It is essentially vital, even as all objects (as objects) are essentially fixed and dead.

Coleridge goes on to distinguish sharply between the secondary imagination and mere fancy, which is "no other than a mode of memory emancipated from the order of time and space" and is (though this he does not say) what Bacon meant by imagination and Hobbes by his undifferentiated imagination and fancy. Fancy, like the understanding, moves on the level of the phenomenal: it is confined to the world of dead objects, of *natura naturata*. Imagination, like reason, rises to the noumenal: indeed it would seem that imagination and reason differ only in the mode of their operation and the form of their expression: they are alike concerned with nature as a living force, with *natura naturans*, and art's imitation of nature in this sense is the genuinely creative activity of the secondary imagination.

In the second passage, Coleridge contrasts with the products of "an unenlightened generalizing Understanding [those of the Imagination] that reconciling and mediatory power which, incorporating the Reason in images of the Sense and organizing as it were the flux of the Senses by the permanence and self-encircling energies of the Reason, gives birth to a system of symbols, harmonious in themselves and consubstantial with the truths of which they are the conductors."

From this too brief account, it should still be clear that for Coleridge the reaction against the empirical tradition, and what he called the "mechanical philosophy," had important religious grounds and implications, and no less important implications for poetry. It has countered the assumptions of Bacon and his disciples, which religious—indeed all serious—poets could escape only by ignoring, has restored poetry to its proper dignity, and has boldly asserted that the imagination is an organ of truth.

To some details of Coleridge's theory, as finally formulated, Wordsworth demurred, but in general he makes it his own: indeed in a sense it was his anyway, for (in one aspect of the matter) Coleridge was casting into philosophic form what Wordsworth had experienced. As Wordsworth in *The Prelude*, whose subtitle is *The Growth of a Poet's Mind*, approaches the conclusion of his argument, he reverts to love as a beneficent force operative in the life of man, and not without its premonitions in the life of nature, and continues:

> . . . but there is higher love
> Than this, a love that comes into the heart
> With awe and a diffusive sentiment;
> Thy love is human merely; this proceeds
> More from the brooding soul, and is divine.
> This love, more intellectual cannot be
> Without Imagination, which, in truth,
> Is but another name for absolute strength
> And clearest insight, amplitude of mind,

> And reason in her most exalted mood.
> This faculty hath been the moving soul
> Of all our labour. . . .

This is the doctrine as Wordsworth phrased it in the early version of *The Prelude*, completed by 1805. In the revised, and in this instance poetically superior, text printed in 1850, he has not changed his mind about the imagination, but somewhat about the love whose indispensable instrument it is, and he has improved the phrasing. "Intellectual love" is now more adequately described as "spiritual": there is a shift from a Platonic to a Christian context. Moreover, the higher love is not set in simple contrast to earthly: taking a hint from Raphael's words to Adam in *Paradise Lost* (human love "is the scale / By which to heav'nly love thou mayst ascend"), Wordsworth now avers that earthly love may

> . . . by a still higher love
> Be hallowed, love that breathes not without awe;
> Love that adores, but on the knees of prayer,
> By heaven inspired; that frees from chains the soul,
> Lifted, in union with the purest, best,
> Of earth-born passions, on the wings of praise
> Bearing a tribute to the Almighty's Throne.

> This spiritual Love acts not nor can exist
> Without Imagination, which, in truth,
> Is but another name for absolute power
> And clearest insight, amplitude of mind,
> And Reason in her most exalted mood.
> This faculty hath been the feeding source
> Of our long labour: we have traced the stream
> From the blind cavern whence is faintly heard
> Its natal murmur; followed it to light
> And open day; accompanied its course
> Among the ways of Nature, for a time
> Lost sight of it bewildered and engulph'd:

> Then given it greeting as it rose once more
> In strength, reflecting from its placid breast
> The works of man and face of human life;
> And lastly, from its progress we have drawn
> Faith in life endless, the sustaining thought
> Of human Being, Eternity, and God.

In these last lines, there is indeed a considerable deviation from those which they replace. There, the culmination is simply "the great thought / By which we live, Infinity and God," and the accompaniment is less one of religious awe and hope than of Stoic self-dependence. For the rest, the implied summary of the course of the poet's history as traced in the poem is substantially the same in both versions.

*The Prelude* elaborates in great detail the basic pattern of the poet's development sketched in *Tintern Abbey*, and of course it adds important elements. The period of boyhood is no longer dismissed in the phrase "with its glad animal motions": amidst them, the power of nature to chasten and to awe, and to furnish sudden impulses to the imagination, is emphasized; the question of reminiscence is raised (it seems as if "the soul / Remembering *how* she felt, but *what* she felt / Remembering not, retains an obscure sense / Of possible sublimity"), but the emphasis falls on the immediate impact of natural objects and its generative power. In the period of youth, with its conscious delight in— its intoxication with—the beauties of nature, a new experience is added:

> Magnificent
> The morning was. . . .
> The solid mountains were as bright as clouds,
> Grain-tinctured, drenched in empyrean light;
> And in the meadows and the lower grounds,
> Was all the sweetness of a common dawn,

Dews, vapours, and the melody of birds,
And Labourers going forth into the fields.
     . . . to the brim
My heart was full; I made no vows, but vows
Were then made for me: bond unknown to me
Was given, that I should be, else sinning greatly,
A dedicated spirit. On I walk'd
In blessedness, which even yet remains.

Another dawn, that of the French Revolution:

Bliss was it in that dawn to be alive
But to be young was very heaven—

and the time of darkness and dismay that followed (the latter alone mentioned in *Tintern Abbey*) are given full treatment; then the return to nature, but with sobered and maturing mind, and finally that view of the imagination which we have considered: responsive to the life of nature and humanity and operating as the instrument of spiritual love; and now at last the poet is ready to fulfill the vows made for him (as he felt) on that morning years before. The whole course of his life to the moment of setting down the record—and he no doubt realizing thereby even more clearly than before the total significance of its pattern—has been at once psychologically intelligible and, as he has come to feel, directed to a beneficent end. By what? By nature? By imagination? By God? The Wordsworth of the first version of *The Prelude* scarcely pauses to inquire. Is not the Presence operative alike in "all thinking things, all objects of all thought"—if the mind is keyed to apprehend it? There is in the experiences themselves, and in the interpretation which the poet puts upon them, a constant sense of significance, of reverence and awe, and the recognition of a spiritual power, immanent if not transcendent, which controls the life of things and the response of the poet. These are the elements of religious (but not yet of Christian) experience present and potent in the earlier poetry of Wordsworth.

There is certainly a higher percentage of dross to gold in the poetry written after 1807 than in the earlier verse (which is also markedly uneven). But it is absurd to assume that this is due to a change in Wordsworth's opinions, or that the change is prompted by mere prejudice and is necessarily either naïve or insincere. In fact the decline was mainly due to some failure of immediate and vital response, of which the poet was acutely conscious as early as the *Immortality* ode, and would have occurred irrespective of any change in his opinions. The result has been, however, to allow one school of critics to brush aside the compensations in human sympathy and philosophic insight which the poet also recognized, and, worse still, to ignore the good poetry (though of a somewhat different order) of which he was on occasion capable in his later years. Thus they have tended to dismiss *The Excursion*, the *Ecclesiastical Sonnets*, and the *Evening Voluntaries* in one general condemnation, and to explain the later version of *The Prelude* (whose poetry is not always inferior to the earlier) as a disingenuous tampering with the record undertaken from prudential motives. But this is prejudice or propaganda, not criticism. And there is (we may add) nothing to choose between it and the heresy hunting of another type of critic who condemns the naturalism of the early poems and complains of the insufficiency of Anglo-Catholic doctrine and sacramental imagery in the later. Our business here is neither to praise nor to blame, but (so far as we are able) to understand.

Essential to an understanding of Wordsworth's experience, and to a fair appraisal of the revisions introduced in *The Prelude*, is a sympathetic reading of *The Excursion*. For there in essence are all Wordsworth's later attitudes and beliefs. In view of the intended relation of the two poems, the simplest explanation of the revisions in The Prelude is that their purpose is to bring it into closer harmony with its sequel. If his views changed after 1805, and while he was at work on The Excursion, if he thought that he now saw more clearly whither his long education at the hands of nature had all the while been leading him, what more natural—what indeed more necessary for truth and art—than to bring into clearer relief the direction and the goal?

Wordsworth, it will be remembered, chose to preface The Excursion with a brief account of the scheme in which the un-published Prelude and the largely unwritten Recluse were to be its companions and its setting—or as he described it, perhaps with a vague memory of George Herbert's The Temple, the whole like a Gothic church with The Prelude as its antechapel; and, most significantly, he quotes the conclusion of the first book of The Recluse, where (in some of the grandest lines he ever wrote) the conscious reminiscences are of Milton. Like his great predecessor, he will assert eternal Providence, but by direct re-flection "On Man, on Nature, and on Human Life," a task not less onerous or less requiring aid of the Heavenly Muse:

> For I must tread on shadowy ground, must sink
> Deep—and, aloft ascending, breathe in worlds
> To which the heaven of heavens is but a veil.
> All strength—all terror, single or in bands,
> That ever was put forth in personal form—
> Jehovah—with his thunder, and the choir
> Of shouting Angels, and the empyreal thrones—
> I pass them unalarmed. Not Chaos, not
> The darkest pit of lowest Erebus, . . .
>                 can breed such fear and awe
> As fall upon us often when we look
> Into our Minds, into the Mind of Man—

My haunt, and the main region of my song.
—Beauty—a living Presence of the earth,
Surpassing the most fair ideal Forms . . .
                              —waits upon my steps. . . .
                              Paradise, and groves
Elysian, Fortunate Fields . . .
                    why should they be
A history only of departed things,
Or more a fiction of what never was?
For the discerning intellect of Man,
When wedded to this goodly universe,
In high and holy passion, shall find these
A simple produce of the common day.
    I long before the blissful hour arrives,
Would chant, in lovely peace, the spousal verse
Of this great consummation:—and by words
Which speak of nothing more than what we are,
Would I arouse the sensual from their sleep
Of Death, and win the vacant and the vain
To noble raptures; while my voice proclaims
How exquisitely the individual Mind
(And the progressive powers perhaps no less
Of the whole species) to the external World
Is fitted:—and how exquisitely, too . . .
The external World is fitted to the Mind;
And the creation (by no lower name
Can it be called) which they with blended might
Accomplish. . . .

That Wordsworth should have quoted these lines written
years earlier proves that he regarded The Excursion as in no
sense a recantation, but merely that he sees more clearly than
before the goal toward which all his experience and his intuition
were pointing and that what their exposition; his "high argument"—as he calls it—echoing Milton's phrase, requires an extension, not a retraction, of his terms of reference.

Though not less certainly a personal record, The Excursion
differs in plan and method from The Prelude. Save as narrator,

the poet seldom intervenes. The Wanderer and in measure the Pastor speak for him, and more remotely the Solitary reflects a past phase, the nadir, of his experience. What was affirmed in *The Prelude* is not here denied, but it is qualified and adjusted to beliefs now more definitely Christian. The power of nature to bless and to restore is as firmly asserted as ever, but is seen now as what, though perhaps unrecognized, it has always been: a possible channel and instrument of grace. The virtues of simplicity of life and heart are confirmed by a sense of Heaven's approval. In the words of the Pastor,

> . . . innocence is strong,
> And an entire simplicity of mind
> A thing most sacred in the eye of Heaven;
> That opens, for such sufferers, relief
> Within the soul, fountains of grace divine;
> And doth commend their weakness and disease
> To Nature's care, assisted in her office
> By all the elements that round her wait
> To generate, to preserve, and to restore.

There will be a further step to take in the *Evening Voluntaries*, when the hard lesson of Christian humility has been fully learned and innocence of mind itself is seen to depend on the grace of God:

> But who *is* innocent? By grace divine,
> Not otherwise, O Nature, we are thine.

There was much more of continuity, with a measure of redirection, than of conscious repudiation in Wordsworth's development. When as early as *Tintern Abbey*, he had felt the Presence permeating "All thinking things, all objects of all thought," he had entered upon a genuinely religious experience—none the less genuine for being incomplete. The next step was a strong emphasis upon moral obligation; and though the heresy hunters who raise the cry of "pantheism" against the earlier phase will find the *Ode to Duty* more Stoic than Christian, this also realizes a religious experience, and one that leaves its imprint on all that follows. Duty is addressed as "stern Daughter of the Voice of God." The palpable echo of Milton's "God so commanded, and left that command / Sole daughter of his voice" is significant: what Milton applies to the single prohibition in Eden, Wordsworth transfers to the inner law by which man must now be guided if he is to achieve what Milton called the "paradise within thee happier far"; and the paradisal suggestion is carried over, for the address to Duty continues: thou

> . . . dost wear
> The Godhead's most benignant grace; . . .
> Flowers laugh before thee in their beds
> And fragrance in thy footing treads;
> Thou dost preserve the stars from wrong;
> And the most ancient heavens, through thee, are fresh and strong.

The last couplet reminds us neither of Milton nor of the Stoics, but of Kant's comparison of the cosmic and the moral law. If the position reached in the *Ode to Duty* betokens a surrender of the "uncharted freedom" of earlier days, it also throws a light back on those effects of admonitory awe in the presence of nature experienced in boyhood and recorded in *The Prelude*, while at the same time it points forward to the religious ethic of *The Excursion* and the later poems, where

> . . . sense is made
> Subservient still to moral purposes,
> Auxiliar to divine.

While concentrating on the human situation ("the Mind of Man / My haunt and the main region of my song"), Wordsworth finds in the world of nature types and symbols of moral and religious truths; and ever and anon he reminds himself and us of the cosmic setting; for, like the shell whose "murmurings . . . expressed / Mysterious union with its native sea," it carried, through the imagination, to "the ear of faith"

> Authentic tidings of invisible things;
> Of ebb and flow, and ever-during power;
> And central peace, subsisting at the heart
> Of endless agitation.

But more often the note is local and domestic. Near the end of *The Excursion* there is a scene which is in its way symbolic:

> Alert to follow as the Pastor led,
> We clomb a green hill's side; and as we clomb,
> The Valley, opening her bosom, gave
> Fair prospect, intercepted less and less. . . .
>            —far off,
> And yet conspicuous, stood the old Church-tower,
> In majesty presiding over fields
> And habitations seemingly preserved
> From all intrusion of the restless world. . . .

The localized but unimpeded vision; the domestic landscape of fields and habitations; the peace and permanence of the English scene; and the church tower, not obtrusive, yet a constant and essential feature of the scene—nothing could more completely strike the note of the later and conservative Wordsworth.

It was back toward their historic English inheritance that Wordsworth and Coleridge alike had slowly turned in their disillusion with Continental radicalism, whose ironic outcome had been the excesses of the French Revolution and the Napoleonic reign of tyranny and conquest. To oversimplify a long and complicated process, they had closed their Rousseau and opened their Burke. They came to conceive of liberty in national and historic, and no longer in abstract and universal, terms. As did Burke (and before him, Hooker), they saw the English

Church as distinct but inseparable from the English State, and recognized in the revealed religion which it taught the completion and crown of natural religion and the safeguard of those principles of natural and Christian ethics which, ideally, the State embodied. Without attempting to pass judgment, we should be able to recognize in their later conservatism a consistent ideal and the essentially English form of conservative Romanticism.

From Coleridge the philosopher, it demanded that vast reappraisal of mind and nature which was his unfinished life work; in Wordsworth, the center and vehicle were still his poetry. We have touched lightly on their reciprocal relation. It is also apparent in their attitudes to the English Church and State: in Coleridge's *Constitution of the Church and State*, one segment of his reappraisal which he managed to complete; and in Wordsworth's *Ecclesiastical Sonnets*, which embody his sense of the Church's ethos as revealed in her history, her doctrine, and her liturgy.

The *Ecclesiastical Sonnets* are indeed the fullest and most eloquent testimony to the *via media* in English poetry: like Jewel and Hooker, whom they praise,

> In doctrine and communion they have sought
> Firmly between the two extremes to steer.

But, more than that, they breathe the spirit of comprehension, of tolerance and charity, of rationality and reverence, of liberty grounded in order, which is the mark of the *via media* at its most characteristic and best. Insistent on the central truths for which the Reformation stood and its martyrs—Ridley, Latimer, and Cranmer—died, the poet can spare a tribute of admiration and pity for Fisher and More, can condemn the dominant motives in the dissolution of the monasteries, and, more important, can

appreciate the riches of a purified Catholic tradition, as in the
sonnet on the Virgin:

> Mother! whose virgin bosom was uncrost
> With the least shade of thought to sin allied;
> Woman! above all women glorified. . . .
> Thy Image falls to earth. Yet some, I ween,
> Not unforgiven the suppliant knee might bend,
> As to a visible Power, in which did blend
> All that was mixed and reconciled in Thee
> Of mother's love with maiden purity,
> Of high and low, celestial and terrene!

Unequivocal in his condemnation of Puritan fanaticism and the
devastation it wrought, he can still recognize the principle of
obedience to conscience, be it in the Pilgrim Fathers, the evicted
Nonconformists, or the Scottish Covenanters, though his own
ideal is realized in the more humane and rational piety of the
Church's saints and sages, celebrated by Izaak Walton with a
pen "Dropped from an angel's wing." Nor is he without sympathy for the Restoration divines, including the Cambridge
Platonists. Though in an age of license,

> Yet Truth is keenly sought for, and the wind
> Charged with rich words poured out in thought's defence;
> Whether the Church inspire that eloquence,
> Or a Platonic Piety confined
> To the sole temple of the inward mind. . . .

And with them he couples Milton, one

> . . . who builds immortal lays,
> Though doomed to tread in solitary ways,
> Darkness before and danger's voice behind;
> Yet not alone, nor helpless to repel
> Sad thoughts; for from above the starry sphere
> Come secrets, whispered nightly to his ear;
> And the pure spirit of celestial light
> Shines through his soul. . . .

The middle way, as Wordsworth understood it, was not one of exclusion but a commanding position from which to recognize and incorporate the virtues that lay on either hand; and he contrasts with "opposites and fierce extremes" "the golden mean, and quiet flow / Of truths, that soften hatred, temper strife." He is responsive to all the aids to devotion that the Church supplies, in her great cathedrals and humble parish churches, in "the precious Cross" (a symbol dear to Wordsworth, as to Donne), in the sacraments, and in the beloved liturgy, whose

> . . . way before us lies
> Distinct with signs, through which in set career,
> As through a Zodiac, moves the ritual year
> Of England's Church.

But characteristically—of both the poet and the Church—the final emphasis falls on none of these things but simply on personal communion with Christ:

> Glory to God! and to the Power who came
> In filial duty, clothed with love divine,
> That made his human tabernacle shine
> Like Ocean burning with purpureal flame;
> Or like the Alpine Mount, that takes its name
> From roseate hues, far kenned at morn and even,
> In hours of peace, or when the storm is driven
> Along the nether region's rugged frame!
> Each prompts—Heaven urges; let us seek the light,
> Studious of that pure intercourse begun
> When first our infant brows their lustre won;
> So, like the Mountain, may we grow more bright
> From unimpeded commerce with the Sun,
> At the approach of all-involving night.

If the imagery, significantly drawn from nature, is put to symbolic use, it is also, we may be sure, rich in personal memories for Wordsworth and a link with his earliest religious experience.

Nor—to pass beyond the *Sonnets* to the *Evening Voluntaries* —need he rely on memory alone. Viewing the calm of sky and waters, but hearing the while "the earth voice of the mighty sea," he imagines in contrast sea and sky in storm; and in both he finds types of the "ways of God to men"; and the poem concludes:

> Thou Power supreme! who, arming to rebuke
> Offenders, dost put off the gracious look,
> And clothe thyself with terrors like the flood
> Of ocean roused into his fiercest mood,
> Whatever discipline thy Will ordain
> For the brief course that must for me remain;
> Teach me with quick-eared spirit to rejoice
> In admonitions of thy softest voice!
> Whate'er the path these mortal feet may trace,
> Breathe through my soul the blessing of thy grace,
> Glad, through a perfect love, a faith sincere
> Drawn from the wisdom that begins with fear,
> Glad to expand; and, for a season, free
> From finite cares, to rest absorbed in Thee!

There are memories here too from earlier days (perhaps of *Peele Castle*, and of the line, "Listen! the mighty Being is awake . . ."); but the occasion of the poem is the prospect from a "high part of the coast of Cumberland," and the day "Easter Sunday" and the poet's "sixty-third birthday." There is no reference, however (such as one might have expected), to the great festival in the Church's "ritual year": our attention is directed solely to nature, to God's ways to men, and to the poet's response to them.

As our whole treatment has implied, while Wordsworth made an impressive contribution to religious poetry, Coleridge's was almost wholly to religious thought. The flowering of his poetic talent was brief and uncertain, and he never adequately illustrates in his poems his profound insights into either religion or poetry. But since we have noticed from his early period his *Religious Musings*, that poem so adequately described as "desultory," it is only fair, before leaving the subject, to revert for a moment to his one religious poem of any permanent worth, which comes at the end of his brief flowering. The *Hymn before Sunrise* records, as in the presence of Mont Blanc (though Coleridge was never actually there), an experience of elation and transcendence suggestive of Wordsworth and a sense of the mighty forces present, faintly anticipatory of Shelley's in the same scene. But both impressions are subordinated to the traditional theme of Nature's glorifying her Creator: "Earth, with her thousand voices, praises God":

> O dread and silent Mount! I gazed upon thee,
> Till thou, still present to the bodily sense,
> Didst vanish from my thought: entranced in prayer
> I worshipped the Invisible alone. . . .
>
> Awake, my soul! not only passive praise
> Thou owest! . . .
>              Awake, my heart, awake!
> Green vales and icy cliffs, all join my Hymn.
>
> Thou first and chief, sole sovereign of the Vale!
> O struggling with the darkness all the night,
> And visited all night by troops of stars. . . .
> Who sank thy sunless pillars deep in Earth?
> Who filled thy countenance with rosy light?
> Who made thee parent of perpetual streams?
>
> And you, ye five wild torrents fiercely glad!
> Who called you forth from night and utter death,
> From dark and icy caverns called you forth,
> Down those precipitous, black, jaggèd rocks,
> For ever shattered and the same for ever?
> Who gave you your invulnerable life,
> Your strength, your speed, your fury, and your joy,
> Unceasing thunder and eternal foam?

In many respects Shelley is the antithesis of Wordsworth and Coleridge; he represents the radical current in the Romantic movement, the source of whose ideas is found in the eighteenth century and which reacts against that century chiefly in its mode of expression, demanding for and from poetry more of imagination and emotion than its poets, sober and less inspired, could command. But the distinction between content and form is never more than a critical convenience. Expression charged with emotion may carry the poet beyond the affirmations warranted by the philosophy he professes; imagination may break through the limits that philosophy seeks to impose; and the final outcome may be the drastic modification or the abandonment of the philosophy itself. Something like this occurs in Shelley, who responds in some degree to Wordsworth's poetic treatment of nature and Coleridge's views on the imagination, antithetical as both are to the materialism which he commences by professing and tries to accommodate to poetry in Queen Mab—a materialism which finds free expression in the notes but already begins to suffer a change in the poem.

In Mont Blanc he is led to recognize or to hypostatize a power in nature, which is far indeed from the beneficent immanent Presence of Tintern Abbey, but still a power:

> Mont Blanc yet gleams on high;—the Power is there,
> The still and solemn power of many sights,
> And many sounds, and much of life and death. . . .
>        The secret Strength of things
> Which governs thought, and to the infinite dome
> Of heaven is as a law, inhabits thee!
> And what were thou, and earth, and stars, and sea,
> If to the human mind's imaginings
> Silence and solitude were vacancy?

"Things" still govern "thought"—yet not absolutely. The imagination is not yet granted its office as an organ of truth, but its voice refuses to be silenced, and it has in fact the last word. One is not perhaps very far from Wordsworth's sense of what the mind sees and what it half-creates; farther (as already implied) from his immanent Presence, and utterly remote of course from Wordsworth's later subordination of nature to religion or of Coleridge's in the imagined presence of this very scene.

The passage would be of less significance if it did not betoken the beginning of a crucial change of direction in Shelley's thought and at the same time suggest the limits of that change, not always recognized by critics. Another landmark is *Adonais,* his poem on the death of Keats. There the influence not of emotion and imagination only but of a consciously adopted poetic genre comes into play. Directed and sustained by the traditional pattern of the pastoral elegy, with its accretion of Christian assumptions, Shelley can go a good deal further—but not, be it noted, in the direction of Christianity:

> He lives, he wakes—'tis Death is dead, not he;
> Mourn not for Adonais.—Thou young Dawn,
> Turn all thy dew to splendour, for from thee
> The spirit thou lamentest is not gone. . . .
>
> He is made one with Nature: there is heard
> His voice in all her music, from the moan
> Of Thunder, to the song of night's sweet bird;
> He is a presence to be felt and known
> In darkness and in light, from herb and stone,
> Spreading itself where'er that Power may move
> Which has withdrawn his being to its own;
> Which wields the world with never wearied love,
> Sustains it from beneath and kindles it above.

But this is not the end. For the final apotheosis nothing but a Platonic conception will suffice:

The One remains, the many change and pass;
Heaven's light forever shines, Earth's shadows fly;
Life, like a dome of many-coloured glass,
Stains the white radiance of Eternity,
Until Death tramples it to fragments. . . .
The massy earth and sphered skies are riven!
I am borne darkly, fearfully, afar;
Whilst burning through the inmost veil of Heaven,
The soul of Adonais, like a star,
Beacons from the abode where the Eternal are.

One may think of this affirmation as a matter of imagery—
as a way of saying that Keats's poetry having been must ever be.
But it is more than that: it is the result of a profound change
in Shelley's outlook, which carried him from his early materialism to its antithesis, Platonic idealism, and from militant atheism
toward the most religious of pagan philosophies, as is confirmed
by his whole treatment of poetry in its relation to truth in the
*Defence of Poetry*, written in the same year as *Adonais*. In the
*Defence of Poetry*, it is plain that for Shelley the ultimate reality
is an ideal and unchanging world of ideas, the source of whatever of truth, beauty, and goodness, of harmony and love, are
apprehended by us, and that the office of the poet is to penetrate
by means of his imagination, the great organ of truth, to this
ultimate reality and make it visible. On the violence done to
distinctions that Plato is so careful to draw, we need not pause
(for Shelley's idealism, like his earlier materialism, is his own).
But that this much-modified Platonism carries Shelley nearer to
Christianity must be questioned. No doubt his unwavering hu-
manitarianism (no new product of his later thinking) brings
him (as it has brought many others) into relation with one part
of the Gospel's teaching: namely, the Second Commandment;
and the pattern of Christian thought, translated into humanitarian terms, helped to supply him with his own kind of apoc-

alyptic vision, as seen in the conclusion of *Prometheus Unbound*. But his hostility to historic Christianity remains, and his desire, like Blake's, to invert the pieces of the pattern is unmistakable in the remarks on Dante and Milton in the *Defence*. Nor is there any suggestion that, like Wordsworth and Coleridge, he learned the lesson of Christian humility or the absolute dependence of man and nature upon God. This is not to say, however, that a poem such as *Adonais* or *Prometheus Unbound* does not embody—that is, realize—a species of religious experience by uniting it very effectively with a genuine aesthetic experience.

In thus concentrating our attention on three of the great Romantics, we must not forget that the poetry of orthodoxy—that is, of an orthodoxy undisturbed by the currents and countercurrents of contemporary thought—continued to flow in a steady stream of devotional verse, increased in volume by the Evangelical revival, which had not yet spent all its force. Here the emphasis fell on salvation through faith and on the personal religious experience held to be its seal. The Oxford Movement had not yet renewed the complementary emphasis on the corporate life of the Church, on liturgy and sacrament, thus rounding out and balancing the dual Anglican inheritance. Some union of the two is implied in Coleridge's late poem on his baptismal birthday, but with the Evangelical emphasis predominant.

The largest body, however, of orthodox religious verse took the form of hymns, a form in which the English Church has been especially prolific. It is a commonplace of literary criticism that the hymn in general takes a low rank as poetry, being tied to a limited range of ideas and to conventional (that is to say, traditional) imagery and diction, and prone (especially under

Evangelical influence) to sentimentality. The first two conditions are indeed inevitable; the last is no necessity, but, where it occurs, a defect. Like any other poem written to be set to music and sung on a more or less public occasion, the hymn cannot be fairly judged in isolation from its setting and its purpose and use. It is at least permissible to ask whether, if one could place beside the whole body of English hymns the whole body of secular lyrics written to be set to music and performed, the hymns might not sustain the comparison fairly satisfactorily.

One of the great needs of the English, as of other Reformed Churches, was an adequate hymnal for public worship. The first attempt was to supply it from a Scriptural source, and from Sternhold and Hopkins (1562) to Tait and Brady (1798), metrical paraphrases of the Psalms abound and are for the most part quite deplorable. Poetic talent seemed to find little scope and achieve little effect even when the poet was Milton (for there is some point in Landor's comment that Milton was never so much a regicide as when he raised his hand and smote King David). And this is the more remarkable when one considers the riches of the original as seen in the prose rendering of either the Authorized or the Prayer Book version. But from the late seventeenth century onward the hymn (as we know it) commenced to supply more adequately the need, and we have briefly mentioned in passing the contribution thereto by Addison, Charles Wesley (on whom, indeed, we might profitably have paused), and Cowper. But it is to the nineteenth century that we owe the majority of the best and best-loved English hymns, including after the Oxford Movement some translations of hymns of the earlier Church. Since we shall not find occasion to return to the subject, and since precise period is here of secondary importance, we may simply recall eight or ten of the best-known examples—most of which escape the charge of sentimentality, bear little relation to party, and move along the common road of Christian doctrine and worship: "Abide with Me" and "Praise, My Soul, the King of Heaven" (Lyte); "Holy, Holy, Holy, Lord God Almighty" (Bishop Heber); "The Church's One Foundation" (Stone); "Jerusalem the Golden" (Neale); "Eternal Father Strong to Save" (Whiting); "Fight the Good Fight" (Monsell); "O Word of God Incarnate" and "For All the Saints" (Walsham How).

Strictly within our present (the Romantic) period falls a famous collection of devotional verse which anticipates by a few years, but has its intimate connection with, the Oxford Movement. John Keble's *Christian Year* stands to the nineteenth century in much the same relation as does George Herbert's *The Temple* to the seventeenth; and there is some common ground not between the books only but between their authors. After a brilliant university career, Keble (who did not, however, have Herbert's demon of worldly ambition to contend with) retired to the ministry of a country parish. He was a fine scholar, a profound admirer of Hooker's *Laws of Ecclesiastical Politie*, of which he produced the standard modern edition, and devoted to the British Church, subscribing no doubt to every word of Herbert's poem in her praise. Like *The Temple*, *The Christian Year* was published just as that Church was entering on a period of special difficulty and danger, but, unlike *The Temple*, it was to prove not a consolation merely but a rallying point.

Like its predecessor, *The Christian Year* responds, with some reserve, to the current of poetry in its day: in about the same degree as Herbert's is "Metaphysical" poetry, Keble's is "Romantic." It is responsive to nature, drawing many of its images therefrom and applying them symbolically, and it does not eschew emotion (which Keble, in his lectures, declared to be the essence of poetry); but, as with Herbert, imagery and emotion alike are moderated and attuned to his religious themes and to a type of piety unmistakably Anglican. In the Advertisement to The Christian Year, Keble, significantly, writes:

Next to a sound rule of faith, there is nothing of so much consequence as a sober standard of feeling in matters of practical religion: and it is the peculiar happiness of the Church of England, to possess, in her authorized formularies, an ample and secure provision for both. . . . The object of the present publication will be attained, if any person find assistance from it in bringing his own thoughts and feelings into more entire unison with those recommended and exemplified in the Prayer Book.

The Christian Year enjoyed immediate and continued success (with, it is said, some 160 editions in its first fifty years). As the title implies, the poems are attached to the dates in the Church's calendar (her "ritual year") and lectionary. But Keble shares with Herbert not only his devotion to the English Church, and its specifically Catholic inheritance, but that immediacy of personal religious experience which is also part of her inheritance and gives a distinctive character to the best poems in both volumes.

We can illustrate this character and at the same time briefly indicate the relation of the Christian Year to the Oxford Movement. For that movement, while ecclesiastical, and even in its earlier stages political in character (as the Wesleyan and Evangelical revivals were not) was also deeply religious in its fundamental motives, as is clearly seen in both Keble and Newman. It was to Keble's famous sermon on national apostasy, preached at Oxford in 1833, that Newman always looked back as the effective beginning of the Oxford Movement; but it was the yet earlier *Christian Year* that helped to mold the religious belief and experience of Newman himself, to transform intellectual principles to religious.

In his *Apologia pro Vita sua*, Newman tells us that he derived from his reading of Butler's *Analogy of Religion* two principles which continued to underlie much of his teaching: first, that there was an analogy between the separate works of God, between the order of nature and the order of grace, and that the lower order stood to the higher in a sacramental relation, as (to adopt the Prayer Book's definition of a sacrament) "the outward and visible sign of an inward and spiritual grace"; and, secondly, that probability is the guide of life, that in matters of belief assent can be grounded only on a graduated scale of probabilities, and that converging probabilities, which must always fall short of demonstration, of certainty (which is a quality of propositions) might still beget *certitude* (which is a state of mind). But something was lacking to make these principles fully operative in a religious sense, and it was found in what Newman called the "religious teaching, so deep, so pure, so beautiful" of Keble's *Christian Year*. The firmness of assent, it seemed, did not depend on the probabilities alone, but on these as they were put to account by faith and love. Faith and love are directed by a person (the believer) to a Person (God), and in the vision of God they live. This truth linked itself to one of Newman's earliest intuitions, when he was yet quite unpracticed in speculative thought—namely, that there were two and only two entities whose reality it was impossible for him to doubt: himself and his Creator. So the argument from probability became an argument from personality; and Keble's poetry brought this home to him. And it also exhibited, by its simple symbolic use of natural imagery, the principle of analogy, as it in turn was put to account by faith and love.

In illustration, and to suggest the quality of Keble's verse (which is certainly higher in religious than in poetic value), we may quote from two poems. First, from *Septuagesima Sunday*, as illustrating what we may read in the book of nature and apply by analogy:

> There is a book, who runs may read
>    Which heavenly truth imparts,
> And all the lore its scholars need,
>    Pure eyes and Christian hearts. . . .
>
> The glorious sky embracing all
>    Is like the Maker's love,
> Wherein encompass'd, great and small
>    In peace and order move.
>
> The Moon above, the Church below,
>    A wondrous race they run,
> But all their radiance, all their glow,
>    Each borrows of its Sun.
>
> The Saviour lends the light and heat
>    That crowns His holy hill;
> The saints, like stars, around His seat,
>    Perform their courses still.
>
> The saints above are stars in Heaven—
>    What are the saints on earth?
> Like trees they stand whom God has given,
>    Our Eden's happy birth.
>
> Faith is their fix'd unswerving root,
>    Hope their unfading flower,
> Fair deeds of charity their fruit,
>    The glory of their bower. . . .
>
> Two worlds are ours: 'tis only Sin
>    Forbids us to descry
> The mystic heaven and earth within,
>    Plain as the sea and sky.

Thou, who hast given me eyes to see
And love this sight so fair,
Give me a heart to find out Thee,
And read Thee everywhere.

Secondly, as illustrating the argument from, and to, personality,
we turn to *St. Bartholomew's Day*, where the book referred to,
and described as a mirror, is of course the Bible:

Hold up thy mirror to the sun,
And thou shalt need an eagle's gaze,
So perfectly the polish'd stone
Gives back the glory of his rays:

Turn it, and it shall paint as true
The soft green of the vernal earth,
And each small flower of bashful hue,
That closest hides its lowly birth.

Our mirror is a blessed book,
Where out from each illumin'd page
We see one glorious Image look
All eyes to dazzle and engage,

The Son of God: and that indeed
We see Him as He is, we know,
Since in the same bright glass we read
The very life of things below.—

Eye of God's word! where'er we turn
Ever upon us! thy keen gaze
Can all the depths of sin discern,
Unravel every bosom's maze:

Who that has felt thy glance of dread
Thrill through his heart's remotest cells,
About his path, about his bed,
Can doubt what spirit in thee dwells?

"What word is this? Whence know'st thou me?"
All wondering cries the humbled heart,
To hear thee that deep mystery,
The knowledge of itself, impart. . . .

"The child-like faith, that asks not sight,
　　Waits not for wonder or for sign,
Believes, because it loves, aright—
　　Shall see things greater, things divine.

"Heaven to that gaze shall open wide,
　　And brightest angels to and fro
On messages of love shall glide
　　'Twixt God above and Christ below."

So still the guileless man is blest,
　　To him all crooked paths are straight,
Him on his way to endless rest
　　Fresh, ever-growing strengths await.

God's witnesses, a glorious host,
　　Compass him daily like a cloud;
Martyrs and seers, the sav'd and lost,
　　Mercies and judgments cry aloud.

Yet shall to him the still small voice,
　　That first into his bosom found
A way, and fix'd his wavering choice,
　　Nearest and dearest ever sound.

And here we find also illustrated that immediacy of religious experience, realized through the poem, which we have remarked as common to Keble and George Herbert (as seen, for example, in *The Collar*), and which belongs to what we may call the Evangelical element in the composite Anglican tradition.

If Keble is the poet of the Oxford Movement, Newman is its philosopher, deeply concerned with the nature and grounds of belief; and in this connection he makes, in one of his Oxford sermons, a penetrating distinction, which embodies his own form of the criticism of reason narrowly conceived. Explicit reason, or the process of formal reasoning, he explains, is an acquired art, and its legitimate function is no more than to give, so far as they are capable of receiving it, logical form to convictions reached by a very different process, that of implicit reason, which is not an art, but the living process of thought itself:

The mind ranges to and fro, and spreads out, and advances forward. . . . It passes from point to point, gaining one by some indication; another on a probability; then availing itself of an association; . . . then committing itself to some popular impression, or some inward instinct, or some obscure memory; and thus it makes progress not unlike a climber on a steep cliff, who . . . ascends how he knows not himself, by personal endowments and by practice rather than by rule.

Newman is not thinking of this distinction in its bearing on poetry; but its bearing on religious poetry is plain and important. It is in fact twofold. If explicit reason can cast convictions into logical form, the imagination can bestow upon them poetic form; but, more than that, it can enter into the process at an earlier stage (as is implied in Newman's glancing reference to impressions, associations, and an inward instinct) and thus help to reach the convictions; for if poetry is in one aspect, and very definitely, an art, it is in another a mode of apprehension.

Though his chief fame, and rightly, is that of a religious thinker, Newman also wrote religious poetry. One meditative lyric which, though not so intended, has become one of the Church's best-loved hymns: "Lead Kindly Light." The deeply religious experience which it realized for Newman also had its part to play in preparing the leader of the Oxford Movement. After abandoning the rather narrow Evangelicalism in which he was brought up, and experiencing the intellectual stimulus of Oriel College, where religious liberalism on the whole prevailed, he had visited the Continent and in Sicily had almost died of an attack of fever. In his long convalescence, and on the slow voyage home, he had engaged in much searching of heart, and it was then that he wrote the poem, with its moving and revealing lines:

> I was not ever thus, nor prayed that Thou
>     Shouldst lead me on.
> I loved to choose and see my path, but now
>     Lead Thou me on!
> I loved the garish day and, spite, of fears,
> Pride ruled my will: remember not past years.

Some thirty-five years later, Newman published his finest poem, *The Dream of Gerontius*, but this belongs to a later phase of his and the century's religious development.

# → VII ←

## THE VICTORIAN AGE: 1840–1900

I N COMPARISON with our own, the Victorian age presents two
different aspects. In one view, it looks like a period of peace
and stability to which we may look back with a degree of nostalgia if also with a slightly superior tolerance for its naïveté and
complacency. But this is a superficial view. It was, as a closer
scrutiny reveals, the seed ground of the twentieth century. It
marked the beginnings of many of our specific problems and
more generally of that sudden heightening of the tempo of
change which has been mounting ever since.

In the practical sphere, the Industrial Revolution altered the
face of the country, multiplied its population, and did much to
make the nineteenth England's century. Political followed economic change and the Reform Bill of 1867 was decisive in the
transition from constitutional to democratic monarchy, and in-
sured that political democracy would in its turn pave the way
to economic. If the impression of peace and stability is not
altogether delusive—and it is not—the reasons are not hard to
discover. The first is a cultural inheritance able to withstand the
shock of change; the second, a remarkable adaptability witnessed
by the Reform Bill, itself a phase of the great English discovery
which I will call (in contradistinction to the Marxist pattern)

the class peace—a peace which recognizes the possibility of war and the imperative need of adjustment to avoid it.

Change was not confined to the practical sphere. It was also to assail the foundations of traditional culture and beliefs. Here we find among the leaders of Victorian thought, instead of complacency, an astonishing activity of the critical spirit. Nowhere is this so apparent as in the type of literature in which the Victorian is pre-eminent among all periods, the literature of thought and opinion, with its galaxy of great names, Carlyle, Ruskin, Newman, John Stuart Mill, T. H. Huxley, Matthew Arnold, and a strong supporting cast of only lesser note; but in degree, the critical spirit also permeates the genres in which the age achieved high, though not the highest, quality: poetry and the novel. A special mark of Victorian thinking, which has its obvious bearing on stability, is that the criticism was, on the whole, constructive: rarely is its conservatism merely reactionary and anti-intellectual or its radicalism emotional and intent to destroy. Where the Victorian radical rejected traditional sanctions, he sought for others to put in their place, and in their name supported the reforms which he advocated. The conservative recognized the need for adaptation. And the liberal, from his standing ground between the two, engaged in both processes.

Early in the period John Stuart Mill distinguished between a radical tradition stemming from Bentham and a conservative which he associated with Coleridge. Retrospect permits some modification and elaboration of this distinction. The radical tradition was grounded in the English Empiricism of the eighteenth century. This philosophy also furnished a basis for the great advance in scientific thought in the new century, but in the process it gradually underwent a notable transformation. For the biological sciences counteracted the tendency of earlier

Empiricism to rely on analysis of the static, and substituted for it natural history and the century's master idea of development. This idea was not the product of the biological sciences alone. Indeed Mill, who could hardly foresee the dominance of biology and its transformation of Empiricism, rather associated development and a historical outlook with Coleridge, where they were combined with a Transcendentalism in reaction against the Empiricists' analysis of mind and motive. As the century proceeded, the idea of development or evolution became the common mark of every school of thought, extended its influence to politics and religion, and—at least to the less critical—seemed to warrant the rooted Victorian belief in progress, where the charge of naïveté and complacency is no doubt justified.

Narrowing our view now to the religious issue and forces playing upon it, we may emphasize, in the first place, the skepticism and naturalism inherent in the Empirical tradition, already apparent in the later eighteenth century and unmistakable in the writings of Bentham and James Mill, and, secondly, note how these tendencies were fortified by the conception of organic evolution culminating in the publication, in 1859, of Darwin's *On the Origin of Species*. Not only did it present masses of new evidence in support of the conception; it furnished what seemed a convincing account of how the development had occurred. By its apparent sufficiency, the Darwinian hypothesis won the day for evolution. The results for religious thought were immediate and far-reaching.

Though attempting to account only for the origin of species and not the origin of life, Darwin's work was a triumph for naturalism, and in the controversy that ensued it sharpened the line of cleavage between science and religion. It seemed to dispose once and for all not only of a literal reading of the first chapter of Genesis, already undermined by a study of the geological record, but of the compromise sought in a series of special "Creations," which had been advanced to meet the evidence of that record. Further, though Darwin was slow to make the inference specific, it was recognized that, if true at all, his evolutionary theory applied likewise to the descent of man, with a series of disturbing consequences for human dignity and for the soul as an immortal entity.

If all this seemed in the highest degree damaging to revealed religion as commonly conceived, the character of Darwin's hypothesis was equally damaging to natural religion and to any form of teleology. For its three cardinal points were "accidental variation" (which meant no more than variation whose cause was unknown, but "words," as Bacon said, "like the Tartar's bow shoot back upon the understanding of the wisest"), the "struggle for existence," and the "survival of the fittest"; and these postulates with the resulting picture of animate nature as the theater of perpetual warfare, suffering, and waste dealt the "argument from design" a blow from which it has never recovered. The picture of nature was not of course wholly new: Tennyson's description of nature "red in tooth and claw" and marked by almost incredible waste, careless not of the individual only but of the type, pre-dated On the Origin of Species. Darwin, however, had made these disturbing facts not concomitants but the very essence of his scheme. True to his character, he had sought to reassure the shocked reader by declaring that death was quick, no fear was felt, and the healthy and the happy survived; but his exponent and defender Huxley would have nothing to do with such attempts at mitigation, declaring that only the dullness of our senses prevented us from hearing the continuous cries of terror and agony from the animal world. Nor was this all: Huxley also insisted on the amorality of the process ("fittest" did not mean "best") and its incompatibility with any form of teleology (accounting for progress in the past, it gave no assurance of progress in the future or of any designed end). An avowed agnostic (and, he claimed, the inventor of the term), Huxley was in philosophy the disciple of Hume; and he carried on the war in behalf of science and against religion on all fronts.

Nor was this the only crisis with which religion was faced. At about the same time, the results of German research and criticism in the text and history of the Bible began to make their weight felt in England, where such studies had lagged behind those of the Continent, and where Christian apologetics had long rested confidently on the letter of the Old and New Testaments. Not unknown to advanced thinkers (for example, George Eliot had already translated Strauss's *Leben Jesu*), the substitution of the historical and natural for the dogmatic and supernatural now received a new impetus and diffusion from Renan's popular *Vie de Jésus* (1863).

A candid but cautious response both to Biblical criticism and to the new facts advanced by science was given by the group of Broad Church clergymen (the lineal descendants of the Cambridge Platonists and Latitudinarians of the seventeenth century) in their famous volume of *Essays and Reviews* (1860), which ran through edition after edition and provoked, as was to be expected, heated controversy. Baden Powell, professor of mathematics at Oxford, fully allowed—indeed asserted—the claim of science to speak for matters of ascertained fact and welcomed *On the Origin of Species* as a "work which must soon bring about an entire revolution of opinion in favour of the grand principle of the self-evolving powers of nature"; nor did he seem at all alarmed by the features of that work to be emphasized by Huxley, though no one could yet assert, as would a writer in *Lux Mundi* (the Anglican manifesto of twenty-five years later) that the "evolution which at first was supposed to have destroyed teleology is found to be more saturated with teleology than the view which it superseded" (for that was the result of a reaction against Darwin and in favor of creative and purposive evolution represented by, among others, Samuel Butler). If Baden Powell spoke of and for natural science, Benjamin Jowett, Regius Professor of Greek and later to become the influential Master of Balliol, applied to the interpretation of Scripture the principles developed in the study of classical texts.

The purpose of *Essays and Reviews* was to effect a reconciliation of science, including the science of history, with religion by distinguishing in the Bible between what had been taken for statements of fact but could no longer be accepted as such and the profound truths of the spirit which its religious and moral teaching embodied. This too was the work taken in hand by Matthew Arnold in *Literature and Dogma* and *St. Paul and Protestantism*, which went further, however, and sought to disengage the ethical content of the Bible from the dogmatic structures imposed upon it by theologians. The result was an extremely attenuated definition of religion ("morality touched by emotion") and of the Deity ("a Power not ourselves making for righteousness") and a reduction of Scripture to a body of literature marked by that quality of "high seriousness" shared by the best poetry from Homer onward: all of which issued in the conviction that more and more poetry would take the place of religion, a conclusion which T. S. Eliot has deplored as equally detrimental to religion and to poetry.

Be that as it may, what one really has in Arnold is an example of a mode of thought best described not as religious but as humanistic and presenting indeed some marked analogies with the later Humanism of Irving Babbitt, though less precise in its formulations. In the preface to *Last Essays on the Church and Religion*, Arnold writes:

It will generally . . . be admitted that all experience as to conduct brings us to the fact of two selves . . . contending for the mastery in man, the one a movement of first impulse and more involuntary, leading us to gratify any inclination that may solicit us, and called generally a movement of man's ordinary or passing self . . . the other, a movement of reflection and more voluntary, leading us to submit inclination to some rule, and called generally a movement of man's higher or enduring self. . . .

And Arnold adds that while the serious-minded may express the experience in different terms, they all agree "that for a man to obey the higher self . . . is happiness and life for him; to obey the lower is death and misery." This may serve to remind us of the strong current of thought which set in against the rising tide of naturalism, and which took a variety of forms and was manifested not only in Arnold and (in his *Idea of a University*) Newman but in John Stuart Mill (who repudiated "nature" as an ethical norm) and, most surprisingly, in T. H. Huxley (who, in his Romanes Lectures on Evolution and Ethics, was driven to recognize beside the cosmic or evolutionary process common to nature the ethical process peculiar to man, whose aim was to exclude the cosmic process from human society). The effect was a constructive effort to reassert traditional values in ethics and culture on a basis not of dogma but simply of human experience. In Arnold, it could form a tenuous alliance with religion against the common enemy. In Huxley, it left his hostility to religion unassuaged. With Mill, George Eliot, and others, it led to the adoption (with some reservations) of Comte's so-called religion of humanity.

Arnold's concern for culture and his sense of its relation to religion (in however attenuated a form) give evidence of some common ground with the liberal interpreters and defenders of religion in the period. They were all humanists, and directly or indirectly they looked back to Coleridge. For him, idealism in the form which he partly adopted, partly excogitated, from Kant and the post-Kantians but also from Plato and the Platonic tradition, was the necessary philosophical basis for a reassertion first of natural, then of revealed, religion, and therewith of all the traditional values of a mature and viable culture as these were embodied in the Church and State and in philosophy, poetry, and the arts. What Coleridge sought was a culture based on religion and a religion permeated by culture. In his view of Scripture he already adumbrated something of the attitude to be manifested by Jowett and his contemporaries, and his whole philosophy was deeply imbued with the idea of mind and nature as living organisms marked by development. Thus he paved the way for the later or neo-Hegelian phase of British idealism which was the dominant philosophy of the liberal defenders of religion in the last third of the century. Up to a point this philosophy served them well, though ultimately (as may be seen in F. H. Bradley) it raised issues difficult to reconcile with revealed religion and a personal Deity.

For the time being, the tide seemed in some degree to have turned in favor of religion. There is nothing apologetic or diffident in the tone of *Lux Mundi*, which could also, as we have seen, aver that evolution was entirely compatible with a basic teleology. But a different vista is disclosed if we turn to the writings of Walter Pater. Underlying his aesthetic theory, as set forth in his *Renaissance*, is a complete surrender to all the negations which science suggested respecting the individual life and, art excepted, its values. More, perhaps, than he could have desired, Pater came into his own in the 1890's, which in many ways mark the effective end of the Victorian period, and was eagerly adopted by the writers of the decadence, while Pater himself was modifying his initial position, writing on religion and even Christianity (though with a heavily aesthetic bias) in *Marius the Epicurean*, and recognizing in his essay on style a category beyond "good literature"—namely, "great literature," distinguished by something like Arnold's highly serious treatment of religious and moral themes.

Again, we notice in Clough the lassitude and indecision which were the heritage of a loss of faith, and in Arnold's poetry, as opposed to the constructive note of his prose, a profound nostalgia, later echoed against a yet bleaker background by Hardy. In Tennyson, we find a hesitant, and in Browning, an assertive, preoccupation with the severely shaken belief in personal immortality. Yet a large poetic reconstruction inspired by a faith in nature and a species of natural religion was possible to Bridges (for though it appeared in the next century, his *Testament of Beauty* is plainly the work of a Victorian); and the faith of the Churches could still give to many an unimpaired sense of security which finds expression in Bridges' friend Gerard Manley Hopkins, who paradoxically seems in some ways to belong more to our century than his own.

Of the theory of poetry in the Victorian period, it is unnecessary to speak at any length; it struck out no new line comparable to that of Coleridge on the imagination. It inherited from the Romantics a sense of the importance of poetry and the high calling of the poet. Poetry was (in Arnold's famous phrase) a "criticism of life": its value lay in the powerful and beautiful application of ideas to life. The poet (as Wordsworth had averred) was a man speaking to men, but a man endowed in unusual degree with sensibility, who had thought and felt deeply. All this entailed a heavy emphasis upon content, upon what was said as well as on how it was said, and on the public character and responsibilities of the poet. These were beliefs common to Tennyson and Browning as poets, and to Arnold as critic, and they were, it would seem, very generally shared by a large body of their readers. Against these assumptions the aesthetic schools reacted: first, Rossetti and the Pre-Raphaelites (with Swinburne openly flaunting his paganism and making, it would almost seem, a responsibility of irresponsibility) and later, the poets of the 'nineties.

With this brief sketch of the period, we may turn to an equally brief consideration of some Victorian poets. Not all the phases of the change in religion which we have noticed can be here illustrated. We must pass over the relatively new phenomenon of a poetry directed against religion or dedicated to a Godless world as seen in the truculent paganism of Swinburne and his equally truculent essay in humanism ("Glory to man in the highest for man is master of things"), or in the avowed atheism of B. V. (James Thomson) in *The City of Dreadful Night*, or in the sad pessimism of Thomas Hardy, not untouched by nostalgia for a lost faith, as in *The Impercipient* (At a Cathedral Service):

> That with this bright believing band
>   I have no claim to be,
> That faiths by which my comrades stand
>   Seem fantasies to me,
> And mirage-mists their Shining Land,
>   Is a strange destiny.
>
> Why thus my soul should be consigned
>   To infelicity,

Why always I must feel as blind
    To sights my brethren see,
Why joys they've found I cannot find,
    Abides a mystery. . . .

Enough. As yet disquiet clings
    About us. Rest shall we.

We need spare only a glance at the religion of humanity, which
produced little of note but George Eliot's bleakly noble *Choir
Invisible:*

O may I join the choir invisible
Of those immortal dead who live again
In minds made better by their presence: live
In pulses stirred to generosity,
In deeds of daring rectitude, in scorn
For miserable aims that end with self,
In thoughts sublime that pierce the night like stars,
And with their mild persistence urge man's search
To vaster issues. . . .

                    This is life to come,
Which martyred men have made more glorious
For us who strive to follow. May I reach
That purest heaven, be to other souls
The cup of strength in some great agony,
Enkindle generous ardour, feed pure love,
Beget the smiles that have no cruelty—
Be the sweet presence of a good diffused,
And in diffusion ever more intense.
So shall I join the choir invisible
Whose music is the gladness of the world.

Nor need we pause on Clough's weary quest and bewilderment
relieved by an occasional note of resolve ("Is there no second
life? / Pitch this one high"), but may turn directly to Arnold.

While modestly admitting the superiority of Tennyson's and
Browning's poetic talent to his own, Arnold could claim that his
poems were more representative of the main movement of mind

in their age. No poem better illustrates one phase of this movement of mind than *Dover Beach*. It touches religion only in a negative way, but it is one of the great poems of the period and can be quoted as poetry and not merely as historical document:

> The sea is calm to-night.
> The tide is full, the moon lies fair
> Upon the straits;—on the French coast, the light
> Gleams and is gone; the cliffs of England stand,
> Glimmering and vast, out in the tranquil bay.
>
> Come to the window, sweet is the night-air!
> Only, from the long line of spray
> Where the sea meets the moon-blanched sand,
> Listen! you hear the grating roar
> Of pebbles which the waves draw back, and fling,
> At their return, up the high strand,
> Begin, and cease, and then again begin,
> With tremulous cadence slow, and bring
> The eternal note of sadness in.
>
> Sophocles long ago
> Heard it on the Aegean, and it brought
> Into his mind the turbid ebb and flow
> Of human misery; we
> Find also in the sound a thought,
> Hearing it by this distant northern sea.
>
> The Sea of Faith
> Was once, too, at the full, and round earth's shore
> Lay like the folds of a bright girdle furled.
> But now I only hear
> Its melancholy, long, withdrawing roar,
> Retreating, to the breath
> Of the night-wind, down the vast edges drear
> And naked shingles of the world.
>
> Ah, love, let us be true
> To one another! for the world, which seems
> To lie before us like a land of dreams,
> So various, so beautiful, so new,
> Hath really neither joy, nor love, nor light,

Nor certitude, nor peace, nor help for pain;
And we are here as on a darkling plain
Swept with confused alarms of struggle and flight,
Where ignorant armies clash by night.

The same basic situation is presented in another phase in *Stanzas from the Grande Chartreuse*. Having described the great monastery as seen at evening in its wild Alpine setting, and the life within its walls, ascetic, dedicated to pain and mortification, and utterly alien to the modern world, the poet proceeds:

All are before me! I behold
The House, the Brotherhood austere!
    And what am I, that I am here?

For rigorous teachers seized my youth,
And purged its faith, and trimmed its fire,
Show'd me the high, white star of Truth,
There bade me gaze, and there aspire.
Even now their whispers pierce the gloom:
*What dost thou in this living tomb?*

Forgive me, masters of the mind!
At whose behest I long ago
So much unlearned, so much resign'd—
I come not here to be your foe!
I seek these anchorites, not in ruth,
To curse and to deny your truth;

Not as their friend, or child, I speak!
But as, on some far northern strand,
Thinking of his own Gods, a Greek
In pity and mournful awe might stand
Before some fallen Runic stone—
For both were faiths, and both are gone.

Wandering between two worlds, one dead,
The other powerless to be born,
With nowhere yet to rest my head,
Like these, on earth I wait forlorn.
Their faith, my tears, the world deride—
I come to shed them at their side.

The most positive note that Arnold can achieve is evoked by the memory of his father, as recalled fifteen years after his death, in *Rugby Chapel*, the only poem of Arnold's, and that by a certain indulgence, included in the *Oxford Book of Christian Verse*. Here it is the power of faith and hope, and not the substance of the things believed and hoped for, that receives all the emphasis. In the long march of mankind through the Alpine wilderness,

> . . . —A God
> Marshalled them, gave them their goal.
> Ah, but the way is so long!

many fall under the weight of weariness and despair, and all would perish were it not for the select few of whom his father was an example:

> Then, in such hour of need
> Of your fainting, dispirited race,
> Ye like angels appear,
> Radiant with ardor divine!
> Beacons of hope, ye appear!
> Languor is not in your heart,
>
> Weakness is not in your word,
> Weariness not on your brow.
> Ye alight in our van! at your voice,
> Panic, despair, flee away.
> Ye move through the ranks, recall
> The stragglers, refresh the outworn,
> Praise, re-inspire the brave!
>
> Order, courage, return.
> Eyes rekindling, and prayers,
> Follow your steps as ye go.
> Ye fill up the gaps in our files,
> Strengthen the wavering line,
> Stablish, continue our march,
> On, to the bound of the waste,
> On, to the City of God.

Arnold's poems tell of course but half the story. There remains the more constructive effort of his prose referred to above. The poems, it may be said, ask the questions for which in the prose he attempts to find the answers, and express the emotions which in the prose must be brought into order. It is there too that Arnold refuses to commit himself merely to the fact as apprehended by the senses and the reason or to a faith that responds wholly to imagination and the heart but demands a union of the two, which he designates as "imaginative reason."

Something like "imaginative reason" might be a fair description of the power at work in the poetry of Tennyson. It records the intense struggle to mediate between the need for faith as he feels it and the facts as science and scholarship present them; and there can be no doubt of the vital role of poetry in attaining as well as expressing the positions reached. Pre-eminently this would seem to be true of *In Memoriam*. There, in section after section, the poet can be seen objectifying his doubts and seeking some secure ground of affirmation. Not the composition of the individual parts only but their organization into a cumulative whole, however and whenever it took place, must also be recognized as an experience at once aesthetic and religious—a new and comprehensive uniting of the religious content with an artistic form, related (though less immediately than *Lycidas* or *Adonais*) to the long tradition of the monody. To demonstrate this would require a detailed analysis of *In Memoriam*, which cannot be attempted here. We must content ourselves with a brief statement of the questions which recur in Tennyson's religious thought and are central to the experiences not simply recorded but realized in the poem.

The first is the problem of the soul's survival after death.

Immortality, sealed and guaranteed by Christ's Resurrection, was a fundamental dogma of the Christian creed, assumed without question in the religious poetry of an earlier day. In Deism and in natural religion generally, and in poetry deriving from such sources in the eighteenth century, it had receded but not disappeared. But now in the nineteenth century it came under double question from the naturalistic account of man given by science and from the skeptical or merely critical examination of Scripture. The degree of importance attached to personal survival in itself, and as essential to the rest of religious belief, differed from individual to individual. With Tennyson, as also with Browning, it seems to have been paramount; with Arnold far less important—but then in Arnold religious belief is much attenuated. In Tennyson there is a good deal of speculation about the soul's history (with some suggestion of the doctrine of pre-existence, and more about its possible transmutations after death with even its ultimate, though not immediate, absorption into the Divine). Of these speculations, A. C. Bradley, in his commentary on *In Memoriam*, finds it impossible to determine how many were matters of belief to Tennyson, or in precisely what degree. It is sufficient, Bradley continues, if we take immortality to mean "the conscious and indefinitely prolonged life of the soul beyond death. For this was to him undoubtedly a matter of fixed belief, and of importance so great that life without belief in it seemed to him to have neither sense nor value. We must remember also that immortality was to his mind a fact of the same order as the existence of a God of love. . . ." These are facts which cannot be "known" in the sense that material phenomena are known ("For knowledge is of things we see") or proved to be fact by strict process of reasoning from such knowledge ("For nothing worth proving"—that is, nothing of ultimate value and importance—"can be proven"): they are matters not of knowledge but of faith. Of faith, however, based on what? Not on the authority of Scripture or Church, though Tennyson will on occasion (as in the Prologue to *In Memoriam*) refer to the dogmas of the Trinity, of Creation, and of the Resurrection; and though he remained a member of the Church and found support in her services, he would (in his own words) "cling to faith beyond the forms of faith." If not on knowledge or what reason can infer from what we certainly "know," and if not on dogma and the two authorities on which dogma can rest, on what then? Primarily on inward experience, and among various inward experiences, pre-eminently of love so strong, so indestructible, that it seems to demand perpetuation both of itself and of its object. That is why *In Memoriam* is so central in Tennyson's religious experience. When, confronted by the impossibility of proof, the heart replies "I have felt," we must not (as Bradley wisely reminds us) take this to mean, "I have felt the desire for immortality," but "I have had experiences beyond the scope of sense perception and reasoned inference"—in a word, the experience of love—and it is on this experience that the belief is grounded not only in immortality but in God as a God of love. Though Tennyson was almost as well equipped in the philosophy of his day as he was in science (Huxley, forgetting Goethe, declared him the best equipped of any poet since Lucretius), though he knew something at first hand of the idealism represented in English literature by Coleridge and Carlyle, he did not put forward a claim for such experience and the resulting conviction, as indeed a form of knowledge, and that the highest accessible to the mind because supplied by the mind itself, and on this knowledge base a superstructure of argument.

Rather he considered that the conditions of finite knowledge bar any full comprehension of the infinite. The result would have seemed to him just one more system among many.

> Our little systems have their day;
>> They have their day and cease to be:
>> They are but broken lights of thee,
> And thou, O Lord, art more than they.

It was not only man's mortality viewed in isolation that presented a problem which faith must transcend since it could not solve, but the whole spectacle of nature as Tennyson, even before On the Origin of Species, had learned to know it; and here the second question emerges: how to reconcile such a spectacle with a God of love.

> Are God and nature then at strife,
>> That Nature lends such evil dreams?
>> So careful of the type she seems
> So careless of the single life. . . .

> I falter where I firmly trod,
>> And falling with my weight of cares
>> Upon the great world's altar-stairs
> That slope through darkness up to God. . . .

> "So careful of the type?" but no.
>> From scarped cliff and quarried stone
>> She cries, "A thousand types are gone:
> I care for nothing, all shall go.

> "Thou makest thine appeal to me:
>> I bring to life, I bring to death:
>> The spirit does but mean the breath:
> I know no more." And he, shall he,

> Man, her last work, who seem'd so fair,
>> Such splendid purpose in his eyes,
>> Who roll'd the psalm to wintry skies,
> Who built him fanes of fruitless prayer,

> Who trusted God was love indeed,
>     And love Creation's final law—
>     Tho' Nature, red in tooth and claw
> With ravine, shriek'd against his creed—
>
> Who loved, who suffer'd countless ills,
>     Who battled for the True, the Just,
>     Be blown about the desert dust,
> Or seal'd within the iron hills?

To this situation Tennyson evinces two immediate responses. One is an indignant sense of the anomaly in the conclusion to which nature points. (The anomaly, by the way, was equally apparent to John Stuart Mill and T. H. Huxley, though they did not link it with the question of immortality as Tennyson does, and they supplied of course quite different answers to the problem.) Tennyson's other response is again the appeal to inner experience against the evidence—itself of necessity inconclusive—of outer fact:

> I stretch lame hands of faith . . .
>                     and call
> To what I feel is Lord of all,
> And faintly trust the larger hope.

The word "faintly" is itself testimony to Tennyson's honest report of his own feelings. One effect that In Memoriam achieves is to enable him to remove or much to qualify that "faintly."

Here emerges the third question (of primary importance for Tennyson in his public office of poetic teacher): What is the relation to human aspiration and conduct of, on the one hand, nature as it is seen to be and, on the other, of God as he impresses himself upon the heart and mind? In the matter of nature, Tennyson has no doubts or reservations. He is well aware of the counsel of ruthless self-assertion, of force and cunning, that can be derived from nature if she is adopted as model and guide, and he anticipates the conclusion that Huxley reached in *Evolution and Ethics:* we must in ourselves "let the ape and tiger die." But what is implied in the service of God? That, for Tennyson, is a more difficult question, and appears to demand a distinction between the exceptional case—that of the saint—and the moral demands of human society. Here, it would seem, our best clue to Tennyson's belief is found, as my colleague F. E. L. Priestley has suggested, in the *Idylls of the King*, and the place of the quest of the Holy Grail therein.

The *Idylls*, taken as a whole, may be read as a moral allegory —a poem which in scope and intention, even up to a point in method, invites comparison with the *Faerie Queene*. Like Spenser's poem, it adopts as a vehicle the chivalric romance, with the legendary King Arthur as hero of the whole; on the level of allegory or example, it permits of a variety of applications, to the individual but also to society; and while its reference is primarily moral and political, there is both an encompassing and an internal religious reference. Speaking of its meaning in application to the individual, Tennyson said, "By Arthur I always meant the soul and by [the knights of] the Round Table the passions and capacities of a man"; and again: "Birth is a mystery and death is a mystery, and in the midst lies the tableland of life and its struggles and performances. It [the whole poem] is not the history of one man or of one generation, but of a whole cycle of generations." So much for the moral and, in lesser degree, religious implications. The social and political lie nearer the literal surface and are more readily perceived. Arthur's kingdom is a Christian social order which must raise a people to its level, check, guide, and protect them and, at the same time, defend itself against its enemies from without, against whatever menaces its own existence. The instrument for these purposes, the institutions of the social order, are the Knights of the Round Table. But, alas, there are also enemies within the order: flaws, weaknesses and betrayals in the very instrument which the King has devised. The inroads of corruption are plain at point after point—for example, in the cynical worldliness of Gawain, the betrayal of Merlin by Vivien, pre-eminently in the illicit love of the noble Lancelot for Arthur's queen, which she returns only to repent too late. The order collapses from betrayal within more than from assailment without. And now what is the place of the quest of the Grail in this general situation and setting?

That the Holy Grail—the cup used by Christ and the Disciples at the Last Supper—here symbolizes Christian idealism in its highest form admits of no doubt. That its appearance to the Knights, if they could understand it, is an incentive and a rebuke seems as clear. The Grail appears to all who are present, but veiled, not fully revealed. And from different motives, honest if mistaken, even in some cases hypocritical, all take an oath to go in quest of it. But only to the pure in heart, only to the person of true vocation, is the vision of the Grail unveiled vouchsafed—only, that is, to Galahad. And only to him, and perhaps to Percivale, does the imperative command really come to forsake all else and follow the holy symbol. The irony of the whole episode is inescapable: the taking of the vow results in the depletion of Arthur's instrument of order and beneficent rule—the collapse of the Round Table, already of course menaced from within, indeed doomed, but it is not easy to resist the inference that the doom is precipitated by the vision and the mistaken or false response of the many to it. At the conclusion, when a tithe of the Knights have straggled back, King Arthur speaks (his words reported by the good Percivale, who saw the

vision of the Grail indeed, but afar off, and has now withdrawn
from the world in a monastic order):

> "And spake I not too truly, O my knights? . . .
> To those who went upon the Holy Quest,
> That most of them would follow wandering fires,
> Lost in the quagmire?—lost to me and gone,
> And left me gazing at a barren board,
> And a lean Order—scarce returning a tithe—
> And out of those to whom the vision came
> Any greatest hardly will believe he saw; [Lancelot]
> Another hath beheld it afar off, [Percivale]
> And, leaving human wrongs to right themselves,
> Cares but to pass into the silent life.
> And one hath had the vision face to face, [Galahad]
> And now his chair desires him here in vain,
> However they may crown him otherwhere.
> "And some among you held that if the King
> Had seen the sight he would have sworn the vow:
> Not easily, seeing that the King must guard
> That which he rules, and is but as the hind
> To whom a space of land is given to plow,
> Who may not wander from the allotted field
> Until his work be done; but, being done,
> Let visions of the night or of the day
> Come, as they will; and many a time they come
> Until this earth he walks on seems not earth . . .
> But vision . . .
> In moments when he feels he cannot die,
> And knows himself no vision to himself,
> Nor the high God a vision, nor that One
> Who rose again: ye have seen what ye have seen."
> So spake the King: I knew not all he meant.

Thus Percivale. We may perhaps see a little further—or at
least isolate some of the elements in the king's speech. The call
to action, doing the duty that lies nearest to you, Carlyle's gospel of work, with some latent Protestant distrust of ascetic with-
drawal, a distrust shared with Spenser and Milton—these are

plain to read. So is the distrust, not of vision, but of the vision-
ary, of seeing dimly and not understanding. Of vision in its
proper relation, and duly understood, there is no distrust: it is,
Tennyson holds, a pledge to the heart which can say, despite all
conflicting evidence, "I have felt." And the description of vision
here, and elsewhere in Tennyson, is interesting: the fading out
of sense, the obliterating of material things, leaving only the
soul aware of itself in an added spiritual dimension—an experience with some parallel in Wordsworth and Newman. In Tennyson, characteristically, it is closely tied to the idea of the soul's
survival. In the *Idylls*, the idea of survival expresses itself in two
forms: Arthur does not die—he is borne mysteriously away; and
he—that is, at the lowest, though not least, his kingdom or what
it stands for—will come again and this is the more emphatic
affirmation, but the Arthur of the poem is also an individual who
utters, though "all [his] mind is clouded with a doubt," his personal hope.

In the disturbed state of religious belief in the Victorian
period, it is not surprising that Tennyson's instinctive clinging
to faith, while giving full recognition to the forces making for
honest doubt, had a strong appeal, and was perhaps taken to be
more intellectually profound and reassuring than in reality it was.
His clinging to time-honored forms while seeking to face the
consequences of advancing knowledge in every field betokens
some affinity with the much more philosophical leaders of the
Broad Church party; and it was at Jowett's request that he supplied the anthem for use in the Balliol chapel (from his *De Pro-
fundis*):

Hallowed be Thy Name—Halleluiah!—
   Infinite Ideality!
   Immeasurable Reality!
   Infinite Personality!
Hallowed be Thy Name—Halleluiah!

In Browning's preoccupation with religion, as in most other respects, he presents interesting points of comparison and contrast with Tennyson. Basic in his thought and poetry are his intense vitality and his eager interest in human phenomena, especially those of individual characters, seen against the backdrop of history and not least in their religious responses. Thus we have an Arab physician commenting on Lazarus whom Christ had raised from the dead, a dying Apostle—Saint John—talking of miracles and their function in winning belief, a Hellenistic polymath dismissing Saint Paul and his message; somewhat less directly involving religious issues, a pagan bishop of the Renaissance ordering his tomb, a grammarian counting on an eternity in which to perfect and apply what he has learned, an artist talking of the relation of flesh and spirit; more directly again, a modern worldly ecclesiastic considering the problems of faith, and—without a specified persona—one viewing in imagination three modern responses to Christianity: that of the Methodist chapel, of Saint Peter's at Rome, and of German Biblical scholarship; these the most important among others, to which may be added the imagined song of David before Saul and the mature comment on life of the aged Rabbi Ben Ezra. The degree to which the interest centers on the character of the speaker and his period differs in the different poems; but the particular theme discussed is always of interest to Browning himself, and the device of dramatic treatment is a means to gain freedom in discussing it and to let Browning's own conclusions be borne in upon the reader without being presented as formal conclusions or his own. And among the dominant themes are two of the major preoccupations of Tennyson: immortality, and a God of love. The intense belief in personal immortality and the form of continued activity and progression which it takes are both characteristic—indeed, in some sort the product of Browning's intense vitality; and once he resorts to more direct statement and argument in his own person—in *La Saisiaz*, which may be thought of as Browning's *In Memoriam*—but how different in intellectual texture and in tone!

Everywhere Browning gives the impression of thinking with greater energy and logical coherence than Tennyson. The latter meditates and feels; Browning thinks and argues—in this respect at least he would have been a poet after Dryden's own heart. On the second theme, of a God of love, Browning encounters less difficulty than does Tennyson. Though widely learned, he was less preoccupied with scientific knowledge than was his contemporary, and with the picture of nature which science presented; his emphasis falls rather on the beauty and goodness of the natural world and natural impulse as they may be put to use by the individual. Indeed, his interest centers in the individual; and it is significant that in his conception of progress he reverts to an earlier and markedly Christian view: for him, progress means not the progress of the race or of society but of the individual soul. Though he is fully conscious of evil, he sees it generally as littleness of spirit—as timidity, meanness, worldliness, not as self-assertion, cruelty, or lustfulness—and not as a result of the Fall (as did more orthodox religious thinkers) or of man's emergence from the brute (as did Tennyson and others impressed by evolutionary theory). If Browning lies more open to the charge of optimism than does Tennyson, the root is in his temperament. Despite the dramatic form which they generally adopt, Browning's poems are at bottom no less personal than Tennyson's and, like his, embody a union of religious and poetic experience.

The most purely emotional—the least intellectual and argumentative of the religious poems—is *Saul*, embodying the imagined song of David when summoned to try the effect of his music on the mad king. The first nine sections were printed in 1845; all the rest of the poem was added ten years later—and it is in this conclusion that the religious experience of David is found. Commencing with pastoral tunes, he goes on to the songs of country folk at their labor, and of funeral and marriage, thence to the keen animal pleasures of the out-of-door life, of the climber, the swimmer, the hunter, and finally with a reference to Saul himself—his youthful prowess in war, his escape, the sense of God's providence (the only specifically religious note in the poem as first composed), the pride in his achievements, the growing power, and at last the kingdom:

Till lo, thou art grown to a monarch; a people is thine;
And all gifts, which the world offers singly, on one head
                                     combine. . . .
High ambition and deeds which surpass it, fame crowning them—all
Brought to blaze on the head of one creature—King Saul!

Here is a poem of energy and imagination, but of no particular religious significance. Then, ten years later, the superstructure is added, built on the first nine sections as base. Taking up the song anew, David sings now of the fame that shall be Saul's and his place in history; and gradually the mad king comes to himself, with a gesture of gratitude. By God's help, David has succeeded in his labor of love. And it is in David's (now prophetic) reflections on the event that the element of religious experience —David's experience—enters. The song itself is ended, but its sweeping rhythm persists through the singer's excited thoughts and words. He looks back at the life of man, and of Saul, as he had sung them, and confirms their meaning:

           . . . I spoke as I saw,
I report as a man may of God's work—all's love, yet all's law.

But it is not in this that the clue lies, or not until it is united with another experience—namely, David's own labor of love for Saul: the outpouring of love is a reflection of God's love. Man's love is coupled with weakness, but the Almighty's with power. Yet something more is needed. Is there in the Godhead the capacity not only of loving but of being beloved? There is:

> He who did most, shall bear most; the strongest shall
>            stand the most weak.
> 'Tis the weakness in strength, that I cry for! my flesh,
>            that I seek
> In the Godhead! I seek and I find it. O Saul, it shall be
> A Face like my face that receives thee; a Man like to me,
> Thou shalt love and be loved by, for ever: a Hand like this
>            hand
> Shall throw open the gates of new life to thee!
>            See the Christ stand!

This too is the conclusion of the subtler and dramatically more interesting *Epistle of Karshish*. On his travels to collect medical lore, the Arab Physician has encountered Lazarus. The meeting has made a strong impression on him, of which he is half-ashamed. He is interested in the state of mind of one who has, or imagines that he has, returned from the dead, though he tries to convince himself that Lazarus is simply mad. He ends with an apology for having dwelt at such length on this case:

> Nor I myself discern in what is writ
> A good cause for the peculiar interest
> And awe indeed this man has touched me with.
> Perhaps the journey's end, the weariness
> Had wrought upon me first.

But it is more than Lazarus himself that has stirred Karshish and struck him with awe, and this deeper appeal bursts out at last in the postscript.

The very God! think, Abib; dost thou think?
So the All-Great were the All-Loving too—
So, through the thunder comes a human voice
Saying, "O heart I made, a heart beats here!
Face my hands fashioned, see it in myself!
Thou hast no power, nor mayst conceive of mine,
But love I gave thee, with myself to love,
And thou must love me who have died for thee!"
The madman saith He said so: it is strange.

A *Death in the Desert*, which lacks the character interest of *Karshish*, also bears less directly upon religious experience and more upon intellectual problems in religion in Browning's own day. Yet the same theme of love is also there. Saint John, at the point of death, insists on the literal truth of the Gospel account of Christ's life and miracles. These he saw. But he suggests that miracles were of use only to convince the simple and uninformed who could be reached in no other way. Their need is past, and they may cease. Men must achieve belief on higher grounds. The events indeed took place; but more important than the past events is the ever-present truth they signified.

To me, that story—ay, that Life and Death
Of which I wrote "it was"—to me it is;
—Is here and now: I apprehend naught else.
Is not God now i' the world His power first made?
Is not his love at issue still with sins
Visibly when a wrong is done on earth?
Love, wrong, and pain, what else see I around?
Yea, and the Resurrection and Uprise
To the right hand of the Throne—what is it beside,
When such truth, breaking bounds, o'er floods my soul. . . .
I saw the power; I see the Love once weak,
Resume the Power: and in this word 'I see,'
Lo, there is recognized the Spirit of both
That moving o'er the spirit of man unblinds
His eye. . . .

> life, with all it yields of joy and woe
> And hope and fear . . .
> Is just our chance of the prize of learning love,
> How love might be, hath been indeed, and is. . . .

This does not mean, I think, that Browning has relaxed his hold on the factual basis of the Christian creed; for Saint John in the poem insists upon it, and refutes the facile inference that just as man discovered fire and presently the myth grew up that fire, being a heavenly element, Prometheus stole it thence, so the truths of the Gospel being in very deed truth, the events were another myth imposed upon them. But it means that he values the truths above the events; and (though his Saint John talks more like Browning than like Saint John) it seems clear that in selecting this evangelist to enforce the lesson, he did not mistake his man. Incidentally, the poem enables us to gauge Browning's attitude toward German Biblical criticism: the repudiation of "myth" as explanation is a comment on Strauss and his school, and he makes Saint John foresee the denial of his authorship of the Fourth Gospel. Nor was he more friendly to *Essays and Reviews*, as appears in his very inferior poem *Gold Hair*, interesting only as driving Browning (whose dismissal of evil often seems too facile) back upon the doctrine of Original Sin.

For Browning, as we have said, personal immortality was of the utmost importance as idea and accepted fact. As idea, because for him, he avers, speaking in his own person:

> There is no reconciling wisdom with a world distraught,
> Goodness with triumphant evil, power with failure in the aim,
> If—(to my own sense, remember though none other felt the
> same)—
> If you bar me from assuming earth to be a pupil's place—
> And life with all its chances, changes, just probation space,
> Mine for me.

Moreover, dependent upon the idea were certain ethical and aesthetic principles to which Browning recurred: the idea of progression applied not to nature or society but to the individual; of aspiration, rather than the attainment of a limited objective, as the test of value; and of imperfection as the inevitable result of the unlimited objective, in which sense "Imperfection means perfection hid." These ideas are not peculiar to Browning: they are an inheritance from Romanticism and found also in Ruskin and others. They are kin to, though not identical with, the Victorian idea of indefinite progression in its various forms, and emotionally at least, with the spirit of Ulysses' last voyage in Tennyson and the poet's counsel, to "follow the gleam." In *Old Pictures in Florence*, Browning applies the principle to the judgment of Christian art, as contrasted with classical—much to the disadvantage of the classical, as in Ruskin:

> Growth came when, looking your last on them all,
>     You turned your eyes inwardly one fine day
> And cried with a start—What, if we so small
>     Be greater and grander the while than they?
> Are they perfect of lineament, perfect of stature?
>     In both, of such lower types are we
> Precisely because of our wider nature;
>     For time, theirs—ours for eternity.
>
> Today's brief passion limits their range;
>     It seethes with the morrow for us and more.
> They are perfect—how else? they shall never change:
>     We are faulty—why not? we have time in store.

And so for Browning, "a man's reach should exceed his grasp / Or what's a Heaven for?" But the idea of immortality cannot remain an idea. If it is to be effective, it must be assumed to be a fact; and in such lyrics as *Prospice* and the *Epilogue to Asolando*, Browning asserts the fact with an energy and assurance as characteristic of him as the "feeling" and "hope" so touchingly expressed by Tennyson in *Crossing the Bar*. Characteristic too is the conception entertained of the hereafter:

> Bid him forward, breast and back as either should be.
> "Strive and thrive," cry, "Speed, — fight on, fare ever
> There as here."

The "this worldly" attitude in religion could hardly go further than to conceive the hereafter so completely in terms of the here and now. But Browning is not content with mere lyric assertion: he will argue the matter through in *La Saisiaz*. For he delights in argument, and even on this vital issue and in the presence of bereavement he will give the mind free if not quite unrestricted play.

Browning is, then, like Tennyson, a Christian poet—but more definite in his commitment. Some sort of turning point seems to have been reached in the poem *Christmas Eve and Easter Day* (1850): hitherto his work has been theistic but hardly Christian in any definite sense. Then comes the imagined experience of this central poem, and it is presumably after it that he is able to add the conclusion of *Saul* and write the *Epistle of Karshish*. In *Christmas Eve* the unspecified persona of the poem, who speaks in the first person throughout—is it the poet or an imagined projection?—takes shelter from the weather in a Dissenting chapel, whose earnest, illogical, indeed illiterate, preacher and bedraggled congregation are realistically described. Then the intruder, intellectually and aesthetically offended, finds himself outside the building once more and in its desolate surroundings. And moving before him is a robed figure. It is Christ, who, unrecognized, has been with the squalid congregation gathered in his name. The poet—we will call him the poet—duly humbled, grasps the hem of the garment and is borne afar: first, to Rome and the Christmas Eve Mass in Saint Peter's, also described with realism, and not without some Protestant commentary, but here also Christ enters; next to a German university, the seat of advanced Biblical scholarship, and a lecture, also realistically described, which in the manner foreseen by Saint John, denies the fact, reduces the Christian story to myth, but ends by exhorting the auditors to hold fast to the values enshrined in the myth. Here the poet is uncertain whether Christ has entered or not. Then suddenly, back in the chapel—and disapproving glances suggest that the poet has slept hrough the preacher's long sermon, now mercifully drawing to a close. But the experience, be it dream or not, has been real. It has taught him humility and tolerance and, more than that, faith:

> I can but testify
> God's care for me—no more can I—
> It is but for myself I know. . . .
> I only knew he named my name.

There is also the second decision to abide by and with the folk of the chapel—less important than the first, but significant nevertheless. Browning's religion is essentially of the more extreme Protestant variety, and Evangelical in feeling if not precisely in doctrine. Middle roads are not for him, and religion and culture are two quite separate entities. He does not even mention the national Church, where, in city and rural parish throughout England, Christmas Eve was also being celebrated— not, one may hope, without the presence of Christ. Unlike Tennyson, he has no affinity with the Broad Church party or with that strain in the Anglican tradition which, from Coleridge onward, it especially treasured—namely, the union of Christianity and humanism and the civilizing mission of the Church.

Since the middle of the seventeenth century, it has been possible in our rapid survey to speak without distortion of religious poetry in its relation to Anglicanism with but slight reference to Protestant Dissent and none at all to Roman Catholicism. But now a body of Roman Catholic verse begins again to appear, in part the work of converts who followed Newman to Rome. In poetry itself, Newman again led the way with his longest and best poem, *The Dream of Gerontius.* This vision of a soul at the hour of death, of its departure from the body, and its conveyance by its guardian angel (not without a promise of final beatitude) to the cleansing fires of purgatory, moves within the controlling and supporting framework of Roman Catholic doctrine. But it is more than a doctrinal treatise in verse; it is an extended meditation, marked by a vividly imagined experience, a range of religious thought, and an effective structural pattern. In its choruses it presents the demonic as well as the angelic point of view. It reminds us at times of Milton, and it strikingly anticipates T. S. Eliot in its presentation of Christ as the surgeon who probes the wound in order to heal. *The Dream of Gerontius* exhibits a religious sensibility able to draw on a tradition long unexploited in English poetry and at the same time able to establish contact with the century in which the poet writes. For Newman, who had already applied the idea of development to Christian doctrine, now applies it to the history of mankind and gives us his version of a God-guided evolution. Of man after the Fall, the angel chorus sings:

> Above him now the angry sky,
>   Around the tempest's din;
> Who once had angels for his friends,
>   Had but the brutes for kin.
>
> O man! a savage kindred they;
>   To flee that monster brood
> He scaled the seaside cave, and clomb
>   The giants of the wood.

With now a fear, and now a hope,
    With aids which chance supplied,
From youth to eld, from sire to son,
    He lived and toiled and died. . . .

And quickened by the Almighty's breath
    And chasten'd by His rod,
And taught by angel-visitings,
    At length he sought his God;

And learn'd to call upon His Name,
    And in His faith create
A household and a father-land,
    A city and a state.

Glory to Him who from the mire,
    In patient length of days,
Elaborated into life
    A people to His praise!

Here, though the doctrine is different, we are unmistakably in the world of Tennyson, as we are not with those whom Newman influenced.

His influence of course, direct or indirect, was not confined to converts to Rome, but operated strongly in the Church he loved and left. It can be traced in two of the best religious poets of the century: the Anglican Christina Rossetti, who found in the Catholic revival within the Established Church her spiritual home and an incentive to both piety and poetry; and Newman's convert Gerard Manley Hopkins, who sought his in the Roman Catholic Church and the discipline of the Jesuit order with spiritual security indeed but with some restriction upon the free expression of his much greater poetic talent.

In Christina Rossetti we recognize a pure and deep vein of personal religion which in her best work unites with a genuine poetic talent to realize a union of beauty with unexpected power. Intensely introspective, she laments the fainting of the inward flame of love and the shadow cast by the intrusive self. This is the source of a tension whose resolution is and can only be Christ, and it is in and by the poems that the tension is objectified and its resolution realized. The kind of experience, its quiet intensity, and even the mode of expression carry us back in memory from Victorian poetry to something more like that of George Herbert. On Good Friday, as she contemplates the Redeemer's suffering, she reproaches herself for her lack of response—her heart, she says, is a stone—but this is not the end:

> Yet give not o'er,
>> But seek thy sheep, true Shepherd of the flock;
>> Greater than Moses, turn and look once more
> And smite a rock.

Or again:

>> I love and love not; Lord, it breaks my heart
>>> To love and not to love.
>> Thou veiled within thy glory, gone apart
>>> Into thy shrine, which is above,
>> Dost thou not love me, Lord, or care
>>> For this mine ill?—
>> *I love thee here or there,*
>>> *I will accept thy broken heart, lie still.*

And finally:

>> God strengthen me to bear myself,
>> That heaviest weight of all to bear,
>> Inalienable weight of care.
>>
>> All others are outside myself;
>> I lock the door and bar them out—
>> The turmoil, tedium, gad-about.
>>
>> I lock the door upon myself,
>> And bar them out; but who shall wall
>> Self from myself, most loathed of all? . . .

God harden me against myself,
This coward with pathetic voice
Who craves for ease, and rest, and joys:

Myself, arch-traitor to myself,
My hollowest friend, my deadliest foe,
My clog whatever road I go.

Yet One there is can curb myself,
Can roll the strangling load from me,
Break off the yoke and set me free.

What we may call the accident (though it was not altogether an accident) of posthumous publication, coming as it did just when a marked reaction against long-established conventions of imagery, diction, and meter was about to set it, has combined with the startling originality of Hopkins' own practice to remove him from his Victorian setting and bracket him securely in the minds of most readers with the post-Georgian poets of our own century—an interesting but in part distorting association. His refusal to publish in his lifetime resulted from the rigorous discipline of his order and his own scruples of conscience, which also severely curtailed his poetic production. It is idle to conjecture what in other circumstances he might have achieved. The hard-won submission to the inward and outward discipline was necessary to the man, and formed the inescapable condition of the religious and aesthetic experience realized (or sometimes failing of realization) in the poems.

At first the "Habit of Perfection" (to adopt the title of one of his earlier poems) seemed not too hard:

Elected Silence, sing to me
And beat upon my whorlèd ear,
Pipe me to pastures still and be
The music that I care to hear.

Shape nothing, lips; be lovely-dumb:
It is the shut, the curfew sent
From there where all surrenders come
Which only makes you eloquent.

Be shellèd, eyes, with double dark
And find the uncreated light:
This ruck and reel which you remark
Coils, keeps, and teases simple sight. . . .

O feel-of-primrose hands, O feet
That want the yield of plushy sward,
But you shall walk the golden street
And you unhouse and house the Lord.

And, Poverty, be thou the bride
And now the marriage feast begun,
And lily-coloured clothes provide
Your spouse not laboured-at nor spun.

But such happy facility and finality were in part delusive. The
acute, sensuous perception which underlay the remrakable evocative power of many of his poems was not so easily subordinated
to, or united with, his profound religious motivation. The fragment *Epithalamion* breaks down as soon as it attempts to effect
the union (and at the moment when we glimpse the significance
of the title) and trails off in a few dejected phrases marked by a
total depletion of energy.

Hark, hearer, hear what I do; lend a thought now, make believe
We are leafwhelmed somewhere with the hood
Of some branchy bunchy bushybowered wood,
Southern dene or Lancashire clough or Devon cleave,
That leans along the loins of hills, where a candycoloured,
    where a gluegold-brown
Marbled river, boisterously beautiful, between
Roots and rocks is danced and dandled, all in froth and
    waterblowballs, down.
We are there, when we hear a shout
That the hanging honeysuck, the dogeared hazels in the cover

Makes dither, makes hover
And the riot of a rout
Of, it must be, boys from the town
Bathing: it is summer's sovereign good. . . .

Enough now; since the sacred matter that I mean
I should be wronging longer leaving it to float
Upon this gambolling and echoing-of-earth note—

And then the broken phrases of a forced effort of symbolism, ending in mid-sentence. How different from the glad song of Browning's David pulsing with energy to its triumphant close! How different indeed from Hopkins himself at his best!

Sometimes he achieves a happy union of the sensuous with the symbolic—the obvious and plainly stated symbolic, as in *The Blessed Virgin Compared to the Air We Breathe*; sometimes, as in *The Windhover* (the best thing, he thought, that he had ever written) with a symbolism so concealed as to require the dedication "To Christ Our Lord" to give us the needed hint:

I caught this morning morning's minion, kingdom of daylight's
    dauphin, dapple-dawn-drawn Falcon, in his riding
Of the rolling level underneath him steady air, and striding
High there, how he rung upon the rein of a wimpling wing
In his ecstasy! then off, off forth on swing,
    As a skate's heel sweeps smooth on a bow-bend: the hurl and
    gliding
Rebuffed the big wind. My heart in hiding
Stirred for a bird,—the achieve of, the mastery of the thing!

Brute beauty and valour and act, oh, air, pride, plume, here
    Buckle! And the fire that breaks from thee then, a billion
Times told lovelier, more dangerous, O my chevalier!

No wonder of it: shéer plód makes plough down sillion
Shine, and blue-bleak embers, ah my dear,
    Fall, gall themselves, and gash gold-vermilion.

Hopkins' response to nature is always vivid and is always brought into some relation with his religion, whether through the medi-

um of symbolism (as in the instances cited) or less often directly, as in *God's Grandeur:*

> The world is charged with the grandeur of God.
>     It will flame out, like shining from shook foil;
>     It gathers to a greatness, like the ooze of oil
> Crushed. Why do men then now not reck his rod?
> Generations have trod, have trod, have trod;
>     And all is seared with trade; bleared, smeared with toil;
>     And wears man's smudge and shares man's smell: the soil
> Is bare now, nor can foot feel, being shod.
>
> And for all this, nature is never spent;
>     There lives the dearest freshness deep down things;
> And though the last lights off the black West went
>     Oh, morning, at the brown brink eastward, springs—
> Because the Holy Ghost over the bent
>     World broods with warm breast and with ah! bright wings.

But nature is not the only subject of his evocative power. In *The
Bugler's First Communion,* sensuousness, human sympathy, religious zeal, and priestly function achieve a perfect harmony;
while in starkest contrast with all that we have quoted, he can
present the deepest loathing of self, in a poem to be compared
and contrasted with Christina Rossetti's (quoted above) on the
same theme:

> I wake and feel the fell of dark, not day.
> What hours, O what black hours we have spent
> This night! what sights you, heart, saw; ways you went!
> And more must, in yet longer light's delay.
>     With witness I speak this. But where I say
> Hours I mean years, mean life. And my lament
> Is cries countless, cries like dead letters sent
> To dearest him that lives alas! away.
>
>     I am gall, I am heartburn. God's most deep decree
> Bitter would have me taste: my taste was me;
> Bones built in me, flesh filled, blood brimmed the curse

Selfyeast of spirit a dull dough sours. I see
The lost are like this, and their scourge to be
As I am mine, their sweating selves; but worse.

Nature, but in another and sterner aspect, inevitably has its
place in the most widely known, the most ambitious, but not
perhaps the most perfect of Hopkins' poems. *The Wreck of the
Deutschland* (1876) is significant as the first full application of
Hopkins' distinctive theories of diction and meter: the free
elaboration and compounding of words, always with a native
English base, the union of heavy stress with alliteration, and the
now famous "sprung rhythm"—all of them the product of a
creative backward look at the home-born tradition of English
poetry. These, of course, are matters not to be paused on here
save to notice a strong vein of English patriotism in Hopkins as
in some other converts to Rome, and (more important) the
shaping of a vehicle for his poetic experience. This said, we may
turn to the poem and the complex experience realized by it, in
which the response to nature has its inevitable place.

*The Wreck of the Deutschland* is still a difficult poem,
though its rhythm and diction are now a minor part of the difficulty. Chiefly the difficulty resides in the diversity of thought
and emotion to which the disaster gave rise—or perhaps mainly
gave release. The suggestion of Hopkins' superior that he should
commemorate in verse the wreck (in which, with many other
victims, five Franciscan nuns, expelled from Germany, perished)
allowed the breaking of his long silence, and (as one can hardly
refrain from inferring) the pent-up emotions of years found
what was for the poet their foreordained mode of expression.

Part I, a prelude of ten stanzas, makes no overt reference to
the disaster. Instead, it presents, couched in an excited throng of
evocative phrases, a highly introspective account of the soul's

experience under the power and terror of God till it surrenders
itself to Christ the suffering Saviour and finds, beneath the
power and the terror, God's love and mercy and its own salvation.

> Thou mastering me
> God! giver of breath and bread;
> World's strand, sway of the sea;
> Lord of living and dead;
> Thou hast bound bones and veins in me, fastened me flesh,
> And after it almost unmade, what with dread,
> Thy doing: and dost thou touch me afresh?
> Over again I feel thy finger and find thee.
>
> I did say yes
> O at lightning and lashed rod;
> Thou heardst me truer than tongue confess
> Thy terror, O Christ, O God:
> Thou knowest the walls, altar and hour and night:
> The swoon of a heart that the sweep and the hurl of thee trod
> Hard down with a horror of height;
> And the midriff astrain with leaning of, laced with fire of
>     stress.

But what has this to do with the wreck of the *Deutschland?* A
good deal, as is borne in upon us as Part II (the final twenty-five
stanzas) evolves. Nothing but a detailed analysis stanza by stanza, if that, could exhaust the relation—a task impossible here.
Enough if I can make evident, with appropriate quotations, the
structural pattern. After a potent stanza on death ("storms bugle
his fame") comes the deliberately prosaic account of the ship's
sailing from Bremen; then the pitiless aspect of nature the de-
stroyer:

> Into the snows she sweeps,
> Hurling the haven behind,
> The Deutschland, on Sunday; and so the sky keeps,
> For the infinite air is unkind,
> And the sea flint-flake, black-backed in the regular blow,

Sitting Eastnortheast, in cursed quarter, the wind;
  Wiry and white-fiery and whirlwind-swivellèd snow
Spins to the widow-making unchilding unfathering deeps.

    She drove in the dark to leeward,
    She struck—not a reef or a rock
  But the combs of a smother of sand: night drew her
    Dead to the Kentish Knock;
  And she beat the bank down with her bows and the ride
    of her keel:
  The breakers rolled on her beam with ruinous shock;
    And canvas and compass, the whorl and the wheel
Idle for ever to waft her or wind her with, these she
    endured. . . .
And frightful a nightfall folded rueful a day
Nor rescue, only rocket and lightship, shone,
    And lives at last were washing away:
To the shrouds they took,—they shook in the hurling
  and horrible airs. . . .

    They fought with God's cold—
    And they could not and fell to the deck
  (Crushed them) or water (and drowned them) or rolled
    With the sea-romp over the wreck.
Night roared, with the heart-break hearing a heart-
    broke rabble,
The woman's wailing, the crying of child without check. . . .

Here the experience of one of the five nuns enters the theme, is
central for seven stanzas (a fifth of the whole poem), and is to be
resumed at the end. Given the occasion, its prominence is natural, and it is necessary to the structural pattern. What is understandable but certainly not necessary is the intrusion of an alien
and disruptive note of sectarian polemic, almost entirely absent
from English religious poetry since the mid-seventeenth century.
But, setting aside this blemish, we recognize at once the relation
implied between the terror of the divine power as manifested in
the storm and as experienced in the spiritual crisis remembered

and re-enacted in Part I: in both, terror gives place to illumination, to a knowledge of God's underlying, overriding mercy and
love. This is what the nun, like the poet, is able to realize; for
the first experience is the necessary prelude to the second. And
there is the other function, of contrast this time, with those
who, lacking the first experience, can feel only terror at the
approach of doom. For them the poet has his word of compassion and, though not of assurance, yet of hope in the infinite love
and mercy of God:

> Heart, go and bleed at a bitterer vein for the
>   Comfortless unconfessed of them—
> No, not uncomforted: . . .
>
>   With a mercy that outrides
>   The all of water, an ark
> For the listener; for the lingerer with a love glides
>   Lower than death and the dark;
> A vein for the visiting of the past-prayer, pent in
>   prison,
> The-last-breath penitent spirits—the uttermost mark
>   Our passion-plungèd giant risen,
> The Christ of the Father compassionate, fetched in the
>   storm of his strides.

A closer analysis would reveal the interrelation of images, and
with it the remarkable density of the poetic texture. What has
perhaps been sufficiently suggested is the basic structural pattern, in part peculiar to the poem, in part conforming to the
tradition of Christian elegy—but even here with a difference; for
while the triumphant apotheosis is reserved for the regenerate
(the only subject elsewhere of Christian elegy), hope is extended to the rest. In its way The Wreck of the Deutschland extends the range of Christian elegy as did, in its own very different way, Lycidas. But to name Lycidas is to remind ourselves of
the astonishing difference in diction, imagery, and rhythm be-

tween the two poems, and indeed between Hopkins' work and everything that had preceded it, and (despite the warning with which we commenced) to sharpen our sense of his affinity with the poets of the twentieth century, into whose company by posthumous publication he was thrust.

This publication was initiated by Robert Bridges, with whom Hopkins was linked in friendship and in their common interest in poetic technique, though no two could be more dissimilar in life and outlook as will appear when we turn to *The Testament of Beauty*. On the way, however, we must spare a glance at Francis Thompson, the only poet of the 1890's demanding notice in so swift a survey. Though no one can question the importance of religion in the later life of this Roman Catholic poet, it would now be generally conceded that his poetry is of a lower order, lacking the simplicity and fortifying restraint of Christina Rossetti's and the originality and concentrated power of Hopkins'. In Thompson, there is the recurrent danger that a genuine religious experience shall be dissipated rather than captured in the flow of words and imperfectly integrated images. Insofar as his powers and limitations can be illustrated in a single quotation, we may call in evidence the concluding lines of his most ambitious poem, the *Ode to the Setting Sun*, with its twofold response to natural phenomena and classic myth and its desire to see in both types of the Redeemer and of the death and Resurrection of the redeemed:

> If with exultant tread
>  Thou foot the Eastern sea,
>  Or like a golden bee
> Sting the West to angry red,
> Thou dost image, thou dost follow
>  That King-Maker of Creation,
> Who, ere Hellas hailed Apollo,
>  Gave thee, angel-god, thy station;

Thou art of Him a type memorial.
　　Like Him thou hang'st in dreadful pomp of blood
　　　　Upon thy Western rood;
　　And His stained brow did vail like thine to night,
　　　　Yet life once more Its light,
And, risen, again departed from our ball,
But when It set on earth arose in Heaven.
Thus hath He unto death His beauty given:
And so of all which form inheriteth
　　The fall doth pass the rise in worth;
For birth hath in itself the germ of death,
　　But death hath in itself the germ of birth.
It is the falling acorn buds the tree,
The falling rain that bears the greenery,
　　The fern-plants moulder when the ferns arise.
For there is nothing lives but something dies,
And there is nothing dies but something lives.
　　Till skies be fugitives,
Till time, the hidden root of change, updries,
Are Birth and Death inseparable on earth;
For they are twain yet one, and Death is Birth.

In his best poem, *The Hound of Heaven*, the intensity of the religious experience comes nearest perhaps to imposing the required concentration, and the hurrying phrases convey vividly the effect of pursuit and flight—the blind and twisting flight of the soul and the relentless pursuit of the divine love:

I fled Him, down the nights and down the days;
　　I fled Him, down the arches of the years;
I fled Him, down the labyrinthine ways
　　Of my own mind; and in the mist of tears
I hid from Him, and under running laughter.
　　　　Up vistaed hopes I sped;
　　　　And shot, precipitated,
Adown Titanic glooms of chasmed fears,
　　From those strong Feet that followed, followed after.
　　　　But with unhurrying chase,
　　　　And unperturbèd pace,

Deliberate speed, majestic instancy,
  They beat—and a Voice beat
  More instant than the Feet—
'All things betray thee, who betrayest Me.'

Sometimes, however, Thompson is capable of striking a simpler and purer, though less powerful note, as in *The Kingdom of God*:

Not where the wheeling systems darken
And our benumbed conceiving soars!—
The drift of pinions, would we hearken,
Beats at our own clay-shuttered doors.

The angels keep their ancient places;—
Turn but a stone, and start a wing!
'Tis ye, 'tis your estrangèd faces,
That miss the many-splendoured thing.

But (when so sad thou canst not sadder)
Cry;—and upon thy so sore loss
Shall shine the traffic of Jacob's ladder
Pitched betwixt Heaven and Charing Cross.

Yea, in the night, my Soul, my daughter,
Cry, — clinging Heaven by the hems;
And lo, Christ walking on the water
Not of Gennesareth, but Thames!

To return to Bridges and *The Testament of Beauty*: despite a lifelong friendship and a common interest in experiments in diction and rhythm, there is far more to contrast than compare with Hopkins. The contrast is signalized in Bridges' confession that in *The Wreck of the Deutschland* "both subject and treatment" were distasteful to him. For his taste was classical; his expression reserved; his religion Anglican: he would have much more sympathy with the religion of Jowett and the other authors of *Essays and Reviews* than with that of his friend. This we may plainly infer from *The Testament of Beauty*.

Though the work of Bridges' old age and not published till 1929, there is good reason for giving it the final place—and a place of honor—in our brief treatment of Victorian poetry. For despite the originality of its carefully calculated diction and rhythm, the range and directness of its thought and the confidence of its affirmations separate it decisively from the new poetry of the 1920's and 1930's and establish its kinship with that of the major Victorians, while the stress on beauty, recorded in the title and present throughout the poem, establishes some link with the aestheticism of the later Victorians. Where the more immediate quest of Tennyson and Browning is for truth and goodness, that of Bridges is for beauty—but a beauty which subsumes the other two, and in its higher reaches is spiritual and one with wisdom. At the same time Bridges is typical of Victorian thought in a scientific approach to nature, which in his case unites with and supports his quest for beauty. He accepts without question the idea of organic evolution, but not in its Darwinian, rather in the later, phase which, reverting to an earlier conception, reads purpose back into the process. For Bridges it all culminates in the master work of nature: man and his development as a civilized being. Indeed, for a long time before he arrived at its present title, we are told, he thought and spoke of the poem as his *De hominum natura*, in allusion to his great predecessor Lucretius, but also with a difference fully borne out by his thought—*The Testament of Beauty* is at once an essay on man and essentially, though not exclusively, a religious poem.

It has too, as this description reminds us, sources and analogues which go back beyond the Victorian age. There is a strong element of Platonism in Bridges' thought, though he adapts it freely to his purpose, exalting the idea of the beautiful rather than of the good, to the supreme place and making it subsume other values, throwing all his emphasis on immanence rather than transcendence, and putting his own interpretation upon Plato's image of the charioteer and the two horses. We have spoken of *The Testament of Beauty* as an essay on man; allowing for Bridges' much deeper grounding in science, and in science of a later age when the emphasis has shifted to biology, it is not altogether fanciful to see some analogy with Pope's poem of that title, and yet more with the ethical-descriptive poetry of the eighteenth century as it is represented in the seemingly discursive and yet unified effort of Thomson's *Seasons*. After all, Bridges' emphasis on beauty has more in common with the aestheticism of one of Thomson's masters—the eighteenth-century Platonist, Shaftesbury, who approximated the moral and religious to the aesthetic faculty—than with that of Pater and his disciples. Nor is *The Testament*, especially in Book I, without intermittent suggestions of the subjectivism that dominates Wordsworth's *Prelude*, the last of the great ethical-descriptive poems in that tradition. But all these analogues are partial and fleeting, and the *Testament of Beauty* is at once eclectic and a profoundly original poem.

It is in effect a series of meditations on nature and the life of man as the aging poet has learned to view them and their relation:

> 'Twas late in my long journey, when I had clomb to where
> the path was narrowing and the company few,
> a glow of childlike wonder enthral'd me, as if my sense
> had come to a new birth purified, my mind enrapt
> re-awakening to a fresh initiation of life;
> with like surprise of joy as any man may know
> who rambling wide hath turn'd, resting on some hill-top
> to view the plain he has left, and see'th it now out-spredd
> mapp'd at his feet, a landscape so by beauty estranged
> he scarce will ken familiar haunts. . . .

So he begins the first book, which traces the rise of man's specific powers in reason, and pre-eminently in love and the response to beauty, and finds premonitions of these powers in the lower creatures, distinguishing man from nature indeed but refusing to separate him therefrom. Strong in his faith in the predominance of beauty and goodness in nature and man, and insistent on the need for faith in them both and in the God of natural religion, he yet recognizes the presence of evil and ugliness and the failure to rise to the true meaning of life, and ascends (like Hooker) from natural to revealed religion:

> So it was when Jesus came in his gentleness
> with his divine compassion and the great Gospel of Peace,
> men hail'd him WORD OF GOD, and in the title of Christ
> crown'd him with love beyond all earth-names of renown.
>     For He, wandering unarm'd save by the Spirit's flame,
> in few years with few friends founded a world-empire
> Wider than Alexander's and more enduring;
> since from his death it took its everlasting life.
> HIS kingdom is God's kingdom, and his holy temple
> not in Athens or Rome but in the heart of man.
> They who understand not cannot forget, and they
> who keep not his commandment call him Master and Lord.
> He preach'd once to the herd, but now calleth the wise,
> and shall in his second Advent, that tarried long,
> be glorified by the Greeks that come to his feast:
> But the great Light shineth in great darkness, the seed
> that fell by the wayside hath been trodden under foot,
> thatt which fell on the Rock is nigh wither'd away;
> While loud and louder thro' the dazed head of the SPHINX
>     the old lion's voice roareth o'er all the lands.

Thus the first meditation, introductory to the whole, ends.

We cannot here begin to suggest the range of observation and thought which the poem embraces, the constant reference to the phenomena of nature and of the life of man, wherein the higher is securely based upon the lower, the spiritual upon the physical, with an ascending beauty as the master clue and reconciliation— not opposition and rejection—the spirit of the whole. The final passage of the fourth book—the coda, as it has been called, of the whole poem—sums up what has been said of love as it ascends, from the animal to the human, and from the human to the divine (the "scale," as Milton said, "By which to heav'nly love thou mayst ascend") and closely linked with love (as in Spenser) the social principle of friendship. But how, asked the ancient philosopher, can there be friendship between God and man, so great is the disparity?

> From this dilemma of pagan thought, this poison of faith,
> Man-soul made glad escape in the worship of Christ;
> For his humanity is God's Personality,
> and communion with him is the life of the soul. . . .
>                       Christ yet walketh the earth,
> and talketh still as with those two disciples once
> on the road to Emmaus—where they walk and are sad;
> whose vision of him then was his victory over death,
> thatt resurrection which all his lovers should share,
> who in loving him had learn'd the Ethick of happiness;
> whereby they too should come where he was ascended
> to reign over men's hearts in the Kingdom of God.
>   Our happiest earthly comradeships hold a foretaste
> of the feast of salvation and by thatt virtue in them
> provoke desire beyond them to out-reach and surmount
> their humanity in some superhumanity
> and ultimat perfection: which, howe'er 'tis found
> or strangely imagin'd, answereth to the need of each
> and pulleth him instinctively as to a final cause. . . .

And here we may leave the Victorians, who, whatever their limitations in thought and poetry, certainly had not lost the gift of largeness of vision.

# ᛫᛭ VIII ᛭᛫

## THE TWENTIETH CENTURY

W<small>HEN</small> B<small>RIDGES</small> published *The Testament of Beauty,* the kaleidoscopic (and cataclysmic) changes that were to mark the new century were already well under way. The dominant emphasis was shifting once more from the biological to the physical and mathematical sciences—the age of Darwin was giving place to the age of Einstein. At first the opened vistas seemed, to some at least, to suggest new possibilities for natural religion and even, it was said, for a reassertion of the shattered belief in miracles. But the hope (or was it merely the attention?) soon faltered in face of a variety of contending influences.

The First World War had shaken Europe, and even England, to the foundations. The momentary elation of victory, the escape from horror, and the accompanying hope of a new order could not conceal from the thoughtful the predicament of society. Nor could the license of the gay 'twenties (fruit at once of war and the relief from war, and encouraged by a misreading of the new psychology, for this was the age of Freud as well as of Einstein) long distract the most thoughtless. The great depression (more shocking perhaps to prosperous America than to prostrate Europe) only emphasized that predicament. Disillusion, already widespread, swept like a wave over thinking and generous minds, and Karl Marx reaped a belated harvest—or shall we vary the metaphor and say that there was a rush of business at his agency for fellow travelers?

Worse, however, was to follow. The Second World War brought terror and carnage to the civil population: they too, it was commonly said (and no one can better the hackneyed phrase), were now in the front line. While their courage and fortitude must indeed in retrospect enhance the dignity of man and rekindle hope in his future, the reckless folly of leaders, the docile gullibility of followers, and the fanatic cruelties could not but suggest very different thoughts and serve to reinforce at least one negative dogma: Original Sin. Spurred on in part by a final disillusion, with communism this time, as merely another form of tyranny, and twin brother to fascism, there was some recoil toward more or less dogmatic Christianity, especially in its Anglo-Catholic and Roman Catholic forms, while Protestantism, though with some renewed attention to its theological bases, redoubled its sociological emphasis and its alliance with democracy—whatever precisely that protean term might mean. But the extent of the recoil toward Christianity, and its record in literature, can easily be exaggerated. Though Western man is still living, more than he is often aware, on the accumulated capital of the Christian centuries, there is some (but by no means complete) excuse for calling our century the post-Christian, even a post-religious, era.

All this is familiar enough, and on a casting up of accounts sufficiently depressing. If the buoyancy of the old man Bridges and any effort of synthesis comparable to his are still possible, they have not yet appeared.

When Bridges published his *Testament*, poetry was already taking a new direction, comparable in its effect to those earlier

257

signals of new directions given successively by Spenser, Donne, Dryden, and Wordsworth. The day of the Georgians was over. There had been small residuum of religion in their work. When they experienced the shock of war, as many of them did in the trenches, the recoil had been not toward religion but toward disillusion and satire. But the shock, while visible in theme and attitude, left no striking mark on form or diction, save to infuse a note of realism already well developed in the novel. Now, however, under various influences, in which the war played little or no direct part, drastic changes in poetic form and effect, and in critical theory, were taking shape, and poetry and criticism of the kind referred to in my introductory chapter as replacing the traditional were commencing to emerge.

To the influences producing the change, it is unnecessary here to revert, save as they might bear more or less directly on the possible revival of religious poetry. Initially, the impulse seemed to be indifferent to religion and to follow that will-o'-the-wisp, pure poetry. It was, for example, the "unified sensibility" of the Metaphysicals, and the techniques by which they gave it expression (seen in the secular poetry of Donne and his school), that chiefly appealed in his earlier phases to T. S. Eliot, and this was accompanied by an attack (adumbrated by Pound and soon joined by Leavis) on the poetry of Milton, which was dedicated almost wholly to religious themes, though the attack was not, overtly at least, on his religious poetry as such. It is idle to seek to impose on the new poetic and criticism any positive unity of motive, but it seems safe to say that the approach was aesthetic and psychological and not at all religious. This approach received indubitable illustration in I. A. Richards as he surrendered the whole realm of truth to science and left poetry to present only pseudo-statements, which under the hand of the poet were somehow to retain their emotive power for the reader and to produce an effect at once aesthetic and therapeutic. (This theory, which belongs to the empirical tradition and stems from Bacon, Richards attempted to unite with Coleridge's observations on the imagination by divesting them of their metaphysical and religious foundation.) William Empson found the essence of poetry to lie in a use of language which exploited its inherent ambivalence, or what he called "ambiguity," and from this it was an easy step to discover that the true poetic effect was one of irony.

Here American voices commenced to swell the critical chorus (not without some counterpoint) which had found its origin in the duet of two Americans, Pound and Eliot—though Eliot by his own choice must now be treated as an English poet and critic. Fully developed, the New Criticism may perhaps be described as an American superstructure on an Anglo-American base, into which some elements were built from Imagist, Symbolist, and other aesthetic sources, none of them particularly religious, and some quite evidently anti-religious, in their associations. The resulting poetic (if one indeed can use the singular) was capacious enough to include negative conceptions like the denial of all validity to the poet's intention, and more positive contributions from psychoanalytic theory, whether of Freud or Jung, which approximated poetry to dream. Jung's contribution, coalescing with the findings of cultural anthropology as gathered in Sir James Frazer's famous *Golden Bough*, introduced the idea of archetypal myth and image as the substance of poetry, the key to its meaning, and the source of its emotive power. Here poetry may be thought to reapproach religion, but religion in its most primitive form.

Whether or not the resulting amalgam constitutes a single

coherent theory of poetry, it is clear that the elements that go to its making, singly and in combination, spell a strong reaction against traditional poetry, not only against its mode of expression and inherited techniques but against its addiction (nowhere more evident than in religious poetry) to affirmation on a basis of conceptual thinking. The reaction showed a marked preference for indirection and suggestion, with image and metaphor (always of course essential elements in poetry) operating now without the support of concept and affirmation—even in the form of pseudo-statements.

There would appear to be little enough in all this to foster a revival of religious poetry in any sense understood by earlier poets—by the admired Metaphysicals, for example (not to mention the reprobated Milton)—since in their religious verse they do not eschew affirmation, or rely on image and metaphor to the exclusion of other and supporting modes of expression, or ever seem to doubt the validity of their own intentions and their power to give them effect. Directly and consistently, they draw on a traditional Christian typology: for them Christ is Christ, prefigured by various persons of the Old Testament (and more remotely by a few from classic myth) but still Christ, the only true Redeemer and not an Adonis figure whose Resurrection is traceable to a primitive seasonal myth or fertility ritual. It is hard to avoid the conclusion that the new theory of poetry as it touches religion furnishes abundant escapes from forthright commitment, or that, despite all its efforts to insulate poet and poem from their historical setting, this is a direct result of the condition of religion in our own day.

The re-entry of religion into English poetry when it came (and we should not exaggerate its extent) sprang largely from a revulsion of feeling, shared no doubt by many who were not

poets, and originating in the conviction that in his present predicament man was the helpless prey of forces within him and
without, and that nothing but a return to some kind of religious
conviction and support could save him and give him peace.

Even so traditional, and so traditionally anti-religious, a poet
as A. E. Housman could share and express this feeling—though
not without a characteristic note of astringency and irony—in
one of his most moving poems:

> If in that Syrian garden, ages slain,
> You sleep, and know not you are dead in vain,
> Nor even in dreams behold how dark and bright
> Ascends in smoke and fire by day and night
> The hate you died to quench and could but fan,
> Sleep well and see no morning, son of man.
>
> But if, the grave rent and the stone rolled by,
> At the right hand of majesty on high
> You sit, and sitting so remember yet
> Your tears, your agony and bloody sweat,
> Your cross and passion and the life you gave,
> Bow hither out of heaven and see and save.

But, generally speaking, Housman, like Bridges, belongs in spirit,
and much more than Bridges in technique, to the preceding century, and we must conclude with a brief examination of two
poets of our own day.

If we select as the two T. S. Eliot and W. H. Auden, the
choice will require no apology save to admit that a better-
equipped commentator, with more time at his disposal, would
not be pardoned for omitting the later Yeats. Now, past the mid-
century, Yeats, rather than Eliot (or indeed any other), has been
taken to be the authentic voice of his age in English-speaking
poetry. But, like Blake, Yeats created his own system, and in his
"supernatural order," as it has been called, Christian civilization

is episodic rather than final, whereas Eliot and Auden come to stand in recognizable relation to the Christian tradition. For Eliot, we need not go farther back than *The Waste Land* (1922) to find our starting point in tracing his movement toward Christianity.

It follows that *The Waste Land* is not itself a Christian poem, despite the shadowy presence of Christ in the pointed allusion to the journey to Emmaus in the concluding section. If the more enigmatic allusion to the Hanged Man in the tarot pack (which Eliot is careful to refer to the archetype of the Hanged God in Frazer's *Golden Bough*) is intended also to suggest Christ, it can only be through the archetype, and at this stage in his development the poet might indeed say with Madame Sosotris, "I do not find / The Hanged Man." That is why her pronouncement (bogus though it in general be) can still hint his present danger: he must "Fear death by water" instead of finding the water of life:

> Here, said she,
> Is your card, the drowned Phoenician Sailor,
> (Those are pearls that were his eyes. Look!)

Perhaps the pearls symbolize the preciousness of spiritual vision —realized only when it is too late. Certainly the Church, to which Eliot was ultimately to turn, at this point offers no aid: the chapel, when discovered, is empty and ruinous, and the cock perched on the rooftree is an enigmatic symbol—if of the dawn, then also of Peter's betrayal. If deciphering the symbolism is at some points hazardous, the attempt to discover the precise relation to the poet's experiences and beliefs is yet more so, and can be undertaken only in defiance of his theory of poetry when he wrote the poem and the elaborate devices of depersonalization employed. But we must take the risk.

Nor can *The Waste Land* be described as, even in the broadest sense we have adopted, a religious poem, since it neither invokes nor presupposes an overruling Power. It is ethical and humanistic but marked by profound disillusion with society and with the individual, presented in a series of brief scenes of extraordinary vividness and immediacy—all of them endured, one is to suppose, by the blind Tiresias. Together they sum up the negative attitudes, the perversities, the feebleness, realized in earlier poems, and especially *Gerontion* and *Prufrock*. The first scene turns on the seeming possibility of finding in love a key to the prison house—a key, if it was a key, which the speaker has, however, failed to seize; others present the negation or the debasement of this passion, whether within the married relation or without, imprisoning to the individual and all too typical of modern society (but for Eliot the individual is always prior to society, whose ills are the fruit, almost it would seem the sum of individual deficiencies). Whether the erotic in the sense presented in the first scene really held the key for the poet, whose asceticism is already plain to read, may be doubted. The partial resolution and temporary expedient with which the poem closes speak to the individual in terms of a more abstract and generalized form of love, significantly accompanied by the admonition to control. And the message is Buddhist, not Christian, in source and emphasis: "Give, sympathize, control." That is "what the thunder said" in Sanskrit, prelude to the oncoming life-giving rain, with its promise, paraphrased by Eliot in the notes as "The peace which passeth understanding."

This is humanism, not religion (at least as the West would understand religion), and one may perhaps detect the influence of Eliot's earliest teacher, Irving Babbitt, whose conscious affinities were more with the Buddha than with Christ. But Eliot's humanism is here crossed by other influences, ranging from F. H. Bradley's closed world of the individual soul to Jessie Weston's treatment of the Grail legend, and from Frazer's archetypal myths to Dante's *Inferno* and *Purgatorio*, the latter with its tormenting fire which yet purges and refines. Here at least is some common ground with Newman's *Gerontius*, though no two poems could differ more in manner or in final outlook. The Waste Land is the fallen world (there can be no mistake about that). It is the region of individual and social failure and futility from which Eliot sets out on his Pilgrim's Progress, bearing on his back, like the one-eyed merchant, the burden represented by the blank card which Madame Sosotris is "forbidden to see" but whose nature the poem as it progresses is able in part to reveal. There are hints that the full resolution which the poem does not achieve may reside in a crucified and risen Redeemer, whose Church, however, is now empty and in ruin. The resolution actually reached is of another sort, ethical and humanistic, as we have said: it promises peace, but not as Eliot is to discover the peace envisaged by Dante, "In his will is our peace." In quest of that peace the pilgrimage will go on—but not perhaps to the point of adding to peace the buoyancy, the sense of the burden cast aside forever, attained in their different ways by Bunyan and by Newman. To the historian this is in part explained by differences in individual temper, coupled with differences in the conditions of the age, of both of which we have had abundant evidence in our survey. When the burden fell from him at the Cross, though many were the trials that lay ahead, Bunyan's Pilgrim, we are told, went "merrily" on his way. We must not expect such a response in our poet. But this is to anticipate.

The Christmas poems, *The Journey of the Magi* (1927) and

the *Song for Simeon* (1928), are not central to the pilgrimage, but they illustrate this last point.

In *The Journey of the Magi*, one of the kings of the East remembers, in sharp evocative phrases, the trials of the long journey in the "very dead of winter" and the recurrent sense "That this was all folly"; he remembers their coming down "at dawn" to a valley below the snow line, "smelling of vegetation"—a hint of hope, this union of dawn and spring in winter, but delusive. For "three trees on the low sky" prefigured the three crosses; the "tavern with vine-leaves" spoke of another god, and the six hands "dicing for pieces of silver" multiplied Judas and added the soldiers dicing for the seamless garment of the Crucified. They journeyed on and "at evening" came at last to the place: "it was (you may say) satisfactory." The flatness of the statement is deliberate, and the hint of dubiety, not of the fact but of the outcome, is in the interjected phrase.

> There was a Birth, certainly,
> We had evidence and no doubt. I had seen birth and death,
> But had thought they were different; this Birth was
> Hard and bitter agony for us, like Death, our death.
> We returned to our places, these Kingdoms,
> But no longer at ease here, in the old dispensation,
> With an alien people clutching their gods.
> I should be glad of another death.

This is Eliot's version of the adoring Magi bearing their gifts to the cradle of Christ, and the contrast with earlier Christmas poems, already quoted, is inescapable: the joyous song of the shepherds in Crashaw, the leveling of wise man and shepherd in the common element of faith and love, in Godolphin; the eagerness of the young Milton as he hastens ahead of the Magi ("O run, prevent them with thy humble ode") and the promise of the Saviour's ultimate triumph over all evils:

> Our Babe to show his godhead true
> Can in his swaddling bands control the damnèd crew.

Eliot chooses to have the Magi speak for themselves, and with the benefit of hindsight, though the three lyricists also knew what was to folow—but not of course the predicament of man in Eliot's age.

The Nunc dimittis is indeed an old man's response to the birth, but one compact of affirmation, peace, and quiet joy. In the Song for Simeon, emphasis and tone are altogether different:

> Before the time of cords and scourges and lamentation
> Grant us thy peace.
> Before the stations of the mountain of desolation,
> Before the certain hour of maternal sorrow,
> Now at this birth season of decease,
> Let the Infant, the still unspeaking and unspoken Word,
> Grant Israel's consolation
> To one who has eighty years and no tomorrow. . . .
>
> They shall praise Thee and suffer in every generation
> With glory and derision,
> Light upon light, mounting the saints' stair. . . .
> I am tired with my own life and the lives of those after me,
> I am dying in my own death and the deaths of those after me.
> Let thy servant depart,
> Having seen thy salvation.

Here indeed God's servant is to depart in peace and acquiescence, so that one might say that for Simeon, God's will is his peace; but the joy of the Incarnation is overshadowed by what is to come after.

Ash Wednesday (1930), a more obscure and difficult poem, whose austerity is at least in keeping with the season, has as one of its basic images the "saints' stair" adumbrated in the Song for Simeon. (Again we must ignore much of the imagery and try to indicate simply the development of the main theme. Nor can we do more with sources than remind ourselves of the echo of Dante and Beatrice and the ascent from earthly to spiritual love.) The poem points the way of ascent through renunciation: first of one's ambition and all striving to achieve it, which can only be subject to time and place; secondly, of love and its imagined power to release, as envisaged, and missed, in the first movement of *The Waste Land*; thirdly, of their very memory:

> Because these wings are no longer wings to fly
> But merely vans to beat the air . . .
> Teach us to care [by way of repentance] and not to care
>                     [by way of regret]
> Teach us to sit still.

Thus the first section. The second carries on the idea of renunciation, specifically of the flesh, through the image of the scattered bones picked clean by the three white leopards.

>                     And I who am here dissembled
> Proffer my deeds to oblivion, and my love
> To the posterity of the desert . . .
>                     The Lady is withdrawn
> In a white gown, to contemplation. . . .
> Let the whiteness of bones atone to forgetfulness.
> There is no life in them. As I am forgotten
> And would be forgotten, so I would forget
> Thus devoted, concentrated in purpose. . . .

But it is not the end: rather the beginning. For now, in the third movement, comes the image of the winding stair—that is, at this point the image becomes explicit, for the poet is now "At the first turning of the second stair," and, looking back, sees "the same shape" (himself)

> Struggling with the devil of the stairs who wears
> The deceitful face of hope and of despair.

The movement ends "In the quiet of the desert. This is the land . . . / We have our inheritance." At the second turning he has left this vision behind and proceeded upward, but in the dark. "At the first turning of the third stair," a slotted window reveals a vernal scene and a pastoral figure who "Enchanted the may-time with an antique flute," and brought distraction—a resurgence of emotion from the world he had renounced. But with "strength beyond hope and despair" he presses forward "climbing the third stair": "Lord, I am not worthy / . . . but speak the world only." In the fourth movement, the image of the winding stair ceases to be explicit, but a new view opens, and the Lady (withdrawn, as we have been told, to contemplation) is seen clad "In blue of larkspur, blue of Mary's color":

> White light folded, sheathed about her, folded. . . .
> Through a bright cloud of tears, the years, restoring
> With a new verse the ancient rhyme. Redeem
> The time. Redeem
> The unread vision in the higher dream . . .
>
> The silent sister veiled in white and blue
> Between the yews [symbols at once of death and immortality],
>            behind the garden god,
> Whose flute is breathless, bent her head and sighed but
>            spoke no word
>
> But the fountain sprang up and the bird sang down
> Redeem the time, redeem the dream
> The token of the word unheard, unspoken
>
> Till the wind shake a thousand whispers [of immortal
>            life] from the yew.

The fifth movement (for in effect the poet is still ascending the winding stair) brings the conviction that the word unspoken, unheard, bears a relation to the Word (the Logos), as the world of time and motion, of sensation and restless thought, also bears its relation to the real World, not of time but of eternity, and that the relation of the transient to the permanent is twofold, of contrast or opposition, but also, if we can penetrate to its meaning, of reflection or symbol:

> Still is the unspoken word, the Word unheard,
> The Word without a word, the Word within
> The world and for the world;
> And the light shone in darkness and
> Against the Word the unstilled world still whirled
> About the centre of the silent Word.

But the conviction of what is real and abiding is not the same thing as surrender to the conviction:

> Where shall the word be found, where will the word
> Resound? Not here, there is not enough silence . . .
> For those who walk in darkness . . .
> The right time and the right place are not here
> No place of grace for those who avoid the face
> No time to rejoice for those who walk among noise and
>     deny the voice.

The Lady, the "veiled sister" (or so it would seem) now becomes the symbol of the Church:

> Will the veiled sister pray for
> Those who walk in darkness, who chose thee and oppose
>     thee . . .
> For children at the gate
> Who will not go away and cannot pray:
> Pray for those who chose and oppose . . .
>
> Will the veiled sister between the slender
> Yew trees pray for those who offend her
> And are terrified and cannot surrender.

The final movement (with its implied view from the next step in the winding stair) looks at first like a relapse:

>       . . . though I do not wish to wish these things
> From the wide window towards the granite shore
> The white sails still fly seaward, seaward flying
> Unbroken wings

> And the lost heart stiffens and rejoices
> In the lost lilac and the lost sea voices
> And the weak spirit quickens to rebel
> For the bent golden-rod and the lost sea smell
> Quickens to recover
> The cry of quail and the whirling plover
> And the blind eye creates
> The empty forms between the ivory gates
> And smells renews the salt savour of the sandy earth.

But again this is not the end. Appealing once more to the "blessed sister," now a "holy mother," the meditation reaches its conclusion:

> This is the time of tension between dying and birth . . .
> But when the voices shaken from the yew-tree [symbol of
> death] drift away
> Let the other yew be shaken and reply.
>
> Blessed sister, holy mother . . .
> Suffer us not to mock ourselves with falsehood
> Teach us to care and not to care
> Teach us to sit still
> Even among these rocks,
> Our peace in His will
> And even among these rocks . . .
> Suffer me not to be separated
>
> And let my cry come unto Thee.

The contrast of this poem, both in content and in mode of expression, with those examined earlier is sufficiently evident. Even with the religious poetry of Donne it seems to have little affinity. But we had better postpone any attempt at generalized comment till we have considered, very briefly, the *Four Quartets*.

Though they belong to a period and situation two decades ago and fast receding into history, the *Quartets* are all we are now likely to get by way of summation from the most influential religious poet of our time. They are indeed a summation of a sort, in which earlier themes recur and are more intimately related to the poet's personal experience. Former devices of distancing are abandoned, though not the mode of oblique expression or the resort to implicit (as distinct from explicit) symbols. Yet the increasing subtlety and complexity of the experiences recorded— that is, realized—in and by the poems, and the effort to bring what on the surface seem to be diverse experiences into a single focus, mean that the *Quartets* are more difficult to interpret with completeness and assurance than is *Ash Wednesday*, especially if one is compelled, as we are, to pass over in silence most of the detail, the symbols and the literary and historical echoes.

Often for whole passages the *Quartets* do not appear to be religious poems, but to be concerned rather with psychological states and experiences; but always the resolution—insofar as there is a resolution—is found in religion, in that version of Christianity to which the poet has been brought, though not easily, to adhere. Central among the themes that recur from earlier meditations is that of time—past, present, and future (the past now localized in places that have for the poet special associations)—and (in contrast with time) the timeless, the still point around which time flows. With this is linked the theme of words as subject to time and motion, and (in contrast) the Word (the Logos) as the still point, the timeless. Now words in their subjection to time are viewed in relation to the special problem of the poet in finding a language adequate to his purpose: a reflection of a dominant concern in Eliot's whole career as poet and critic. There is evidence enough of bafflement and struggle. But always the resolution, insofar as there is resolution, is sought in religion. Thus religion and poetry are brought into close relation—a relation as close (though not as simple and unequivocal) as in Dante or Milton, Donne or Herbert; and one could perhaps infer from the *Quartets* a theory of religious poetry. If so, it would assuredly not involve emotive pseudo-statements but would turn on a hard-won and at last "willing suspension of disbelief."

The meditation on time commences with the first line of the first poem, *Burnt Norton*, and turns on the potential, the might-have-been in contrast to what was, and the equal reality and unreality of the two. We do not know whether the children in the rose garden are symbols of earliest memories in "our first world" or whether, like Elia's "dream children," they are symbols of what might have been. It does not matter: they serve to establish the central contrast, and thereby to bring home to us the element of illusion in what we take for real, the perpetual movement of our time-conditioned existence. Reality is found only "At the still point of the turning world," where "past and future" (which dominate our action and suffering, our hope and fear and desire) "are gathered." Yet, while they are thus opposed as illusion to reality, it would be a mistake to assume that time and the timeless, the flux and the still center, have no connection with each other. This is but the first in the series of meditations and, though the resolution is yet to come, there are hints of time's dependence on the timeless.

> Time past and time future
> Allow but a little consciousness.
> To be conscious is not to be in time
> But only in time can the moment in the rose-garden . . .
> Be remembered; involved with past and future.
> Only through time time is conquered.
>
> Words move, music moves
> Only in time; but that which is only living
> Can only die. Words, after speech, reach
> Into the silence. Only by the form, the pattern,
> Can words or music reach
> The stillness. . . .

And (here is the poet's problem):

> Words strain,
> Crack and sometimes break, under the burden,
> Under the tension, slip, slide, perish,
> Decay into imprecision. . . .

> The detail of the pattern is movement. . . .
> Desire itself is movement
> Not in itself desirable;
> Love is itself unmoving,
> Only the cause and end of movement,
> Timeless, and undesiring
> Except in the aspect of time
> Caught in the form of limitation
> Between un-being and being.
> Sudden in a shaft of sunlight
> Even while the dust moves
> There rises the hidden laughter
> Of children in the foliage
> Quick now, here, now, always—
> Ridiculous the waste sad time
> Stretching before and after.

Thus the poem returns at the end to the experience from which it took its beginning, but with some (though a limited) accession of insight. This is the structural principle basic to its pattern (much of which we have perforce passed over in silence). If it achieves no escape from time, no resolution in the stillness, it is a step on the way.

In *East Coker* the scene is the village whence the poet's family had emigrated to America, which thus provides a less accidental and evanescent link with the poet's experience. Here he is concerned not with what might have been but at least initially with what was. The note is struck in the opening words: "In my beginning is my end." But "succession," the historical process, means impermanence, decay, and change, though ghosts of the past still haunt the scene:

> On the summer midnight you can hear the music
> Of the weak pipe and the little drum
> And see them dancing around the bonfire
> The association of man and woman
> In daunsinge, signifying the matrimonie—
> A dignified and commodious sacrament.

This last from the sixteenth-century Elyot's *The Governour*, not without wry suggestion of irony:

> Keeping the rhythm in their dancing
> As in their living in the living seasons
> The time of the seasons and the constellations . . .
> The time of the coupling of man and woman
> And that of beasts.

Perhaps we remember, as we are meant to remember, "that which is only living / Can only die." This is what tradition can tell us, and the limit of what it can tell us. For tradition is of time and temporal experience, and there is

> At best, only a limited value
> In the knowledge derived from experience.
> The knowledge imposes a pattern, and falsifies,
> For the pattern is new in every moment
> And every moment is a new and shocking
> Valuation of all we have been. . . .
> The only wisdom we can hope to acquire
> Is the wisdom of humility. . . .

And in the spirit of humility:

> I said to my soul, be still, and wait without hope
> For hope would be hope for the wrong thing; wait without love
> For love would be love of the wrong thing; there is yet
> > faith
> But the faith and the love and the hope are all in the
> > waiting.

Wait without thought, for you are not ready for thought:
So the darkness will be the light, and the stillness the
                              dancing. . . .

You must go by a way wherein there is no ecstasy.
In order to arrive at what you do not know
   You must go by a way which is the way of ignorance.
In order to possess what you do not possess
   You must go by the way of dispossession. . . .

This is the way, evidently, not only of humility but of renunciation and purgation. And Christianity, as it makes its first overt
entry into these poems, continues and intensifies this note:

> The wounded surgeon plies the steel
> That questions the distempered part;
> Beneath the bleeding hands we feel
> The sharp compassion of the healer's art
> Resolving the enigma of the fever chart. . . .

Such is the secret of the true pattern (and its realization is now
the poet's task, though words and his command of them are always failing him, and "there is only the trying"). Only as the
secret is apprehended does human experience begin to become
intelligible and, reversing this time the premise in the conclusion, can we say, "In my end is my beginning."

   In the third poem, *The Dry Salvages*, the beginning is not in
the life of the poet's forebears but in his own, in this coast
scene of early vacations and, by contrast, at an even earlier date,
his midland home by the Mississippi; but the immemorial sea
and its menace—the "sea voices," the wailing of the siren, the
clanging of the swell-rung bell—dominate the meditation:

> Where is there an end of it, the soundless wailing,
> The silent withering of autumn flowers . . .
> Where is there an end to the drifting wreckage,
> The prayer of the bone on the beach, the unprayable
> Prayer at the calamitous annunciation [of expected disaster]?

275

There is no end, but addition: the trailing
Consequences of further days and hours,
While emotion takes to itself the emotionless
Years of living among the breakage
Of what was believed in as most reliable—
And therefore the fittest for renunciation.

There is only the final addition, age with its failing pride, its resentment at failing powers, and

The silent listening to the undeniable
Clamour of the bell of the last annunciation [death]. . . .

There is no end of it, the voiceless wailing,
No end to the withering of withered flowers . . .
To the drift of the sea and the drifting wreckage,
The bone's prayer to Death its God. Only the hardly,
        barely prayable
Prayer of the one Annunciation [Christ's].

This is the turning point in the pattern of the poem. There is something to be learned and, as we are able, to practice. With age (it may be) the past takes on a new pattern

        . . . and ceases to be a mere sequence—
Or even development: . . . a partial fallacy
Encouraged by superficial notions of evolution,
Which becomes, in the popular mind, a means of disowning
        the past.

We may realize that in its

moments of happiness—not the sense of wellbeing . . .
                but the sudden illumination—
We had the experience but missed the meaning,
And approach to the meaning restores the experience
In a different form. . . .

And

        the past experience revived in the meaning
        Is not the experience of one life only

But of many generations. . . .
Now, we come to discover that the moments of agony . . .
                are likewise permanent
With such permanence as time has.

We may

      Here between the hither and the farther shore
      While time is withdrawn, consider the future
      And the past with equal mind. . . .

                But to apprehend
      The point of intersection of the timeless
      With time, is an occupation for the saint—
      Not occupation either, but something given
      And taken, in a lifetime's death in love,
      Ardour and selflessness and self-surrender.
      For most of us, there is only the unattended
      Moment, the moment in and out of time,
      The distraction fit, lost in a shaft of sunlight . . .
                or music heard so deeply
      That it is not heard at all, but you are the music
      While the music lasts. These are only hints and guesses,
      Hints followed by guesses; and the rest
      Is prayer, observance, discipline, thought and action.
      The hint half guessed, the gift half understood, is
                Incarnation.
      Here the impossible union.
      Of spheres of existence is actual,
      Here the past and future
      Are conquered and reconciled. . . .

And in its light, action takes on a new meaning, and that meaning is freedom. It is no longer

              . . . movement
      Of that which is only moved
      And has in it no source of movement. . . .
              right action is freedom
      From past and future also.

This is the stage in the resolution of time and the timeless reached in the third poem; and it is not in essence qualified by the humble admission:

> For most of us, this is the aim
> Never here to be realized;
> Who are only undefeated
> Because we have have gone on trying;
> We, content at the last
> If our temporal reversion [the body] nourish
> (Not too far from the yew tree [symbol of death, but also
>                     of the hope of immortality])
> The life of significant soil.

At the risk of drastic oversimplification, we may recognize in these three poems a common theme (at bottom metaphysical, though the problem posed is not to be solved by mere metaphysics): the tension between time and the timeless, and in each poem a stage in the resolution of that tension. The first is psychological in its approach: the sway of time which seems so absolute is in measure dispelled by the experience in the garden, by the recognition that what might have been is as real (and unreal) as what was. The second is primarily ethical: the discovery that experience in time may issue in purgation; and here religion (that is, an aspect of Christianity) enters to confirm, indeed to contain, the lesson, in the image of "the wounded surgeon" (Christ of the earthly ministry, culminating in the Crucifixion) and the "sharp compassion of the healer's art." The third approaches the metaphysical level with the implied question: Is there not some point at which time is intersected by the timeless, and which alone can give time its relevance and value? There is: and the answer is found again in Christ, now in the Incarnation. The distinction of the psychological, the ethical, and the metaphysical (though it can be supported from the poems) is here merely a device of exposition; for each approach is grounded in human experience and is in that degree psychological, and (as we have just seen) the religious and the ethical, the contemplative and the active, are intimately related. Let us admit a cumulative difficulty in giving a brief account of these poems. By hint and image each one recalls, gathers up and recalls in a new context, themes which have occurred before—it is not for nothing that the title of the whole is derived from music —but this is something to which only the most detailed analysis, if even that, could do justice. Brevity, which means exclusion, is almost certain in some degree to falsify, and the danger is greater in the final poem. There, on the face of it, the overt reference to religion as the solvent recedes, and we are tempted to imagine that we are back in the area of psychological experience as in the first poem—but this would be an example of the half-truth that falsifies.

This fourth poem centers on two scenes which turn upon the poet's more immediate experience: Little Gidding (which gives its title to the poem), the quiet country setting of the quasi-monastic retreat of Nicholas Ferrar, George Herbert's friend, and a type of religion—Catholic without ceasing to be English; and, in startling contrast to this, wartime London, the agonized London of the air raids. First then, Little Gidding in "Midwinter spring," with sunlight bright but chill, and snow on the hedgerows instead of the blossoming May:

> There are other places
> Which also are the world's end . . .
> But this is the nearest, in place and time,
> Now and in England.

Whatever your purpose in coming, it is "altered in fulfilment":

> You are here to kneel
> Where prayer has been valid. . . .
> And what the dead had no speech for, when living,
> They can tell you, being dead: the communication
> Of the dead is tongued with fire beyond the language
>     of the living.
> Here the intersection of the timeless moment
> Is England and nowhere. Never and always.

The scene shifts to London,

> Near the ending of interminable night
> At the recurrent end of the unending
> After the dark dove with the flickering tongue
> Had passed below the horizon . . .

and to the strange encounter with the ghost of some dead teacher
—concerned like the poet with "speech,"

> . . . and speech impelled us
> To purify the dialect of the tribe
> And urge the mind to aftersight and foresight.

Of his efforts, and of the poet's, he can only say now:

> These things have served their purpose: let them be.
> So with your own, and pray they be forgiven
> By others, as I pray you to forgive
> Both bad and good.

And for the individual himself, it all amounts to nothing unless
experience becomes purgation:

> From wrong to wrong the exasperated spirit
> Proceeds, unless restored by that refining fire
> Where you must move in measure, like a dancer.

Back in the chapel at Little Gidding, the poet reflects on the
memories of a past struggle, of Charles I coming there at nightfall, of Strafford, Charles, and Laud, who perished on the scaf-

fold, and others who died forgotten, and of Milton "who died blind and quiet"—all of whom now, their strife forgotten,

> Accept the constitution of silence
> And are folded in a single party.

"History may be servitude," or it "may be freedom," and

> This is the use of memory:
> For liberation—not less of love but expanding
> Of love beyond desire, and so liberation
> From the future as well as the past.

The meaning of struggle and suffering—its purpose and value if we can apprehend it—in the past, as in the present, is purgation, is the "purification of the motive." Thus to profit by the fire of purgation is to escape the fire of hell. And so back to contemporary London:

> The dove descending breaks the air
> With flame of incandescent terror
> Of which the tongues declare
> The one discharge from sin and error.
> The only hope, or else despair
>   Lies in the choice of pyre or pyre—
>   To be redeemed from fire by fire.
>
>   Who then devised the torment? Love.
> Love is the unfamiliar Name
> Behind the hands that wove
> The intolerable shirt of flame
> Which human power cannot remove.
>   We only live, only suspire
>   Consumed by either fire or fire.

The final movement is toward a moment of illumination in which elements from all four poems are recalled, fall into a pattern, and reach out toward significance. (Not all the echoes of the earlier poems can be caught here because of the enforced brevity of our earlier analysis, but enough perhaps to suggest the pattern.) In the cycle of time, beginning and end are relative terms and not really distinguishable:

> What we call the beginning is often the end
> And to make an end is to make a beginning.
> The end is where we start from.

It is true in the craft of words—the poet's art:

> ... every phrase
> And sentence that is right (where every word is at home,
> Taking its place to support the others ...
> The complete consort dancing together)
> Every phrase and every sentence is an end and a beginning,
> Every poem an epitaph.

And it is true in the life of action, for

> ... any action
> Is a step to the block, to the fire, down the sea's throat
> Or to an illegible stone: and that is where we start. ...
> The moment of the rose [life] and the moment of the
> yew-tree [death but not without sug-
> gestion of a beginning also]
> Are of equal duration.

But time, we are meant to remember, derives its significance only as it is intersected by the timeless, and (in its true significance)

> ... history is a pattern
> Of timeless moments. So, while the light fails
> On a winter's afternoon, in a secluded chapel
> History is now and England.

And so (to come at once to the illumination) what is required of us if we would apprehend the meaning is

> A condition of complete simplicity
> (Costing not less than everything)

and the result is a new confidence (significantly phrased in the words of no intellectual, but of Juliana of Norwich, an English medieval mystic):

> And all shall be well and
> All manner of thing shall be well
> When—

but here the echo is from Dante, though the combination is Eliot's own:

> When the tongues of flame are in-folded
> Into the crowned knot of [purging] fire
> And the fire and the rose are one.

We have been able to do no more than suggest in outline the poet's pilgrimage as it is recorded—that is, realized—in a succession of poems. Like other religious poets, Eliot does not escape the influence of his time and his temperament.

The time is more readily comprehended since it is also ours; and we shall not fail to recognize the difficulties of religion, and hence of the religious poet, therein. Secularism has reached a dominance and a diffusion unknown in the Christian centuries. The climate and conditions of belief have changed. No doubt, by the more thoughtful the hollowness and hopelessness of a merely secular outlook are often felt, and the value of ideas embodied in the Christian tradition, in varying degrees recognized; but as a result of developments at which we have glanced, the "facts" with which those ideas have been so long associated are subject to very general questioning. This is a condition which the poet and his audience cannot escape; and the outcome, when it has not been simply a turning back toward the secular, has been a shift in emphasis from accepted fact to experienced need. Not that the experienced need of religion is not abundantly present in earlier religious poetry, but that the need is met there by a turning to, and reliance on, generally accepted fact and dogma. The change is unmistakable and is characteristic of our century, though premonitions of it must have been evident in our brief discussion of the Victorians. So much for Eliot's time and ours.

The question of temperament is more hazardous. In *The Waste Land* we have the poet's sense of the utter barrenness, the utter futility, of a fevered or lethargic life without purpose and without hope, and the need for an awakening, for a change of outlook and of heart—the need but scarcely the way to their achievement. The Waste Land is our life today, and it is the City of Destruction from which the Pilgrim must escape. But that is as far as the analogy with Bunyan will carry us: the rest is all contrast. Bunyan leaves the City of Destruction behind him, and once the burden has fallen from him at the Cross, he goes (as we have said) though through many a trial and setback, "merrily" on his way. The shadow of the City of Destruction pursues Mr. Eliot, and he has as little of Bunyan's natural buoyancy as of his simplicity of mind and feeling. With Dante, on the other hand, we recognize a natural affinity: the austerity, the sternness, the union of subtle thought with intense feeling, the asceticism, the principle of sublimation through renunciation— the idea, above all, of experience as a purging fire; and from Dante a potent influence can be traced in Eliot's subsequent poetry, in *Ash Wednesday* and again in the *Four Quartets*. The influence is not confined to idea, or to a reading of the human situation and its need, but extends in some degree to the mode of expression. Not that Eliot abandons indirection, but (unless I am mistaken—and I think that the quotations from the later poems will bear me out) he combines with it much more of personal affirmation, and what reads like direct statement, conceptual in character, than is found in the earlier verse; in effect they furnish a basis for his symbolic imagery and a key to its meaning. And this in turn may perhaps be related to his having attained, as did Dante, to what is for him a firm standing ground in a world of uncertainty, of endless flux.

In the attainment, poetry, it seems impossible to doubt, has played its vital role—poetry which, as I have repeatedly insisted, is not simply the record of an experience but its realization. In the poetry we can plainly read that a primary incentive has been a recognition of man's desperate need—a growing conviction that there is no escape from the Waste Land in the limited commitments of humanism, which in its nature cannot transcend man's weakness or the conditions of his predicament. The urgent sense of need points the first step to the solution: to an acceptance of man's utter dependence on God, of the complete surrender of his will to God's, and of humility as the essential condition of all wisdom and virtue, of all stability and peace. We recognize here a traditional religious—indeed, specifically Christian—attitude, which (besides the resistance of the natural man) is, for a variety of reasons, not easy for the intellectual to adopt. There is the problem, prominent in Eliot's meditations, of how any contract can exist between the temporal (the theater of man's experience) and the eternal (the residence of God's power), how time can be intersected by the timeless. As the need points to its answer in a Christian attitude, the emergent difficulty points to its solution in Christianity's central dogma of the Incarnation: here (if one can take the necessary step of faith) time is intersected by the timeless—the Word is made flesh. And everything else follows. Suffering is sanctified, and its purpose made manifest, in the Cross: its purpose (if we will so apply it) is purgation, and the motive of its infliction is love. If human experience points the need, and faith supplies the answer, that answer in turn is not without its verifications in human experience if one can penetrate to their meaning. And in the exploration and ordering of human experience, poetry finds its role. As time depends on the timeless, and pattern, which is ordered movement, on the still point, so words bear their relation to the Word. It is the function of religious poetry (as one must, I think, infer—especially from the *Four Quartets*) to realize these relations and with them the need for faith which human experience manifests and the verifications of faith which it suggests. The task is not an easy one in any age, and certainly not in our own. But for Eliot, facility is no more a characteristic of poetry than it is an outcome of faith. The outcome of faith is humility, self-abnegation, submission to the will of God ("In His Will is our peace"), a degree of insight and a renewed possibility of action and of freedom experienced in action: it is even a measure of reassurance that "All shall be well." But it is not joy. Saint Paul couples joy with the peace of God ("Rejoice in the Lord always . . . And the peace of God, which passeth all understanding, shall keep your hearts and minds . . .); whether it be the result of temperament or of the age, or of both, Eliot does not. The Incarnation is central in his doctrine; but while he does not remain in the state of mind dramatized in his own Magi, neither does he attain to that of Crashaw's shepherds or of Browning's prophetic David.

We have been careful not to exaggerate (as some have tended to do) the extent of the religious revival in our own day. It may well be, however, that the sense of need is greater and more widespread than the attainment; and it is surely significant that the most influential poet of the period *entre deux guerres* should have turned to religion and (despite the narrowing of the audience and the difficulty of the medium) should have struck in so many readers a responsive chord. Among the poets, one at least has taken a similar, but certainly not an identical, road.

In temperament, and to a considerable extent in background

and experience, W. H. Auden (whom in justice we should now regard as an American poet, but we can hardly dispense with him in our survey) differs markedly from T. S. Eliot. If Eliot's pilgrimage from his Waste Land, in the 'twenties, culminated in the years of the Second World War, Auden's was of briefer duration: starting in the 'thirties (not for him an unrelievedly Waste Land but one whose hopes turned out to be illusory), it too reached its perhaps less decisive goal in the war years, but not in the intimate and heart-searching contact with them revealed in the last of the Four Quartets. The difference in temperament may be seen in the influences to which the younger poet responded: Blake, D. H. Lawrence, and Freud, to whom he turned, in a quest for personal liberation, combined to leave a legacy of anti-intellectualism foreign to Eliot. Marxism gave a hope of social and economic amelioration, almost wholly absent from Eliot's interests, and if in his subsequent reaction against its materialism Auden parallels, indeed anticipates, the flight of many of his contemporaries from Marxism to religion, the hope does not perish but finds a new basis. There is, of course, in the poetry of Auden, the influence of Eliot himself and of the literary movement of which he was a central figure; but here again there are differences. One may doubt whether Auden's view of poetry and its function kept pace with Eliot's developing view. If (as has been suggested) he was encouraged to set limits to the significance of art by his reading in Kierkegaard, there was, one may suspect, a basis laid in the theories of I. A. Richards. Whatever influence of Dante there is in his later work may well have been channeled through the poetry of Eliot, but is certainly much less pervasive and profound. And at the point in religious thought and experience where he seems closest to Eliot, in the conception of the Incarnation as the penetrating of time by the timeless, Auden's application as yet lacks the range, subtlety, and consistency of the elder poet. There are other differences. Eliot is much more the thinker. At the same time he has a much stronger sense of tradition. Both facts have their bearing on his attitude toward the Church: he seeks support in her philosophy and in her aids to devotion as he finds them embodied in Anglo-Catholicism. Auden has been called an essential Protestant: an individualist, not indeed without a feeling for communal experience, but finding no essential need or role for the Church therein. But to pursue the comparison one step further, we must recognize in Auden wider human sympathies, greater warmth, a suggestion that the pervasive sense of mankind's weakness springs more directly from a recognition of his own, and some return to the idea that what Christianity offers is indeed tidings of joy.

There are premonitions of the new direction in his discursive *New Year Letter*. There, in what seem perhaps too facile octosyllabics though marked by unflagging energy, he questions both the age and himself, and ends on a note of humility and self-surrender in the prayer:

> Convict our pride of its offence
> In all things, even penitence,
> Instruct us in the civil art
> Of making from the muddled heart
> A desert and a city where
> The thoughts that have to labour there
> May find locality and peace,
> The pent-up feelings their release.
> Send strength sufficient for the day,
> And point our knowledge on its way.
> *O da quod jubes, Domine.*

The premonitions are realized in *For The Time Being: A Christmas Oratorio*. In the title a threefold significance may be recognized: first, the centering on the idea of the Incarnation; secondly, the resort to a dramatic form, but less, it would seem, as a device of distancing than as a recognition of communal experience; thirdly, in a double suggestion in the phrase "For the Time Being"—the obvious one, borne out by the Epilogue, that this is the essential message of Christmas which requires to be completed by others from the Christian year, and is all too apt to fade amid the routine and cares of ordinary life, but the suggestion, too, that the work is a sort of progress report, that there is, or should be, growth in comprehension, more to follow. Again, we must content ourselves with a bare outline of the main theme.

The utterance of the Chorus at the beginning voices the human predicament, essentially that of modern man, and the resolution which it demands—namely, the acceptance of a miracle:

> Alone, alone in a dreadful wood
> Of conscious evil runs a lost mankind,
> Dreading to find its Father lest it find
> The Goodness it has dreaded is not good.
> Alone, alone about our dreadful wood.
>
> Where is the Law for which we broke our own,
> Where now that Justice for which Flesh resigned
> Her hereditary right to passion, Mind
> His will to absolute power? Gone. Gone.
> Where is the Law for which we broke our own? . . .
>
> We who must die demand a miracle.
> How could the Eternal do a temporal act,
> The Infinite become a finite fact?
> Nothing can save us that is possible:
> We who must die demand a miracle.

(We remember Tertullian's *credo quia impossibile est.*)

The miracle begins in the Annunciation. Its outcome and significance commence to be realized in the experience of the Wise

Men (the intellectuals) and the Shepherds (average humanity). To the former, the star which summons them utters its warning, striking a note characteristic of Auden's anti-intellectualism, his conviction (contrary to the long tradition of Christian humanism, but joining another tradition of Christian thought) that revealed truth does not complete but contradicts the strivings of the human reason:

> I am that star most dreaded of the wise,
> For they are drawn against their will to me,
> Yet read in my procession through the skies
> The doom of orthodox sophrosyne. . . .
> Beware. All those who follow me are led
> Onto that Glassy Mountain where are no
> Footholds for logic, to the Bridge of Dread
> Where knowledge but increases vertigo.

The Wise Men have studied, and put their confidence in, natural science (and found its conclusions self-contradictory), in the evolution of mind (and found that it spoke always of past and future, never of the present), in utilitarian ethics (and found that it left no place for affection). To discover how to be "truthful," "living," and "loving" now—in a word, "how to be human"—is the "reason they follow this star." The praise of Caesar and his civilizing power, which breaks in, is the voice of propaganda, with the effect of ironic contrast.

The Chorus returns, to relate what has been learned so far to the question raised at the outset and to point to love as the solution of the individual's, and of society's, problem.

> Our Father whose creative Will
>     Asked Being for us all,
> Confirm it that thy Primal Love
> May weave in us the freedom of
> The actually deficient on
>     The justly actual. . . .

Inflict thy promises with each
   Occasion of distress,
That from our incoherence we
May learn to put our trust in Thee
And brutal fact persuade us to
   Adventure, Art, and Peace.

Presently the Chorus of the Angels will complete the resolution
in idea, toward which the Oratorio has been moving. The birth
of the Child means nothing less than the "ingression of Love";
so that

   . . . after today
The children of men
May be certain that
The Father Abyss
Is affectionate
To all Its creatures.

And this, too, is the dawning of a new hope for society; for

   . . . the new-born Word
Declares that the old
Authoritarian
Constraint is replaced
By His Covenant
And a city based
On love and consent.

But before the truth can become operative, it must be apprehended and accepted. The Wise Men and Shepherds must meet
at the Manger, where (in the Oratorio) Mary sings to the Child
of his human heritage: "an anxiety his Father cannot feel" and
the "Sorrowful Way" of suffering and death—for Bethelehem
implies Calvary.

   With the entry of the Shepherds, two features of the work
which we must not neglect have come, not for the first time, into
play: the insistent contemporary reference—the Shepherds repre-

sent the workers, the "masses" of modern society, as the Wise Men its thinkers; and the recurrent earthiness of tone and phrase. And a kind of balance is struck: if the Wise Men need to be rescued from the impasse of the intellect, the Shepherds also need to escape from that lethargy of thought and feeling bred of ignorance and routine. Love is the solvent of both their ills: it can redeem the talents of the wise and sanctify them in its service, and it can redeem the simple from their "childish way." The Wise Men's journey ends at the Manger; the Shepherds' starts there. And together they can sing, with a note of joy now made explicit:

> O Living Love replacing fantasy,
> O Joy of life revealed in Love's creation;
> Our mood of longing turns to indication:
> Space is the Whom our loves are needed by,
> Time is our choice of How to love and Why.

This is, in a real sense, the culmination of the *Oratorio*. The doctrine has still to be elaborated, and put in its historical context, in the prose "Meditation of Simeon" (Auden's interpretation, more successful than Eliot's, of the *Nunc dimittis*). "The Massacre of the Innocents" (in which Herod appears as the disciple of Caesar, the proponent of secular paternalism—whose issue is inhumanity and despair) and "The Flight into Egypt" bring us back with a shock of calculated anticlimax to our world and its present state; and the Epilogue (as I have called it) recognizes how far is the full potential of the Christmas message from being realized in our lives:

> Once again,
> As in previous years, we have seen the actual Vision
> and failed
> To do more than entertain it as an agreeable
> Possibility; once again we have sent Him away,
> Begging though to remain his disobedient servants.

Yet this is not quite the end. The final Chorus is positive in its
conviction that "He is the Way, the Truth, and the Life."

It has seemed more profitable, here as elsewhere, to deal in
some detail with selected poets and let them, so far as possible,
speak for themselves. Selection, of course, has its dangers; and it
may be well to conclude with a poem more characteristic perhaps, if not of religious poetry, then of poetry in the presence of
religion, in our age. Philip Larkin gives us the thoughts of one
who has wandered into an empty English parish church:

> Once I am sure there's nothing going on
> I step inside, letting the door thud shut.
> Another church: matting, seats, and stone,
> And little books; sprawlings of flowers, cut
> For Sunday, brownish now; some brass and stuff
> Up at the holy end; the small neat organ;
> And a tense, musty, unignorable silence,
> Brewed God knows how long. Hatless, I take off
> My cycle-clips in awkward reverence,
>
> Move forward, run my hand around the font.
> From where I stand, the roof looks almost new—
> Cleaned or restored? Some one would know: I don't. . . .
> Reflect the place was not worth stopping for.
>
> Yet stop I did: in fact I often do,
> And always end much at a loss like this,
> Wondering what to look for; wondering, too,
> When churches fall completely out of use
> What shall we turn them into.

Will superstition survive belief?

> And what remains when disbelief has gone?
> Grass, weedy pavement, brambles, buttress, sky.
>
> A shape less recognizable each week,
> A purpose more obscure. I wonder who
> Will be the last, the very last, to seek
> This place for what it was.

Some antiquarian perhaps or aesthete?

Or will he be my representative.

Bored, uninformed, knowing the ghostly silt
Dispersed, yet tending to this cross of ground
Through suburb scrub because it held unspilt
So long and equably what since is found
Only in separation—marriage, and birth,
And death and thoughts of these—for whom was built
This special shell? For, though I've no idea
What this accoutred frowsty barn is worth,
It pleases me to stand in silence here;

A serious house on serious earth it is,
In whose blent air all our compulsions meet,
Are recognized, and robed as destinies.
And that much never can be obsolete,
Since someone will forever be surprising
A hunger in himself to be more serious,
And gravitating with it to this ground,
Which, he once heard, was proper to grow wise in,
If only that so many dead lie round.

This is not religion; but neither is it an assertion that England
can do without it, or without her historic Church.

# INDEX

Adam (in *Paradise Lost*), 107, 108, 111, 112, 114–17, 119. *See also* Second Adam
Addison, Joseph, 126, 138, 140–41, 197; and Church of England, 140–41
Anglicanism. *See* Church of England
Anglo-Catholicism. *See* Church of England
Aristotle, 4–5, 6, 12, 22, 26, 58
Arnold, Matthew, 2, 12, 207, 211–13, 216–20; and Irving Babbitt, 211–12; and Coleridge, 213; as critic, 215; and humanism, 211–13; and T. H. Huxley, 212; and J. S. Mill, 212; and naturalism, 212; and Newman, 212; and poetry as "criticism of life," 214. Works: *Dover Beach*, 217–18; *Last Essays on the Church and Religion*, 212; *Literature and Dogma*, 211; *Rugby Chapel*, 219; *St. Paul and Protestantism*, 211; *Stanzas from the Grande Chartreuse*, 218
Auden, W. H., 286–93; and Anglo-Catholicism, 288; anti-intellectualism of, 290; and Blake, 287; and Dante, 287; and Eliot, 262, 287–88, 292; and Freud, 287; and Incarnation of Christ, 287–89; and Kierkegaard, 287; and D. H. Lawrence, 287; and Marxism, 287; and Protestantism, 288; and I. A. Richards, 287. Works: *For the Time Being: A Christmas Oratorio*, 288–93; *New Year Letter*, 288

"B. V." *See* Thomson, James (B. V.)
Babbitt, Irving, 263; and Arnold, 211–12; and Eliot, 263
Bacon, Francis, 14, 48, 123, 126–29, 132, 134–37, 209; and Blake, 132–37, 177; and Cambridge Platonists, 128; and Coleridge, 136–37, 177; and Cowley, 88–89, 123, 127; and Donne, 14; and Neoclassicism, 134–37; and Platonism, 128; and Wordsworth, 137. Works: *The New Atlantis*, 89, 126–27
Bartas, Guillaume de Salluste du, 19–20; and Protestantism, 19. Works: *Divine Weeks and Works*, 19; *Job Triumphans*, 19; *Judith*, 19
Beaumont, Joseph, 87; Works: *Morning Hymn to Christ*, 87; *Psyche*, 87
Benlowes, Edward, 87; Works: *Theophila*, 87
Bentham, Jeremy, 168, 207, 208
Berkeley, George, 126; and Coleridge, 174

295